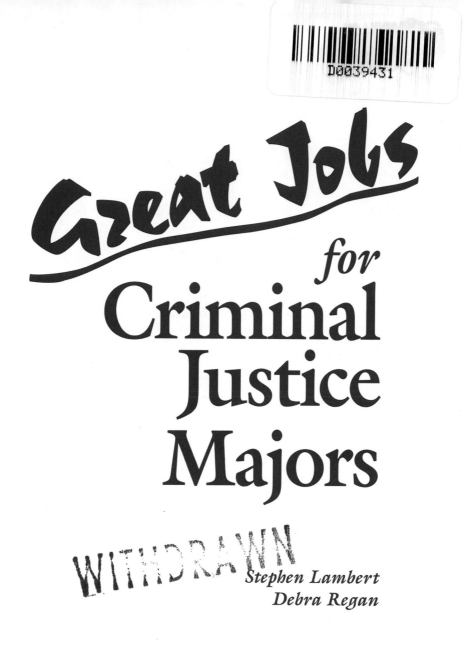

Great Jobs
for
Criminal
Justice
Majors

WITHDRAWN

Stephen Lambert
Debra Regan

VGM Career Books

Chicago   New York   San Francisco   Lisbon   London   Madrid   Mexico City
Milan   New Delhi   San Juan   Seoul   Singapore   Sydney   Toronto

Library of Congress Cataloging-in-Publication Data

Lambert, Stephen E.
      Great jobs for criminal justice majors / Stephen E. Lambert and Debra Regan.
          p.   cm. — (Great jobs for)
      Includes index.
      ISBN 0-658-01063-8
        1. Law enforcement—Vocational guidance—United States.   2. College
graduates—Employment—United States.   3. Job hunting—United States.
I. Regan, Debra.   II. Title.   III. Series.

HV8143.L335   2001
364'.023'73—dc21   00-68499

VGM Career Books

A Division of The McGraw·Hill Companies

6 7 8 9 0   LBM/LBM   0 9 8 7 6 5

ISBN 0-658-01063-8

This book was set in Adobe Garamond
Printed and bound by Lake Book Manufacturing

McGraw-Hill books are available at special quantity discounts to use as premiums and
sales promotions, or for use in corporate training programs. For more information, please
write to the Director of Special Sales, Professional Publishing, McGraw-Hill, Two Penn
Plaza, New York, NY 10121-2298. Or contact your local bookstore.

This book is printed on acid-free paper.

DEDICATION

This book is dedicated to Donald J. Melisi, retired lieutenant, Concord, Massachusetts, Police Department and founder, former professor, and department chair of the criminal justice program at Middlesex Community College, Bedford and Lowell, Massachusetts.

One of the themes of this book is the increasingly high standards of professionalism and personal integrity demanded in today's criminal justice careers. Don Melisi has epitomized these hallmarks in his careers on the force and in academia. His own distinguished career path exemplifies the breadth of opportunity available to talented criminal justice professionals.

His design for the criminal justice program at Middlesex Community College could serve as an example of how to build a quality program. Listening carefully to an advisory board drawn from almost every sector of the criminal justice community described in this book, he assured that his program would guarantee his graduates a full set of options—access to great jobs or further education. His annual Criminal Justice Career Day brought hundreds of students together each year with a wide variety of potential employers for some frank conversations about the future. Students always came away with a new appreciation for the value of their degree program, and employers discovered a wealth of potential job applicants. Perhaps this book can also serve in part as a token of appreciation from the many students who benefited from these special days.

This book is dedicated to Don Melisi not just to honor his professional success but also to honor those personal qualities recognized by friends, colleagues, and students over a lifetime of service. Don's leadership, vision, sensitivity, and compassion, combined with his wonderful sense of humor, will be remembered and appreciated long after his list of achievements and accomplishments has been recited.

CONTENTS

ACKNOWLEDGMENTS

T he following individuals contributed greatly to the writing of this book. To Captain Art Walker of the Keene, New Hampshire, Police Department; Dr. Lynda Pintrich, professor of criminal justice, Middlesex Community College; David Collum, former chief of police, Rindge, New Hampshire; and John E. Clark, chief of security/campus police, Plymouth State College, thank you for sharing your time, experiences, observations, and expertise with us and for leading us in the right direction. Your combined input provided the foundation for *Great Jobs for Criminal Justice Majors*. To our colleagues Rosemary Nichols, director of career planning and placement, Franklin Pierce College, Rindge, New Hampshire, and Sam Allen, director of career services, Saint Anselm College, Manchester, New Hampshire, thank you for providing us with your resources, contacts, and insights into the criminal justice major. To Karen Fuller, public information coordinator, American Probation and Parole Association, and Anne Skove, knowledge management analyst, National Center for State Courts, we extend our appreciation for your quick response to our requests for information. The information you sent was exactly what we needed.

INVESTIGATE THE OPPORTUNITIES

I t's difficult to generalize about the field of criminal justice. Some observers may say, "It's harsh!" Criminal justice majors will remind you of the compassionate and deeply feeling role of juvenile counselors and the impact and difference that their caring, listening skills, and empathy can mean in positively redirecting a young life. Others may say, "It's black-and-white, no room for gray!" Criminal justice majors will tell you that's not entirely true, either. In fact, although the Justice Department announced in 2000 that arrests were up nationwide, over the past decade we have seen a 30 percent decline in the likelihood of convicted criminals going to prison. Why? The American justice system has increased the numbers of offenders receiving probation for drug offenses and drunken driving convictions through specific treatment plans, community supervision, and supervised rehabilitation.

Generalizations are often not fair, and they are particularly hard to make about criminal justice jobs and careers. However, one generalization we can confidently make about criminal justice careers is that they hold *breadth* and *depth* for the graduates of these programs. The five career paths outlined in this book demonstrate the remarkable range of occupations available to the graduate today.

Perhaps no criminal justice career typifies the changes in our systems of justice administration more than *law enforcement*. You've seen reports in newspapers and on television news programs that document these changes: hiring more women and minorities, increased cultural sensitivity, a greater focus on community policing and awareness that law enforcement officials are members of the communities in which they work. You may know, as well, that the educational backgrounds of law enforcement officials have never been so high and that they're getting higher! Entry-level applicants with bachelor's degrees are competing with each other for jobs that before might have gone to associate degree recipients or even high school graduates. Today the supply of job applicants with four-year degrees far outnumbers the positions, so employers can select the "cream of the crop" and fill positions that may not strictly require a bachelor's degree with bachelor's degree candidates.

And once you're on the job, your education is hardly over. Those state trooper vehicles passing you on the highway are more likely than not to contain officers who have passed the bar exam and are licensed attorneys. In management and administration, you'll find that the number of personnel with master's degrees in criminal justice, business management, or other social science fields is on the rise. Law enforcement these days is about brains, not brawn, and law enforcement employers want smart people who have the motivation and self-discipline to continue their education.

Still, all these wonderful changes in professionalism and educational standards, however important to you, are only symptoms of the deeper change going on in law enforcement and the criminal justice system in general. These deeper changes have to do with a new emphasis on legitimacy in law enforcement, and you'll find that emphasized throughout your entry period, during training, and in the daily practice of your career. Here are some of the ways in which law enforcement is working to enhance its own legitimacy:

■ Law enforcement officials are mandated to have high-quality "ordinary" interactions with the public, not just to respond during those times when we depend on law enforcement to provide needed services. Your encounters with the public must now be more than obligatory; they must be ordinary, everyday, common, and consistent occurrences.

■ With whatever organization you choose to affiliate in law enforcement, be it the local police, the FBI, or some branch of state law enforcement, you'll discover a new emphasis on making that organization more visible and more open to public scrutiny, which can be intense. Gone are the days when law enforcement ruled by fiat. The public is interested in being assured that policies, practices, and organizational structures are appropriate.

■ More and more, law enforcement is asking the public to realize that common citizens have a vital role to play in crime control and criminal justice operations. Law enforcement increasingly works alongside and in partnership with citizens for the goals of order and justice.

In the field of *corrections*, opportunities have never been more dynamic. The number of people under correctional supervision stands at an all-time high of 6.3 million at the time of this book's publication. Of this 6.3 million, 1.86 million men and women are literally behind bars. The remainder include the highest number of parolees and probationers in criminal justice history. More than a million of these probationers and parolees are in the big states of Texas and California. Other states with large populations of parolees/probationers include Georgia and Idaho. The scope and numbers of people involved with the criminal justice system have increased substantially over the past twenty years. From just a little over 1 percent of the population in 1980, the offender total has climbed to its current record level of more than 3 percent of all adults. That's one out of every thirty-two men and women.

These probation and parole facts, however, do not mean that prisons are not also working with higher populations. They are. More aggressive and longer sentencing that began in the '90s means overcrowded conditions in many states, with complicated repercussions. Some states have been forced to move prisoners to other states, raising a public outcry from family members, who say these distant sites of incarceration are yet another form of inhumane punishment. In a case in Connecticut in which two prisoners who had been transferred to Virginia died (one a suicide, one of natural causes following a struggle with a guard), the volume of criticism rose to new decibel levels.

These few telling statistics underlie the correspondingly high employment demands of the correctional system. Correctional officers specialize in many areas beyond the obvious category of security. They can develop specialized skills in registration and other administrative procedures, in structured vocational activities, in counseling (both individual and group) and recreation, and—as our statistics for parolees and probationers indicate—in the all-important field of specialized aftercare and treatment programs for reentry into society.

The field of corrections offers wonderful growth and personal development along its varied career tracks. At the working apex of these promotional ladders is the role of warden, filled now by capable men and women whose careers in corrections and whose continuing education in the areas of criminal justice, business management, sociology, and psychology have qualified them for these demanding administrative executive positions. Beyond the job of warden lie many state and regional correctional facility management and commission positions for those who are looking for a career path with true growth and personal potential.

The potential for the role of our *courts* in the justice system is incalculable. It's the arena in which we sort out what has happened and how we will redress any injustice that has been done. It's both an active place and a thoughtful one. This book presents a full range of possible occupations within the courts—some available to you immediately upon graduation, others requiring some additional education and training—and, as in every career path, includes details on more advanced career positions to which you may aspire.

Sadly, the American public receives a false impression of most criminal justice activity through the media. Television dramas, movies, novels, and stories often portray every aspect of the system in a heightened and overly sensationalized manner. For those of us who have actually witnessed courtroom proceedings, the difference between fiction and reality is stunningly obvious! Court processes are methodical and reflective—and surprisingly, not very loud or dramatic in most cases. They are, however, terribly complex and seldom black-and-white.

You know from your sociology and psychology course work that people are motivated by any number of stimuli and that those are different for each of us, ranging from our genetic makeup to our psychological and sociological conditioning. Experts have yet to categorize good and evil as absolutes. Even the "good" person can commit a crime, and the "bad" person is capable of goodness. So, courts aren't about good and bad as much as they are about people and about people coming into conflict with one another. The court's job is to sort it out and determine a fair and equitable resolution.

Courts today, like every other facet of the justice system, are trying hard to change. They've been subject to the same exponential growth that has affected the correctional system. Former Chief Justice Warren Burger once said, "The entire legal profession—lawyers, judges, law teachers—has become so mesmerized with the stimulation of the courtroom contest that we forget that we ought to be healers of conflict." And that's where the changes are occurring today, as we see pilot projects such as neighborhood justice centers or pretrial settlement conferences. The American Bar Association has set up an Alternative Dispute Resolution branch that offers nonadversarial alternatives to the courtroom. This is an exciting time to think about working in the court system.

As with every career path featured in Chapters 10 through 14, your degree in criminal justice gives you enormous scope for your options in the courts. There's good work in court security as either a court security officer or bailiff, and both of these jobs have many interesting duties in addition to their principal charge to maintain the integrity of the courtroom. Like most other employees in the court system, you are very much part of a team in the work you do and the role you play.

Several administrative positions are highlighted as well, some very active and visible, and others more behind-the-scenes and less obvious. Chief among these are the jobs of clerk of court and court administrator. These are critical administrative functions that help to organize and regularize the schedules and work of the court. People in both positions, depending on the size and location of the court, may hear and resolve some disputes themselves. They are significant positions and hold the promise of careers full of constant learning. You'll discover continuing career interest and wonderful possibilities for personal growth and professional development either by moving up from a clerk position to a senior court administrator or by moving to a larger court or into the federal system.

We all are aware of the role of court reporters. They are visible in any depiction, real or fictionalized, of the court. A skilled, demanding, and highly responsible position with excellent financial rewards and career stability, it is an attractive option for many criminal justice majors who are interested in adding to their degrees with the specific training that this position requires. Other attractive features of this work are the distinct possibilities of freelancing with these skills and the ability to be mobile. Both of those are especially attractive options in a society in which many of us move several times in a career and want to be able to find work in our field quickly or need to "stop out" of work or work part-time for personal or family reasons. The work of court reporting makes that possible.

Behind the scenes and not well known to many outside the court are the legal research positions that support the judicial staff and court legal staff through their work in law libraries and on the computer (frequently using database skills or purchased CD-ROM information-database software). They provide the legal definitions, history, precedents, and background that underpin the administration of justice in the courts. If you are fascinated by the law, enjoy reading and problem solving, and have good detective skills, every day on this job will bring you a new set of interesting cases to pursue as you track down the relevant information. It's a quieter type of excitement and challenge, but it's infinitely varied and always surprising.

The final two positions featured in the courts career path, each requiring its own additional education and training, are those of paralegal and lawyer. Each has a natural career relationship to your criminal justice education, is highly visible in the courts, and is apt to set you thinking about the career possibilities. Each is thus attractive in its own way and for its own reasons.

Paralegals are the workhorses of the law profession. Frequently specializing and often paired with a particular attorney, they do the complex and vital research and administrative paperwork for the legal case that the attorney is preparing. Researching items such as past opinions, precedents, and exceptions for mutiple cases is demanding, exciting, and always different. While there are certifications and professional standards for paralegals, there are also many possible routes to this job. Some criminal justice majors may simply begin work with on-the-job training in a law office and develop their skills as they go, gaining expertise through additional professional development seminars or short courses along the way. Others, depending on geography or setting, earn a certificate through a formal program or school to qualify for these jobs.

This career choice can be ideal if you are proficient in research and writing. Paralegal jobs are highly stable and can be very lucrative; most important, you are recognized as being an integral part of the organization. Your work is valued by others, and for you, the rewards include increased competency, professionalism, and income as you grow in the profession.

This growing expertise leads many paralegals to enter law school and become lawyers. We include lawyers in this career path because they are active participants in the court process, and the law degree is hardly a stranger to those with a criminal justice undergraduate degree—and not just in the court setting, either. Many criminal justice professionals in corrections and law enforcement pursue graduate studies in law for the J.D. (Juris Doctor) and the ability to practice law. Likewise, many paralegals find that they are doing work so closely akin to that of the more highly paid attorneys that it becomes important to them to become attorneys themselves. The opportunities that unfold with a law degree are a volume unto themselves!

The issues (and as a result, the careers) surrounding *juvenile justice* and serious and violent juvenile (SVJ) offenses focus on prevention and not punishment. Much has been learned from studies of serious and violent juvenile crime. For example:

- A distinct group of offenders who start early and continue throughout their youth is responsible for a disproportionately high percentage of all juvenile crime. Consequently, if juvenile justice specialists can reach this group, the chances of breaking that cycle would be significantly greater.

- Most offenders younger than twelve are not routinely processed in juvenile court, and services in the community are unfortunately fragmented. Juvenile justice experts must work with other mental health, social welfare, and school officials to redirect these potential offenders.

- The development of delinquent behavior in boys takes place in an orderly fashion, progressing from less serious problems to more significant crimes. Boys tend to progress from conflict with authority to covert actions to overt actions. Once they reach these aggressive stages, it is more difficult to habituate them to healthier behaviors.

Your work may be in a detention center, within the juvenile court system, or in a residential facility for delinquent youth. Regardless of the locale, the work remains the same: inhibiting inappropriate behavior and redirecting it into healthier and more productive channels. Your job will involve either reducing the risk factors that promote bad behavior (such as in a residential facility) or helping to change the way a child responds to these risks (by increasing the child's resilience). Ultimately your work is about promoting positive behavior, health and well-being, and personal success. In addition to resilience, the protective factors you will help to place within the young person's reach will include positive adult and peer relationships that promote bonding. You'll also work to enhance healthy beliefs and clear standards. No pressure!

In all seriousness, can there be more challenging and yet more rewarding work? Nevertheless, you must also be aware that the pressures on those who work in this field, who must serve as daily, hourly, and minute-by-minute role models, are unrelenting. You are not expected to be perfect, but you must be careful, thoughtful, appropriate, empathetic, and infinitely patient—which means that this area of criminal justice is certainly not for everyone. It's a special area of jobs for special people.

The final chapter in this book only hints at the unlimited career horizons possible in *allied business* with your criminal justice degree. Private security and the relatively new field of cybercrime both place the criminal justice degree high on their lists of qualifications. Each of these fields offers personal rewards and professional development and allows you the advantage of staying within your degree field of knowledge but exercising a range of other skills and talents that you may have and want to use.

Contrary to popular belief, private security may be the world's oldest profession! There has always been a need for additional security or investigative work outside of public agencies. Sometimes, that has been the result of public law enforcement agencies being too busy or burdened to provide the necessary resources in a situation (especially older, evidentially weaker cases). Other times, it is simply a matter of the purchaser wanting the extra measure of security, discretion, and privacy that these services ensure. Of even more importance to people considering this work is that they can be assured that the future is bright—although the technological demands of the investigative side of the profession will certainly increase along with its usefulness to the industry.

Private security is really a reflection of our culture. The growing number of secure, gated communities in the United States with their own security forces, the increasing emphasis on corporate security and integrity of office buildings and headquarters, and the continuing need for private investigative work and personal bodyguards assure the entrepreneurial criminal justice major of an incredibly full menu from which to choose the endeavors that best fit your particular skills, aptitudes, and work needs.

Detective services also fill a niche for customers that cannot be met by public practitioners of the law. Private detective services came about and have remained in the marketplace because they fill an important void in criminal justice services. The individuals and organizations who buy private detective services from providers are hoping for discretion, efficiency, and tact as they seek investigative and other services for issues that concern them.

The final area of criminal justice discussed in this career path is cybercrime. If you enjoy computers and perhaps are graduating with some significant computer expertise in addition to your criminal justice degree, you may find the area of cybercrime to be just what you're looking for. A criminal justice education, strong computer skills (and an equally strong desire to learn and know more of this technology), and basic business acumen are what you need to get your foot in the door of an employer that specializes in investigating and uncovering incidents of computer crime.

The impact of computer viruses is not to be underestimated, and their swift detection and, even more important, internal defenses against them are critical. But a virus is only one kind of computer terrorism. So-called computer hackers and crackers have threatened organizations by breaking through password-protected sites and infiltrating supposedly secure computer domains—domains that may contain huge amounts of personal and privileged information. Even the relatively easily solved problems of jamming corporate Internet accounts with enough queries or messages to effect a shutdown can cost businesses (and ultimately consumers) millions of dollars.

Internal issues abound, too. The field of cybercrime may have you investigating employee crimes having to do with misuse of computers for illegal purposes such as pornography or stealing computer time for processing of personal materials. It may involve employees stealing data to use themselves or to sell to a competitor. Increasingly, firms have also been subjected to incidents of personal vandalism during layoffs or discharge procedures that have caused significant damage to the business operation.

These few examples do not begin to do justice to the investigative adventure that cybercrime situations present, nor can this book predict what new criminal endeavors may be prompted by technological advances. It is that very inability to predict the future, the ignorance of what may be around the corner both in computer development and in crimes that seek to take illegal advantage of that technology, that you may find exciting.

However exciting cybercrime may appear to you, it would be too easy and, in fact, wrong to label this the "new frontier" of criminal justice. These are, after all, machines—machines made by people—and what is more infinitely complex than the mind of a man or woman? Without question, cybercrime represents a new and as yet undeveloped area of investigation and criminal activity. But the innovation and dramatic changes going on in law enforcement, in the courts, in the field of juvenile justice, and in corrections are equally dramatic and sometimes startling. If you're seeking a career highly charged with almost a volatile level of change, any of the areas of criminal justice set forth in these pages will fit the bill nicely!

The simple reason for this is that justice is an abstract concept, as are the ideas of good and evil. On television and in comic books, good is rewarded and evil punished. But is that how it really is? No, sometimes in the real world, evil goes unpunished, and very bad things can happen to good people. Or good people conflict with good people, or evil conflicts with evil, because intents are different or perceptions vary. The result is the same. It is not the comic-book good and evil with which you will deal in your career but the harsh truths of the real world—and seeking justice here is far more complicated, frustrating, and mystifying than any fiction.

It is these complexities of human nature, their infinite variety and form, that make the careers in criminal justice so demanding. Cybercrime may be "new," but it joins a long list of social crises that we have yet to solve—including poverty, racism, and organized crime—despite dramatic developmental progress on many fronts. So, it stands to reason that as the challenges proliferate, so do the demands on those who would do battle against these threats to law and order. The careers in criminal justice demand the best people—the smartest, the most creative, the most curious—people who are interested in people. Above all, the careers of criminal justice need people who will work hard against significant obstacles in order to make a true difference in the world for each and every one of us.

PART ONE

THE
JOB SEARCH

CHAPTER ONE

THE
SELF-ASSESSMENT

elf-assessment is the process by which you begin to acknowledge your own particular blend of education, experiences, values, needs, and goals. It provides the foundation for career planning and the entire job search process. Self-assessment involves looking inward and asking yourself what can sometimes prove to be difficult questions. This self-examination should lead to an intimate understanding of your personal traits, your personal values, your consumption patterns and economic needs, your longer-term goals, your skill base, your preferred skills, and your under-developed skills.

You come to the self-assessment process knowing yourself well in some of these areas, but you may still be uncertain about other aspects. You may be well aware of your consumption patterns, but have you spent much time specifically identifying your longer-term goals or your personal values as they relate to work? No matter what level of self-assessment you have undertaken to date, it is now time to clarify all of these issues and questions as they relate to the job search.

The knowledge you gain in the self-assessment process will guide the rest of your job search. In this book, you will learn about all of the following tasks:

- Writing resumes

- Exploring possible job titles

- Identifying employment sites

- Networking

- Interviewing

- Following up

- Evaluating job offers

In each of these steps, you will rely on and often return to the understanding gained through your self-assessment. Any individual seeking employment must be able and willing to express these facets of his or her personality to recruiters and interviewers throughout the job search. This communication allows you to show the world who you are so that together with employers you can determine whether there will be a workable match with a given job or career path.

HOW TO CONDUCT A SELF-ASSESSMENT

The self-assessment process goes on naturally all the time. People ask you to clarify what you mean, you make a purchasing decision, or you begin a new relationship. You react to the world and the world reacts to you. How you understand these interactions and any changes you might make because of them are part of the natural process of self-discovery. There is, however, a more comprehensive and efficient way to approach self-assessment with regard to employment.

Because self-assessment can become a complex exercise, we have distilled it into a seven-step process that provides an effective basis for undertaking a job search. The seven steps include the following:

1. Understanding your personal traits

2. Identifying your personal values

3. Calculating your economic needs

4. Exploring your longer-term goals

5. Enumerating your skill base

6. Recognizing your preferred skills

7. Assessing skills needing further development

As you work through your self-assessment, you might want to create a worksheet similar to the one shown in Exhibit 1.1, starting on the following page. Or you might want to keep a journal of the thoughts you have as you

Exhibit 1.1

SELF-ASSESSMENT WORKSHEET

STEP 1. Understand Your Personal Traits
The personal traits that describe me are:
(Include all of the words that describe you.)

The ten personal traits that most accurately describe me are:
(List these ten traits.)

STEP 2. Identify Your Personal Values
Working conditions that are important to me include:
(List working conditions that would have to exist for you to accept a position.)

The values that go along with my working conditions are:
(Write down the values that correspond to each working condition.)

Some additional values I've decided to include are:
(List those values you identify as you conduct this job search.)

STEP 3. Calculate Your Economic Needs
My estimated minimum annual salary requirement is:
(Write the salary you have calculated based on your budget.)

Starting salaries for the positions I'm considering are:
(List the name of each job you are considering and the associated starting salary.)

STEP 4. Explore Your Longer-Term Goals
My thoughts on longer-term goals right now are:
(Jot down some of your longer-term goals as you know them right now.)

STEP 5. Enumerate Your Skill Base
The general skills I possess are:
(List the skills that underlie tasks you are able to complete.)

The specific skills I possess are:
(List more technical or specific skills that you possess and indicate your level of expertise.)

General and specific skills that I want to promote to employers for the jobs I'm considering are:
(List general and specific skills for each type of job you are considering.)

STEP 6. Recognize Your Preferred Skills
Skills that I would like to use on the job include:
(List skills that you hope to use on the job, and indicate how often you'd like to use them.)

STEP 7. Assess Skills Needing Further Development
Some skills that I'll need to acquire for the jobs I'm considering include:
(Write down skills listed in job advertisements or job descriptions that you don't currently possess.)

I believe I can build these skills by:
(Describe how you plan to acquire these skills.)

undergo this process. There will be many opportunities to revise your self-assessment as you start down the path of seeking a career.

STEP 1 Understanding Your Personal Traits

Each person has a unique personality that he or she brings to the job search process. Gaining a better understanding of your personal traits can help you evaluate job and career choices. Identifying these traits and then finding employment that allows you to draw on at least some of them can create a rewarding and fulfilling work experience. If potential employment doesn't allow you to use these preferred traits, it is important to decide whether you can find other ways to express them or whether you would be better off not considering this type of job. Interests and hobbies pursued outside of work hours can be one way to use personal traits you don't have an opportunity to draw on in your work. For example, if you consider yourself an outgoing person and the kinds of jobs you are examining allow little contact with other people, you may be able to achieve the level of interaction that is comfortable for you outside of your work setting. If such a compromise seems impractical or otherwise unsatisfactory, you probably should explore only jobs that provide the interaction you want and need on the job.

Many young adults who are not very confident about their attractiveness to employers will downplay their need for income. They will say, "Money is not all that important if I love my work." But if you begin to document exactly what you need for housing, transportation, insurance, clothing, food, and utilities, you will begin to understand that some jobs cannot meet your financial needs and it doesn't matter how wonderful the job is. If you have to worry each payday about bills and other financial obligations, you won't be very effective on the job. Begin now to be honest with yourself about your needs.

Inventorying Your Personal Traits. Begin the self-assessment process by creating an inventory of your personal traits. Using the list in Exhibit 1.2, decide which of these personal traits describe you.

Exhibit 1.2

PERSONAL TRAITS

Accurate	Considerate	Fair-minded
Active	Cool	Farsighted
Adaptable	Cooperative	Feeling
Adventurous	Courageous	Firm
Affectionate	Critical	Flexible
Aggressive	Curious	Formal
Ambitious	Daring	Friendly
Analytical	Decisive	Future-oriented
Appreciative	Deliberate	Generous
Artistic	Detail-oriented	Gentle
Brave	Determined	Good-natured
Businesslike	Discreet	Helpful
Calm	Dominant	Honest
Capable	Eager	Humorous
Caring	Easygoing	Idealistic
Cautious	Efficient	Imaginative
Cheerful	Emotional	Impersonal
Clean	Empathetic	Independent
Competent	Energetic	Individualistic
Confident	Excitable	Industrious
Conscientious	Expressive	Informal
Conservative	Extroverted	Innovative

Intellectual	Peaceable	Self-disciplined
Intelligent	Personable	Sensible
Introverted	Persuasive	Sensitive
Intuitive	Pleasant	Serious
Inventive	Poised	Sincere
Jovial	Polite	Sociable
Just	Practical	Spontaneous
Kind	Precise	Strong
Liberal	Principled	Strong-minded
Likable	Private	Structured
Logical	Productive	Subjective
Loyal	Progressive	Tactful
Mature	Quick	Thorough
Methodical	Quiet	Thoughtful
Meticulous	Rational	Tolerant
Mistrustful	Realistic	Trusting
Modest	Receptive	Trustworthy
Motivated	Reflective	Truthful
Objective	Relaxed	Understanding
Observant	Reliable	Unexcitable
Open-minded	Reserved	Uninhibited
Opportunistic	Resourceful	Verbal
Optimistic	Responsible	Versatile
Organized	Reverent	Wholesome
Original	Sedentary	Wise
Outgoing	Self-confident	
Patient	Self-controlled	

Focusing on Selected Personal Traits. Of all the traits you identified from the list in Exhibit 1.2, select the ten you believe most accurately describe you. If you are having a difficult time deciding, think about which words people who know you well would use to describe you. Keep track of these ten traits.

Considering Your Personal Traits in the Job Search Process. As you begin exploring jobs and careers, watch for matches between your personal traits and the job descriptions you read. Some jobs will require many personal traits you know you possess, and others will not seem to match those traits.

··

A police officer's work, for example, is a combination of
sensitivity and action. Being constantly required to make
decisions and to exercise sound judgment means remaining alert and aware at all times. Listening skills are essential in this job, especially during interactions of heightened
emotion or tension. Today's law enforcement officer is an
active participant in community life and is focused more
on prevention than punishment. As a result, the law
enforcement professional today is equally at home presenting a sidewalk safety program to third graders or utilizing the latest investigative techniques in attempting to
solve a crime.

··

Your ability to respond to changing conditions, your decision-making ability, productivity, creativity, and verbal skills all have a bearing on your success in and enjoyment of your work life. To better guarantee success, be sure
to take the time needed to understand these traits in yourself.

STEP 2 Identifying Your Personal Values

Your personal values affect every aspect of your life, including employment,
and they develop and change as you move through life. Values can be defined
as principles that we hold in high regard, qualities that are important and
desirable to us. Some values aren't ordinarily connected to work (love, beauty,
color, light, relationships, family, or religion), and others are (autonomy,
cooperation, effectiveness, achievement, knowledge, and security). Our values determine, in part, the level of satisfaction we feel in a particular job.

Defining Acceptable Working Conditions. One facet of employment is the
set of working conditions that must exist for someone to consider taking a
job.

Each of us would probably create a unique list of acceptable working conditions, but items that might be included on many people's lists are the
amount of money you would need to be paid, how far you are willing to
drive or travel, the amount of freedom you want in determining your own
schedule, whether you would be working with people or data or things, and
the types of tasks you would be willing to do. Your conditions might include
statements of working conditions you will *not* accept; for example, you might
not be willing to work at night or on weekends or holidays.

If you were offered a job tomorrow, what conditions would have to exist
for you to realistically consider accepting the position? Take some time and
make a list of these conditions.

Exhibit 1.3

WORK VALUES

Achievement	Development	Physical activity
Advancement	Effectiveness	Power
Adventure	Excitement	Precision
Attainment	Fast pace	Prestige
Authority	Financial gain	Privacy
Autonomy	Helping	Profit
Belonging	Humor	Recognition
Challenge	Improvisation	Risk
Change	Independence	Security
Communication	Influencing others	Self-expression
Community	Intellectual stimulation	Solitude
Competition	Interaction	Stability
Completion	Knowledge	Status
Contribution	Leading	Structure
Control	Mastery	Supervision
Cooperation	Mobility	Surroundings
Creativity	Moral fulfillment	Time freedom
Decision making	Organization	Variety

Realizing Associated Values. Your list of working conditions can be used to create an inventory of your values relating to jobs and careers you are exploring. For example, if one of your conditions stated that you wanted to earn at least $30,000 per year, the associated value would be financial gain. If another condition was that you wanted to work with a friendly group of people, the value that went along with that might be belonging or interaction with people. Exhibit 1.3 provides a list of commonly held values that relate to the work environment; use it to create your own list of personal values.

Relating Your Values to the World of Work. As you read the job descriptions in this book and in other suggested resources, think about the values associated with each position.

....

For example, the duties of a victim advocate include interviewing clients, building trusting relations, counseling, and referring clients to appropriate community resources for services. Associated values are openness, responsiveness, altruism, problem-solving, and networking skills.

....

If you were thinking about a career in this field, or any other field you're exploring, at least some of the associated values should match those you extracted from your list of working conditions. Take a second look at any values that don't match up. How important are they to you? What will happen if they are not satisfied on the job? Can you incorporate those personal values elsewhere? Your answers need to be brutally honest. As you continue your exploration, be sure to add to your list any additional values that occur to you.

STEP 3   Calculating Your Economic Needs

Each of us grew up in an environment that provided for certain basic needs, such as food and shelter, and, to varying degrees, other needs that we now consider basic, such as cable television, E-mail, or an automobile. Needs such as privacy, space, and quiet, which at first glance may not appear to be monetary needs, may add to housing expenses and so should be considered as you examine your economic needs. For example, if you place a high value on a large, open living space for yourself, it would be difficult to satisfy that need without an associated high housing cost, especially in a densely populated city environment.

As you prepare to move into the world of work and become responsible for meeting your own basic needs, it is important to consider the salary you will need to be able to afford a satisfying standard of living. The three-step process outlined here will help you plan a budget, which in turn will allow you to evaluate the various career choices and geographic locations you are considering. The steps include (1) developing a realistic budget, (2) examining starting salaries, and (3) using a cost-of-living index.

Developing a Realistic Budget.   Each of us has certain expectations for the kind of lifestyle we want to maintain. To begin the process of defining your economic needs, it will be helpful to determine what you expect to spend on routine monthly expenses. These expenses include housing, food, transportation, entertainment, utilities, loan repayments, and revolving charge accounts. A worksheet that details many of these expenses is shown in Exhibit 1.4. You may not currently spend anything for certain items, but you probably will have to once you begin supporting yourself. As you develop this budget, be generous in your estimates, but keep in mind any items that could be reduced or eliminated. If you are not sure about the cost of a cer-

Exhibit 1.4

ESTIMATED MONTHLY EXPENSES WORKSHEET

		Could Reduce Spending? (Yes/No)
Cable	$ _____	_____
Child care	_____	_____
Clothing	_____	_____
Educational loan repayment	_____	_____
Entertainment	_____	_____
Food		
At home	_____	_____
Meals out	_____	_____
Gifts	_____	_____
Housing		
Rent/mortgage	_____	_____
Insurance	_____	_____
Property taxes	_____	_____
Medical insurance	_____	_____
Reading materials		
Newspapers	_____	_____
Magazines	_____	_____
Books	_____	_____
Revolving loans/charges	_____	_____
Savings	_____	_____
Telephone	_____	_____
Transportation		
Auto payment	_____	_____
Insurance	_____	_____
Parking	_____	_____
Gasoline	_____	_____
or		
Cab/train/bus fare	_____	_____
Utilities		
Electric	_____	_____
Gas	_____	_____
Water/sewer	_____	_____
Vacations	_____	_____

		Could Reduce Spending? (Yes/No)
Miscellaneous expense 1	_____	_____
Expense: _____		
Miscellaneous expense 2	_____	_____
Expense: _____		
Miscellaneous expense 3	_____	_____
Expense: _____		

TOTAL MONTHLY EXPENSES: _____

YEARLY EXPENSES (Monthly expenses × 12): _____ _____

INCREASE TO INCLUDE TAXES (Yearly expenses × 1.35): _____ _____ =

MINIMUM ANNUAL SALARY REQUIREMENT: _____ _____

tain item, talk with family or friends who would be able to give you a realistic estimate.

If this is new or difficult for you, start to keep a log of expenses right now. You may be surprised at how much you actually spend each month for food or stamps or magazines. Household expenses and personal grooming items can often loom very large in a budget, as can auto repairs or home maintenance.

Income taxes must also be taken into consideration when examining salary requirements. State and local taxes vary, so it is difficult to calculate exactly the effect of taxes on the amount of income you need to generate. To roughly estimate the gross income necessary to generate your minimum annual salary requirement, multiply the minimum salary you have calculated (see Exhibit 1.4) by a factor of 1.35. The resulting figure will be an approximation of what your gross income would need to be, given your estimated expenses.

Examining Starting Salaries. Starting salaries for each of the career tracks are provided throughout this book. These salary figures can be used in conjunction with the cost-of-living index (discussed in the next section) to determine whether you would be able to meet your basic economic needs in a given geographic location.

Using a Cost-of-Living Index. If you are thinking about trying to get a job in a geographic region other than the one where you now live, understanding differences in the cost of living will help you come to a more informed decision about making a move. By using a cost-of-living index, you can compare salaries offered and the cost of living in different locations with what you know about the salaries offered and the cost of living in your present location.

Many variables are used to calculate the cost-of-living index. Often included are housing, groceries, utilities, transportation, health care, clothing, and entertainment expenses. Right now you do not need to worry about the details associated with calculating a given index. The main purpose of this exercise is to help you understand that pay ranges for entry-level positions may not vary greatly, but the cost of living in different locations *can* vary tremendously.

· ·

If you lived in Pittsburgh, Pennsylvania, for example, and you were interested in working as a police patrol officer, based on average police patrol officer salaries in Pittsburgh, you would plan on earning $34,171 annually. But, let's say you're also thinking about moving to Oakland, California; Burlington, Vermont; or Little Rock, Arkansas. You know you can live on $34,171 in Pittsburgh, but you want to be able to maintain the same lifestyle this salary affords you in the other locations you're considering. How much will you have to earn in those locations to do this? Determining the cost of living for each city will show you.

Many websites, such as Yahoo!'s (http://verticals.yahoo .com/cities/salary.html), can assist you as you undertake this research. Using any search engine, enter the keywords *cost-of-living index*. Several choices will appear. Choose one site, and look for options such as cost-of-living analysis or cost-of-living comparator. Some sites will ask you to register and/or pay for the information, but most sites are free. Follow the instructions, and you will be able to create a table of information like the one shown here.

JOB: POLICE PATROL OFFICER		
City	Base Amount	Equivalent Salary
Pittsburgh, PA	$34,171	
Oakland, CA		$43,520
Burlington, VT		$29,013
Little Rock, AR		$21,921

At the time this comparison was done, you would have needed to earn $43,520 in Oakland, $29,013 in Burlington, and $21,921 in Little Rock to match the buying power of $34,171 in Pittsburgh.

If you would like to determine whether it's financially worthwhile to make any of these moves, one more piece of information is needed: the salaries of police patrol officers in these other cities. One website that contains brief job descriptions and salary information is salary.com (www.salary.com). The "Salary Wizard" will provide you with salary comparisons by city (displayed on a graph) along with links to additional resources such as other salary survey sites. Salary.com reports the following average salaries for a police patrol officer in the selected cities:

City	Actual Salary	Equivalent Salary Needed	Change in Buying Power
Oakland	$39,213	$43,520	− $4,307
Burlington	$32,672	$29,013	+ $3,659
Little Rock	$31,650	$21,921	+ $9,729

If you moved to Oakland and secured employment as a police patrol officer, you would not be able to maintain the same lifestyle that you would have in Pittsburgh, as your annual salary would be worth $4,307 less in buying power. However, if you moved to Burlington, you could expect to enhance your lifestyle. And look at Little Rock! Even though your actual salary as a police patrol officer is $2,521 less than it would be in Pittsburgh, your dollar will go significantly further in Little Rock. Remember, these figures change all the time, so be sure to undertake your own calculations.

• •

You can work through a similar exercise for any type of job you are considering and for many locations when current salary information is available. It will be worth your time to undertake this analysis if you are seriously considering a relocation. By doing so you will be able to make an informed choice.

STEP 4   Exploring Your Longer-Term Goals

There is no question that when we first begin working, our goals are to use our skills and education in a job that will reward us with employment, income, and status relative to the preparation we brought with us to this position. If we are not being paid as much as we feel we should for our level of education or if job demands don't provide the intellectual stimulation we had hoped for, we experience unhappiness and as a result often seek other employment.

Most jobs we consider "good" are those that fulfill our basic "lower-level" needs of security, food, clothing, shelter, income, and productive work. But even when our basic needs are met and our jobs are secure and productive, we as individuals are constantly changing. As we change, the demands and expectations we place on our jobs may change. Fortunately, some jobs grow and change with us, and this explains why some people are happy throughout many years in a job.

But more often people are bigger than the jobs they fill. We have more goals and needs than any job could satisfy. These are "higher-level" needs of self-esteem, companionship, affection, and an increasing desire to feel we are employing ourselves in the most effective way possible. Not all of these higher-level needs can be met through employment, but for as long as we are employed, we increasingly demand that our jobs play their part in moving us along the path to fulfillment.

Another obvious but important fact is that we change as we mature. Although our jobs also have the potential for change, they may not change as frequently or as markedly as we do. There are increasingly fewer one-job, one-employer careers; we must think about a work future that may involve voluntary or forced moves from employer to employer. Because of that very real possibility, we need to take advantage of the opportunities in each position we hold to acquire skills and competencies that will keep us viable and attractive as employees in a job market that not only is technology/computer dependent, but also is populated with more and more small, self-transforming organizations rather than the large, seemingly stable organizations of the past.

It may be difficult in the early stages of the job search to determine whether the path you are considering can meet these longer-term goals. Reading about career paths and individual career histories in your field can be very helpful in this regard. Meeting and talking with individuals further along in their careers can be enlightening as well. Older workers can provide valuable guidance on "self-managing" your career, which will become an increasingly valuable skill in the future. Some of these ideas may seem remote as you read this now, but you should be able to appreciate the need to ensure that you are growing, developing valuable new skills, and researching other employers who might be interested in your particular skills package.

••

If you are weighing a position in the courts system, perhaps starting as assistant clerk, you would gain a far better perspective of this career if you could talk to an
entry-level clerk, a more senior and experienced person
such as a clerk of the court, and finally, a senior management person such as a court administrator. Each will have
a different perspective, unique concerns, and an individual set of value priorities.

••

STEP 5   Enumerating Your Skill Base

In terms of the job search, skills can be thought of as capabilities that can
be developed in school, at work, or by volunteering and then used in specific job settings. Many studies have documented the kinds of skills that
employers seek in entry-level applicants. For example, some of the most
desired skills for individuals interested in the teaching profession are the ability to interact effectively with students one-on-one, to manage a classroom,
to adapt to varying situations as necessary, and to get involved in school activities. Business employers have also identified important qualities, including
enthusiasm for the employer's product or service, a businesslike mind, the
ability to follow written or oral instructions, the ability to demonstrate self-
control, the confidence to suggest new ideas, the ability to communicate with
all members of a group, an awareness of cultural differences, and loyalty, to
name just a few. You will find that many of these skills are also in the repertoire of qualities demanded in your college major.

To be successful in obtaining any given job, you must be able to demonstrate that you possess a certain mix of skills that will allow you to carry out
the duties required by that job. This skill mix will vary a great deal from job
to job; to determine the skills necessary for the jobs you are seeking, you
can read job advertisements or more generic job descriptions, such as those
found later in this book. If you want to be effective in the job search, you
must directly show employers that you possess the skills needed to be successful in filling the position. These skills will initially be described on your
resume and then discussed again during the interview process.

Skills are either general or specific. General skills are those that are developed throughout your college years by taking classes, being employed, and
getting involved in other related activities such as volunteer work or campus
organizations. General skills include the ability to read and write, to perform
computations, to think critically, and to communicate effectively. Specific

skills are also acquired on the job and in the classroom, but they allow you to complete tasks that require specialized knowledge. Computer programming, drafting, language translating, and copyediting are just a few examples of specific skills that may relate to a given job.

To develop a list of skills relevant to employers, you must first identify the general skills you possess, then list specific skills you have to offer, and, finally, examine which of these skills employers are seeking.

Identifying Your General Skills. Because you possess or will possess a college degree, employers will assume that you can read and write, perform certain basic computations, think critically, and communicate effectively. Employers will want to see that you have acquired these skills, and they will want to know which additional general skills you possess.

One way to begin identifying skills is to write an experiential diary. An experiential diary lists all the tasks you were responsible for completing for each job you've held and then outlines the skills required to do those tasks. You may list several skills for any given task. This diary allows you to distinguish between the tasks you performed and the underlying skills required to complete those tasks. Here's an example:

Tasks	Skills
Answering telephone	Effective use of language, clear diction, ability to direct inquiries, ability to solve problems
Waiting on tables	Poise under conditions of time and pressure, speed, accuracy, good memory, simultaneous completion of tasks, sales skills

For each job or experience you have participated in, develop a worksheet based on the example shown here. On a resume, you may want to describe these skills rather than simply listing tasks. Skills are easier for the employer to appreciate, especially when your experience is very different from the employment you are seeking. In addition to helping you identify general skills, this experiential diary will prepare you to speak more effectively in an interview about the qualifications you possess.

Identifying Your Specific Skills. It may be easier to identify your specific skills because you can definitely say whether you can speak other languages, program a computer, draft a map or diagram, or edit a document using appropriate symbols and terminology.

Using your experiential diary, identify the points in your history where you learned how to do something very specific, and decide whether you have a beginning, intermediate, or advanced knowledge of how to use that particular skill. Right now, be sure to list *every* specific skill you have, and don't consider whether you like using the skill. Write down a list of specific skills you have acquired and the level of competence you possess—beginning, intermediate, or advanced.

Relating Your Skills to Employers. You probably have thought about a couple of different jobs you might be interested in obtaining, and one way to begin relating the general and specific skills you possess to a potential employer's needs is to read actual advertisements for these types of positions (see Part Two for resources listing actual job openings).

••••••••••••••••••••••••••••••••••••••

For example, you may be interested in working as a youth counselor in a residential facility. A typical job listing may read, "Responsible for the supervision of juveniles during their daily activities, to include all aspects of daily living, treatment, and education. Provide daily structure for your living unit, provide discipline, and hold residents accountable for their actions. Assist teachers in the classroom. Responsible for the safety and security of the residents. Provide on-the-spot counseling and behavior correction. Implement intervention strategies and complete reports as necessary." If you then used any of a number of general sources of information that describe the job of youth counselor, you would find additional information and other specified duties.

Begin building a comprehensive list of required skills with the first job description you read. Exploring advertisements for and descriptions of several types of related positions will reveal an important core of skills that is necessary for obtaining the type of work in which you're interested. In building this list, include both general and specific skills.

Following is a sample list of skills needed to be successful as a youth counselor. These items were extracted from general resources and actual job listings:

JOB: YOUTH COUNSELOR

General Skills	Specific Skills
Work in a sometimes stressful environment	Maintain behavior log
	Mediate disputes
Supervise activities	Write incident reports
Discipline inappropriate behavior	Design activities
Adjust to changing shift schedules	Facilitate groups
Use a computer	Develop discharge plans
Work outdoors and indoors	Teach personal grooming
Maintain order	Provide counseling
Model appropriate behaviors	Issue instructions and procedures
Ensure safety	
Supervise housing maintenance	Implement intervention strategies
Provide structure	Assist with academics

On a separate sheet of paper, try to generate a comprehensive list of required skills for at least one job you are considering.

The list of general skills that you create for a given career path will be valuable for any number of jobs for which you may apply. Many of the specific skills would also be transferable to other types of positions. For example, developing discharge plans is a required specific skill for some youth counselors, and it would also be required for some parole positions.

● ●

Now review the list of skills that are required for jobs you are considering, and check off those skills that *you know you possess*. You should refer to these specific skills on the resume that you write for this type of job. See Chapter 2 for details on resume writing.

STEP 6   Recognizing Your Preferred Skills

In the previous section you developed a comprehensive list of skills that relate to particular career paths that are of interest to you. You can now relate these to skills that you prefer to use. We all use a wide range of skills (some researchers say individuals have a repertoire of about 500 skills), but we may not particularly be interested in using all of them in our work. There may be some skills that come to us more naturally or that we use successfully time and time again and that we want to continue to use; these are best described as our preferred skills. For this exercise use the list of skills that you created for the previous section, and decide which of them you are *most interested in using* in future work and how often you would like to use them. You might be interested in using some skills only occasionally, while others you would like to use more regularly. You probably also have skills that you hope you can use constantly.

As you examine job announcements, look for matches between this list of preferred skills and the qualifications described in the advertisements. These skills should be highlighted on your resume and discussed in job interviews.

STEP 7 Assessing Skills Needing Further Development

Previously you compiled a list of general and specific skills required for given positions. You already possess some of these skills; those that remain to be developed are your underdeveloped skills.

If you are just beginning the job search, there may be gaps between the qualifications required for some of the jobs you're considering and skills you possess. The thought of having to admit to and talk about these underdeveloped skills, especially in a job interview, is a frightening one. One way to put a healthy perspective on this subject is to target and relate your exploration of underdeveloped skills to the types of positions you are seeking. Recognizing these shortcomings and planning to overcome them with either on-the-job training or additional formal education can be a positive way to address the concept of underdeveloped skills.

On your worksheet or in your journal, make a list of up to five general or specific skills required for the positions you're interested in that you *don't currently possess.* For each item list an idea you have for specific action you could take to acquire that skill. Do some brainstorming to come up with possible actions. If you have a hard time generating ideas, talk to people currently working in this type of position, professionals in your college career services office, trusted friends, family members, or members of related professional associations.

If, for example, you are interested in a job for which you don't have some specific required experience, you could locate training opportunities such as classes or workshops offered through a local college or university, community college, or club or association that would help you build the level of expertise you need for the job.

You will notice in this book that many excellent positions for your major demand computer skills. While basic word processing has been something you've done all through college, you may be surprised at the additional computer skills required by employers. Many positions for college graduates will ask for some familiarity with spreadsheet programming, and frequently some database-management software familiarity is a job demand as well. Desktop publishing software, graphics programs, and basic Web-page design also pop up frequently in job ads for college graduates. If your degree program hasn't introduced you to a wide variety of computer applications, what are your options? If you're still in college, take what computer courses you can before you graduate. If you've already graduated, look at evening programs, continuing education courses, or tutorial programs that may be available commercially. Developing a modest level of expertise will encourage you to be more confident in suggesting to potential employers that you can continue to add to your skill base on the job.

In Chapter 5 on interviewing, we will discuss in detail how to effectively address questions about underdeveloped skills. Generally speaking, though, employers want genuine answers to these types of questions. They want you to reveal "the real you," and they also want to see how you answer difficult questions. In taking the positive, targeted approach discussed above, you show the employer that you are willing to continue to learn and that you have a plan for strengthening your job qualifications.

USING YOUR SELF-ASSESSMENT

Exploring entry-level career options can be an exciting experience if you have good resources available and will take the time to use them. Can you effectively complete the following tasks?

1. Understand your personality traits and relate them to career choices

2. Define your personal values

3. Determine your economic needs

4. Explore longer-term goals

5. Understand your skill base

6. Recognize your preferred skills

7. Express a willingness to improve on your underdeveloped skills

If so, then you can more meaningfully participate in the job search process by writing a more effective resume, finding job titles that represent work you are interested in doing, locating job sites that will provide the opportunity for you to use your strengths and skills, networking in an informed way, participating in focused interviews, getting the most out of follow-up contacts, and evaluating job offers to find those that create a good match between you and the employer. The remaining chapters in Part One guide you through these next steps in the job search process. For many job seekers, this process can take anywhere from three months to a year to implement. The time you will need to put into your job search will depend on the type of job you want and the geographic location where you'd like to work. Think of your effort as a job in itself, requiring you to set aside time each week to complete the needed work. Carefully undertaken efforts may reduce the time you need for your job search.

CHAPTER TWO

THE RESUME AND COVER LETTER

The task of writing a resume may seem overwhelming if you are unfamiliar with this type of document, but there are some easily understood techniques that can and should be used. This section was written to help you understand the purpose of the resume, the different types of resume formats available, and how to write the sections of information traditionally found on a resume. We will present examples and explanations that address questions frequently posed by people writing their first resume or updating an old resume.

Even within the formats and suggestions given, however, there are infinite variations. True, most resumes follow one of the outlines suggested, but you should feel free to adjust the resume to suit your needs and make it expressive of your life and experience.

WHY WRITE A RESUME?

The purpose of a resume is to convince an employer that you should be interviewed. Whether you're mailing, faxing, or E-mailing this document, you'll want to present enough information to show that you can make an immediate and valuable contribution to an organization. A resume is not an in-depth historical or legal document; later in the job search process you may be asked to document your entire work history on an application form and attest to its validity. The resume should, instead, highlight relevant information pertaining directly to the organization that will receive the document or to the type of position you are seeking.

We will discuss four types of resumes in this chapter: chronological, functional, targeted, and digital. The reasons for using one type of resume over another and the typical format for each are addressed in the following sections.

THE CHRONOLOGICAL RESUME

The chronological resume is the most common of the various resume formats and therefore the format that employers are most used to receiving. This type of resume is easy to read and understand because it details the chronological progression of jobs you have held. (See Exhibit 2.1.) It begins with your most recent employment and works back in time. If you have a solid work history or have experience that provided growth and development in your duties and responsibilities, a chronological resume will highlight these achievements. The typical elements of a chronological resume include the heading, a career objective, educational background, employment experience, activities, and references.

The Heading

The heading consists of your name, address, telephone number, and other means of contact. This may include a fax number, E-mail address, and your home-page address. If you are using a shared E-mail account or a parent's business fax, be sure to let others who use these systems know that you may receive important professional correspondence via these systems. You wouldn't want to miss a vital E-mail or fax! Likewise, if your resume directs readers to a personal home page on the Web, be certain it's a professional personal home page designed to be viewed and appreciated by a prospective employer. This may mean making substantial changes in the home page you currently mount on the Web.

We suggest that you spell out your full name in your resume heading and type it in all capital letters in bold type. After all, you are the focus of the resume! If you have a current as well as a permanent address and you include both in the heading, be sure to indicate until what date your current address will be valid. The two-letter state abbreviation should be the only abbreviation that appears in your heading. Don't forget to include the zip code with your address and the area code with your telephone number.

The Objective

As you formulate the wording for this part of your resume, keep the following points in mind.

Exhibit 2.1

CHRONOLOGICAL RESUME

BARBARA O'NEIL

Mungovan Hall   14 Fleming Street
University of Massachusetts–Lowell   Apartment 26A
Lowell, MA 01851   Key West, FL 98766
(603) 555-5555   (723) 555-5555
boneil@xxx.com
(until May 2001)

OBJECTIVE
To obtain a position as Victim Services Specialist.

EDUCATION
Bachelor of Science in Criminal Justice
University of Massachusetts–Lowell
May 2001
Minor: Human Relations

HONORS/AWARDS
Chancellor's Scholar, Spring/Fall Semesters, 2000
Who's Who Among Universities and Colleges, 2001–2002
Greater Lowell Rotary Award—Student of the Year, 1999

RELATED COURSES
Investigative Procedures   Report Writing
Police Operations   Deviant Psychology

EXPERIENCE
Internship: Rosie's Place, Boston, Massachusetts, 2000–2001
Credit-bearing, structured academic internship at this long-established shelter for
homeless women. Provided counseling to indigent women and developed contacts
among several Boston-area social service agencies for referrals. Designed and
implemented "Rosie's Closet"—a new program to provide clean, attractive clothing
to promote self-esteem and a renewed interest in personal grooming. Arranged for
local department stores to donate cosmetics.

continued

Nursing Home Aide: Pleasant View Home for the Aged, Billerica, Massachusetts, 1999–2000

Performed general aide duties, including assisting residents in personal grooming, feeding, delivering meals, changing bed linen, and some light housekeeping. Assisted ambulatory patients with daily exercise and frequently read to patients and contributed to general therapeutic atmosphere.

Waitress: Captain John's Seafood Restaurant, Key West, Florida, 1998–1999

Summer income-production job in one of the city's most prominent eateries. Fast-paced, high turnover of principally a tourist market. Provided quality customer service, resolved disputes, and scheduled day staff.

ACTIVITIES

Center for Gender Resources—student staff volunteer for three years.
Peer Tutor—paid position at the college academic resource center. Provided tutoring and assistance in study skills for criminal justice majors.

REFERENCES

Available upon request.

The Objective Focuses the Resume. Without a doubt this is the most challenging part of the resume for most resume writers. Even for individuals who have decided on a career path, it can be difficult to encapsulate all they want to say in one or two brief sentences. For job seekers who are unfocused or unclear about their intentions, trying to write this section can inhibit the entire resume writing process.

Recruiters tell us time and time again that the objective creates a frame of reference for them. It helps them see how you express your goals and career focus. In addition, the statement may indicate in what ways you can immediately benefit an organization. Given the importance of the objective, every point covered in the resume should relate to it. If information doesn't relate, it should be omitted. You'll file a number of resume variations in your computer. There's no excuse for not being able to tailor a resume to individual employers or specific positions.

Choose an Appropriate Length. Because of the brevity necessary for a resume, you should keep the objective as short as possible. Although objectives of only four or five words often don't show much direction, objectives that take three full lines could be viewed as too wordy and might possibly be ignored.

Consider Which Type of Objective Statement You Will Use. There are many ways to state an objective, but generally there are four forms this statement can take: (1) a very general statement; (2) a statement focused on a specific position; (3) a statement focused on a specific industry; or (4) a summary of your qualifications. In our contacts with employers, we often hear that many resumes don't exhibit any direction or career goals, so we suggest avoiding general statements when possible.

1. General Objective Statement. General objective statements look like the following:

- An entry-level educational programming coordinator position

- An entry-level marketing position

This type of objective would be useful if you know what type of job you want but you're not sure which industries interest you.

2. Position-Focused Objective. Following are examples of objectives focusing on a specific position:

- To obtain the position of conference coordinator at State College

- To obtain a position as assistant editor at *Time* magazine

When a student applies for an advertised job opening, this type of focus can be very effective. The employer knows that the applicant has taken the time to tailor the resume specifically for this position.

3. Industry-Focused Objective. Focusing on a particular industry in an objective could be stated as follows:

- To begin a career as a sales representative in the cruise line industry

4. Summary of Qualifications Statement. The summary of qualifications can be used instead of an objective or in conjunction with an objective. The purpose of this type of statement is to highlight relevant qualifications gained through a variety of experiences. This type of statement is often used by individuals with extensive and diversified work experience. An example of a qualifications statement follows:

....

A degree in criminal justice and four years of progressively increasing job responsibility in the telecommunications industry have prepared me to begin a career as a computer crime analyst with a propriety security firm that values hard work and dedication.

....

Support Your Objective. A resume that contains any one of these types of objective statements should then go on to demonstrate why you are qualified to get the position. Listing academic degrees can be one way to indicate qualifications. Another demonstration would be in the way previous experiences, both volunteer and paid, are described. Without this kind of documentation in the body of the resume, the objective looks unsupported. Think of the resume as telling a connected story about you. All the elements should work together to form a coherent picture that ideally should relate to your statement of objective.

Education

This section of your resume should indicate the exact name of the degree you will receive or have received, spelled out completely with no abbreviations. The degree is generally listed after the objective, followed by the institution name and location, and then the month and year of graduation. This section could also include your academic minor, grade point average (GPA), and appearance on the Dean's List or President's List.

If you have enough space, you might want to include a section listing courses related to the field in which you are seeking work. The best use of a "related courses" section would be to list some course work that is not traditionally associated with the major. Perhaps you took several computer courses outside your degree that will be helpful and related to the job prospects you are entertaining. Several education section examples are shown here:

....

- Bachelor of Science in Criminology, December 2002
  University of Arizona
  Tucson, Arizona

- Bachelor of Science in Interdisciplinary Studies, a self-designed program concentrating in criminal justice and computer science, San Diego State University, San Diego, California, May 2001

■ **Bachelor of Arts in Psychology, State College,**
Durham, New Hampshire, May 2003
Minor: Criminal Justice

An example of a format for a related courses section
follows:

RELATED COURSES

Social Problems	Juvenile Justice
Human Behavior	Criminal Justice Administration
Criminal Law	Constitutional Law

Experience

The experience section of your resume should be the most substantial part
and should take up most of the space on the page. Employers want to see
what kind of work history you have. They will look at your range of experiences, longevity in jobs, and specific tasks you are able to complete. This
section may also be called "work experience," "related experience," "employment history," or "employment." No matter what you call this section, some
important points to remember are the following:

1. **Describe your duties** as they relate to the position you are seeking.

2. **Emphasize major responsibilities** and indicate increases in
   responsibility. Include all relevant employment experiences: summer,
   part-time, internships, cooperative education, or self-employment.

3. **Emphasize skills**, especially those that transfer from one situation to
   another. The fact that you coordinated a student organization,
   chaired meetings, supervised others, and managed a budget leads one
   to suspect that you could coordinate other things as well.

4. **Use descriptive job titles** that provide information about what you
   did. A "Student Intern" should be more specifically stated as, for
   example, "Magazine Operations Intern." "Volunteer" is also too
   general; a title such as "Peer Writing Tutor" would be more
   appropriate.

5. **Create word pictures** by using active verbs to start sentences.
   Describe *results* you have produced in the work you have done.

A limp description would say something such as the following: "My duties included helping with production, proofreading, and editing. I used a word-processing package to alter text." An action statement would be stated as follows: "Coordinated and assisted in the creative marketing of brochures and seminar promotions, becoming proficient in Word."

Remember, an accomplishment is simply a result, a final measurable product that people can relate to. A duty is not a result; it is an obligation—every job holder has duties. For an effective resume, list as many results as you can. To make the most of the limited space you have and to give your description impact, carefully select appropriate and accurate descriptors from the list of action words in Exhibit 2.2.

Exhibit 2.2

RESUME ACTION VERBS

Achieved	Controlled	Explained
Acted	Converted	Facilitated
Administered	Coordinated	Finalized
Advised	Corrected	Generated
Analyzed	Created	Handled
Assessed	Decreased	Headed
Assisted	Defined	Helped
Attained	Demonstrated	Identified
Balanced	Designed	Illustrated
Budgeted	Determined	Implemented
Calculated	Developed	Improved
Collected	Directed	Increased
Communicated	Documented	Influenced
Compiled	Drafted	Informed
Completed	Edited	Initiated
Composed	Eliminated	Innovated
Conceptualized	Ensured	Instituted
Condensed	Established	Instructed
Conducted	Estimated	Integrated
Consolidated	Evaluated	Interpreted
Constructed	Examined	Introduced

Learned	Presented	Scheduled
Lectured	Processed	Selected
Led	Produced	Served
Maintained	Projected	Showed
Managed	Proposed	Simplified
Mapped	Provided	Sketched
Marketed	Qualified	Sold
Met	Quantified	Solved
Modified	Questioned	Staffed
Monitored	Realized	Streamlined
Negotiated	Received	Studied
Observed	Recommended	Submitted
Obtained	Recorded	Summarized
Operated	Reduced	Systematized
Organized	Reinforced	Tabulated
Participated	Reported	Tested
Performed	Represented	Transacted
Planned	Researched	Updated
Predicted	Resolved	Verified
Prepared	Reviewed	

Here are some traits that employers tell us they like to see:

- Teamwork

- Energy and motivation

- Learning and using new skills

- Versatility

- Critical thinking

- Understanding how profits are created

- Organizational acumen

- Communicating directly and clearly, in both writing and speaking

- Risk taking

- Willingness to admit mistakes

- High personal standards

SOLUTIONS TO FREQUENTLY ENCOUNTERED PROBLEMS

Repetitive Employment with the Same Employer

EMPLOYMENT: The Foot Locker, Portland, Oregon. Summer 2001, 2002, 2003. Initially employed in high school as salesclerk. Due to successful performance, asked to return next two summers at higher pay with added responsibility. Ranked as the #2 salesperson the first summer and #1 the next two summers. Assisted in arranging eye-catching retail displays; served as manager of other summer workers during owner's absence.

A Large Number of Jobs

EMPLOYMENT: Recent Hospitality Industry Experience: Affiliated with four upscale hotel/restaurant complexes (September 2001–February 2004), where I worked part- and full-time as a waiter, bartender, disc jockey, and bookkeeper to produce income for college.

Several Positions with the Same Employer

EMPLOYMENT: Coca-Cola Bottling Co., Burlington, Vermont, 2001–2004. In four years, I received three promotions, each with increased pay and responsibility.

Summer Sales Coordinator: Promoted to hire, train, and direct efforts of add-on staff of fifteen college-age route salespeople hired to meet summer peak demand for product.

Sales Administrator: Promoted to run home office sales desk, managing accounts and associated delivery schedules for professional sales force of ten people. Intensive phone work, daily interaction with all personnel, and strong knowledge of product line required.

Route Salesperson: Summer employment to travel and tourism industry sites that use Coke products. Met specific schedule demands, used good communication skills with wide variety of customers, and demonstrated strong selling skills. Named salesperson of the month for July and August of that year.

QUESTIONS RESUME WRITERS OFTEN ASK

How Far Back Should I Go in Terms of Listing Past Jobs?

Usually, listing three or four jobs should suffice. If you did something back in high school that has a bearing on your future aspirations for employment, by all means list the job. As you progress through your college career, high school jobs will be replaced on the resume by college employment.

Should I Differentiate Between Paid and Nonpaid Employment?

Most employers are not initially concerned about how much you were paid. They are anxious to know how much responsibility you held in your past employment. There is no need to specify that your work was as a volunteer if you had significant responsibilities.

How Should I Represent My Accomplishments or Work-Related Responsibilities?

Succinctly, but fully. In other words, give the employer enough information to arouse curiosity but not so much detail that you leave nothing to the imagination. Besides, some jobs merit more lengthy explanations than others. Be sure to convey any information that can give an employer a better understanding of the depth of your involvement at work. Did you supervise others? How many? Did your efforts result in a more efficient operation? How much did you increase efficiency? Did you handle a budget? How much? Were you promoted in a short time? Did you work two jobs at once or fifteen hours per week after high school? Where appropriate, quantify.

Should the Work Section Always Follow the Education Section on the Resume?

Always lead with your strengths. If your education closely relates to the employment you now seek, put this section after the objective. Or, if you are weak on the academic side but have a surplus of good work experiences, consider reversing the order of your sections to lead with employment, followed by education.

How Should I Present My Activities, Honors, Awards, Professional Societies, and Affiliations?

This section of the resume can add valuable information for an employer to consider if used correctly. The rule of thumb for information in this section is to include only those activities that are in some way relevant to the objective stated on your resume. If you can draw a valid connection between your activities and your objective, include them; if not, leave them out.

Granted, this is hard to do. Playing center on the championship basketball team or serving as coordinator of the biggest homecoming parade ever held are roles that have meaning for you and represent personal accomplishments you'd like to share. But the resume is a brief document, and the information you provide on it should help the employer make a decision about your job eligibility. Including personal details can be confusing and could hurt your candidacy. Limiting your activity list to a few significant experiences can be very effective.

If you are applying for a position as a safety officer, your certificate in Red Cross lifesaving skills or CPR would be related and valuable. You would want to include it. If, however, you are applying for a job as a junior account executive in an advertising agency, that information would be unrelated and superfluous. Leave it out.

Professional affiliations and honors should all be listed; especially important are those related to your job objective. Social clubs and activities need not be a part of your resume unless you hold a significant office or you are looking for a position related to your membership. Be aware that most prospective employers' principal concerns are related to your employability, not your social life. If you have any, publications can be included as an addendum to your resume.

The focus of the resume is your experience and education. It is not necessary to describe your involvement in activities. However, if your resume needs to be lengthened, this section provides the freedom either to expand on or mention only briefly the contributions you have made. If you have made significant contributions (e.g., an officer of an organization or a particularly long tenure with a group), you may choose to describe them in more detail. It is not always necessary to include the dates of your memberships with your activities the way you would include job dates.

There are various ways in which to present additional information. You may give this section a number of different titles. Assess what you want to list, and then use an appropriate title. Do not use "extracurricular activities." This terminology is scholastic, not professional, and therefore not appropriate. The following are two examples:

■ ACTIVITIES: Society for Technical Communication, Student Senate, Student Admissions Representative, Senior Class Officer

■ ACTIVITIES:
   • Society for Technical Communication Member
   • Student Senator
   • Student Admissions Representative
   • Senior Class Officer

The position you are looking for will determine what you should or should not include. *Always* look for a correlation between the activity and the prospective job.

How Should I Handle References?

The use of references is considered a part of the interview process, and they should never be listed on a resume. You would always provide references to a potential employer if requested to, so it is not even necessary to include this section on the resume if space does not permit. If space is available, it is acceptable to include one of the following statements:

- REFERENCES: Furnished upon request.

- REFERENCES: Available upon request.

Individuals used as references must be protected from unnecessary contacts. By including names on your resume, you leave your references unprotected. Overuse and abuse of your references will lead to less-than-supportive comments. Protect your references by giving out their names only when you are being considered seriously as a candidate for a given position.

THE FUNCTIONAL RESUME

The functional resume departs from a chronological resume in that it organizes information by specific accomplishments in various settings: previous jobs, volunteer work, associations, and so forth. This type of resume permits you to stress the substance of your experiences rather than the position titles you have held. (See Exhibit 2.3.) You should consider using a functional resume if you have held a series of similar jobs that relied on the same skills or abilities.

The Objective

A functional resume begins with an objective that can be used to focus the contents of the resume.

Specific Accomplishments

Specific accomplishments are listed on this type of resume. Examples of the types of headings used to describe these capabilities might include research, computer skills, teaching, communication, production, management, marketing, or writing. The headings you choose will directly relate to your experience and the tasks that you carried out. Each accomplishment section contains statements related to your experience in that category, regardless of when or where it occurred. Organize the accomplishments and the related tasks you describe in their order of importance as related to the position you seek.

Exhibit 2.3

FUNCTIONAL RESUME

CARLOS HIDALGO

Student Apartment 12   12 Cornwall Street
Michigan State University   Rocky River, OH 44116
Detroit, MI 36754   (212) 555-5555
(216) 555-5555
Fax (216) 555-5556
chidalgo@xxx.com
(until May 2003)

OBJECTIVE

An entry-level court analyst position that allows me to use my problem-solving, computing, and researching skills.

CAPABILITIES

- Effective researcher
- Analytical problem solver
- Experienced software and hardware user

SELECTED ACCOMPLISHMENTS

Effective Researcher: Researched current and accurate sources of information for ongoing projects. Designed survey instruments and developed methods and systems for processing survey data results for twenty-three different projects. Performed numerous short-term research projects based on queries from staff lawyers, judges, and other court officials. Prepared interim reports and executive summaries.

Analytical Problem Solver: Comfortable with problems and enjoy creative, solution-focused thinking. Able to see problems from multiple perspectives and can frequently provide numerous alternatives. Enjoy manipulating database information to reveal relationships and causality.

Experienced Software and Hardware User: Used SPSS and SAS software packages to process data; manipulated digitizers, plotters, and graphics software to create graphics for reports; utilized mainframe and personal computing hardware; comfortable with a variety of ancillary equipment, including scanners, computerized video accessories, and personal memo pads.

AWARDS
Graduated with Honors
Departmental Award for Student Leadership in Criminal Justice
City of Rocky River College Scholarship Award

EMPLOYMENT HISTORY
Research Assistant, Center for Urban Studies, Michigan State University,
Detroit, Michigan, 2001–2003
Library Worker, Putnam, Putnam and Bolles P.A., Rocky River, Ohio,
Summers, 1999–Present

EDUCATION
Bachelor of Science in Justice Administration
Michigan State University, Detroit, Michigan
May 2003

REFERENCES
Provided upon request.

Experience or Employment History

Your actual work experience is condensed and placed after the specific accomplishments section. It simply lists dates of employment, position titles, and employer names.

Education

The education section of a functional resume is identical to that of the chronological resume, but it does not carry the same visual importance because it is placed near the bottom of the page.

References

Because actual reference names are never listed on a resume, a statement of reference availability is optional.

THE TARGETED RESUME

The targeted resume focuses on specific work-related capabilities you can bring to a given position within an organization. (See Exhibit 2.4.) It should be sent to an individual within the organization who makes hiring decisions about the position you are seeking.

The Objective
The objective on this type of resume should be targeted to a specific career or position. It should be supported by the capabilities, accomplishments, and achievements documented in the resume.

Capabilities
Capabilities should be statements that illustrate tasks you believe you are capable of based on your accomplishments, achievements, and work history. Each should relate to your targeted career or position. You can stress your qualifications rather than your employment history. This approach may require research to obtain an understanding of the nature of the work involved and the capabilities necessary to carry out that work.

Accomplishments/Achievements
This section relates the various activities you have been involved in to the job market. These experiences may include previous jobs, extracurricular activities at school, internships, and part-time summer work.

Experience
Your work history should be listed in abbreviated form and may include position title, employer name, and employment dates.

Education
Because this type of resume is directed toward a specific job target and an individual's related experience, the education section is not prominently located at the top of the resume as is done on the chronological resume.

DIGITAL RESUMES

Today's employers have to manage an enormous number of resumes. One of the most frequent complaints the writers of this series hear from students is the failure of employers to even acknowledge the receipt of a resume and cover letter. Frequently, the reason for this poor response or nonresponse is the volume of applications received for every job. In an attempt to better manage the considerable labor investment involved in processing large numbers of resumes, many employers are requiring digital submission of resumes. There are two types of digital resumes: those that can be E-mailed or posted to a website, called *electronic resumes*, and those that can be "read" by a com-

Exhibit 2.4

TARGETED RESUME

AMANDA BAILEY

Redbud Apartments 223
Middlebury College
Middlebury, VT 09878
(802) 555-5555
Fax (802) 555-5556
manda@xxx.com
(until May 2004)

43 London Street
Rosendale, NY 12472
(914) 555-5555

JOB TARGET
Probation Officer with the State of New York

CAPABILITIES
• Comfortable in diverse settings
• Able to communicate effectively to diverse audiences
• Bilingual Spanish/English
• Strong background in community resources
• Skilled writer in a variety of formats

ACHIEVEMENTS
• Sharpshooter Prize, College Gun Club
• Student Assistant Teacher, Tai Kwan Do
• Certified in Lifesaving, CPR, and First Aid
• Appointed to campus student mediation group

WORK HISTORY

2003–present
(part-time)
Practicum, City of Burlington (VT) Police Department
Assigned to Juvenile Division to assist in writing probation plans

2001–present
Staff, Stand Firm Fitness, Middlebury, Vermont
Assist personal trainers in providing services to a variety of clients

2001–2002
Volunteer, Burlington Children's Hospital
Part-time, evenings assisting with children's programming; provided some translation services when requested

continued

2000   Tutor, Academic Resources
                Provided study assistance and language practice for students
                enrolled in Spanish courses

EDUCATION
Bachelor of Science in Criminal Justice, 2004
Middlebury College
Middlebury, Vermont
Minor: Sociology

---

puter, commonly called *scannable resumes*. Though the format may be a bit different from the traditional "paper" resume, the goal of both types of digital resumes is the same—to get you an interview! These resumes must be designed to be "technologically friendly." What that basically means to you is that they should be free of graphics and fancy formatting.

Electronic Resumes

Sometimes referred to as plain-text resumes, electronic resumes are designed to be E-mailed to an employer or posted to a commercial Internet database such as CareerMosaic.com, America's Job Bank (www.ajb.dni.us), or Monster.com.

Some technical considerations:

- Electronic resumes must be written in American Standard Code for Information Interchange (ASCII), which is simply a plain-text format. These characters are universally recognized so that every computer can accurately read and understand them. To create an ASCII file of your current resume, open your document, then save it as a text or ASCII file. This will eliminate all formatting. Edit as needed using your computer's text editor application.

- Use a standard-width typeface. Courier is a good choice because it is the font associated with ASCII in most systems.

- Use a font size of 11 to 14 points. A 12-point font is considered standard.

- Your margin should be left-justified.

- Do not exceed sixty-five characters per line because the word-wrap function doesn't operate in ASCII.

Exhibit 2.5

DIGITAL RESUME

ANDREW TYLER ⟵——————————— Put your name at the
117 Stetson Avenue   top on its own line.
Small School, NV 02459 ——————— Put your phone number
508-555-5555 ⟵   on its own line.
atyler@xxx.com ⟵——————————— Use a standard-width
                                                typeface.

KEYWORD SUMMARY
B.S. Criminal Justice, 2002
Law Enforcement, Corrections,   Keywords make your
Detention Officer, Jail, Security,   resume easier to find in
Weapons Training, Self-Defense,   a database.
Police Officer

EDUCATION ⟵————————————— Capital letters emphasize
Bachelor of Science, Criminal Justice, 2002   headings.
Small State College, Small School, Nevada
Minor: Human Behavior
G.P.A.: 3.0/4.0

RELATED COURSES
Criminal Investigation and Evidence
Courts and Criminal Procedure   No line should exceed
Criminology   sixty-five characters.
Corrections

SKILL TRAINING   End each line by hitting
Certified EMT, Lifesaving, First Aid,   the ENTER key.
CPR, Self-Defense, Triathlete

EXPERIENCE
Pinkerton Security Services, 2001–2002
* Numerous assignments over two years   Use a space between
* Licensed by the state as security guard   asterisk and text.
* Promoted and increase in salary
* Staff training in investigations

continued

Student Representative to Judicial Council, 1999–2001
* Participated in student conduct hearings
* Drafted sanctions document
* Presented to student groups

House Painting, 2000
* Established business with friends

COLLEGE ATHLETICS
* Played on inter-hall sports teams
* Cocaptain of the football team

REFERENCES
Available upon request.

++ Willing to relocate ++ ◄——————— Asterisks and plus signs replace bullets.

- Do not use boldface, italics, underlining, bullets, or various font sizes. Instead, use asterisks, plus signs, or all capital letters when you want to emphasize something.

- Avoid graphics and shading.

- Use as many "keywords" as you possibly can. These are words or phrases usually relating to skills or experience that either are specifically used in the job announcement or are popular buzzwords in the industry.

- Minimize abbreviations.

- Your name should be the first line of text.

- Conduct a "test run" by E-mailing your resume to yourself and a friend before you send it to the employer. See how it transmits, and make any changes you need to. Continue to test it until it's exactly how you want it to look.

- Unless an employer specifically requests that you send the resume in the form of an attachment, don't. Employers can encounter problems opening a document as an attachment, and there are always viruses to consider.

- Don't forget your cover letter. Send it along with your resume as a single message.

Scannable Resumes

Some companies are relying on technology to narrow the candidate pool for available job openings. Electronic Applicant Tracking uses imaging to scan, sort, and store resume elements in a database. Then, through OCR (Optical Character Recognition) software, the computer scans the resumes for keywords and phrases. To have the best chance at getting an interview, you want to increase the number of "hits"—matches of your skills, abilities, experience, and education to those the computer is scanning for—your resume will get. You can see how critical using the right keywords is for this type of resume.

Technical considerations include:

- Again, do not use boldface (newer systems may read this OK, but many older ones won't), italics, underlining, bullets, shading, graphics, or multiple font sizes. Instead, for emphasis, use asterisks, plus signs, or all capital letters. Minimize abbreviations.

- Use a popular typeface such as Courier, Helvetica, Ariel, or Palatino. Avoid decorative fonts.

- Font size should be between 11 and 14 points.

- Do not compress the spacing between letters.

- Use horizontal and vertical lines sparingly; the computer may misread them as the letters L or I.

- Left-justify the text.

- Do not use parentheses or brackets around telephone numbers, and be sure your phone number is on its own line of text.

- Your name should be the first line of text and on its own line. If your resume is longer than one page, be sure to put your name on the top of all pages.

- Use a traditional resume structure. The chronological format may work best.

- Use nouns that are skill-focused, such as *management, writer,* and *programming.* This is different from traditional paper resumes, which use action-oriented verbs.

- Laser printers produce the finest copies. Avoid dot-matrix printers.

- Use standard, light-colored paper with text on one side only. Since the higher the contrast, the better, your best choice is black ink on white paper.

- Always send original copies. If you must fax, set the fax on fine mode, not standard.

- Do not staple or fold your resume. This can confuse the computer.

- Before you send your scannable resume, be certain the employer uses this technology. If you can't determine this, you may want to send two versions (scannable and traditional) to be sure your resume gets considered.

RESUME PRODUCTION AND OTHER TIPS

An ink-jet printer is the preferred option for printing your resume. Begin by printing just a few copies. You may find a small error or you may simply want to make some changes, and it is less frustrating and less expensive if you print in small batches.

Resume paper color should be carefully chosen. You should consider the types of employers who will receive your resume and the types of positions for which you are applying. Use white or ivory paper for traditional or conservative employers or for higher-level positions.

Black ink on sharp, white paper can be harsh on the reader's eyes. Think about an ivory or cream paper that will provide less contrast and be easier to read. Pink, green, and blue tints should generally be avoided.

Many resume writers buy packages of matching envelopes and cover sheet stationery that, although not absolutely necessary, help convey a professional impression.

If you'll be producing many cover letters at home, be sure you have high-quality printing equipment. Learn standard envelope formats for business, and retain a copy of every cover letter you send out. You can use the copies to take notes of any telephone conversations that may occur.

If attending a job fair, either carry a briefcase or place your resume in a nicely covered legal-size pad holder.

THE COVER LETTER

The cover letter provides you with the opportunity to tailor your resume by telling the prospective employer how you can be a benefit to the organization. It allows you to highlight aspects of your background that are not already discussed in your resume and that might be especially relevant to the organization you are contacting or to the position you are seeking. Every resume should have a cover letter enclosed when you send it out. Unlike the resume, which may be mass-produced, a cover letter is most effective when it is individually prepared and focused on the particular requirements of the organization in question.

A good cover letter should supplement the resume and motivate the reader to review the resume. The format shown in Exhibit 2.6 is only a suggestion to help you decide what information to include in writing a cover letter.

Begin the cover letter with your street address twelve lines down from the top. Leave three to five lines between the date and the name of the person to whom you are addressing the cover letter. Make sure you leave one blank line between the salutation and the body of the letter and between paragraphs. After typing "Sincerely," leave four blank lines and type your name. This should leave plenty of room for your signature. A sample cover letter is shown in Exhibit 2.7.

The following guidelines will help you write good cover letters:

1. Be sure to type your letter neatly; ensure there are no misspellings.

2. Avoid unusual typefaces, such as script.

3. Address the letter to an individual, using the person's name and title. To obtain this information, call the company. If answering a blind newspaper advertisement, address the letter "To Whom It May Concern" or omit the salutation.

4. Be sure your cover letter directly indicates the position you are applying for and tells why you are qualified to fill it.

5. Send the original letter, not a photocopy, with your resume. Keep a copy for your records.

6. Make your cover letter no more than one page.

7. Include a phone number where you can be reached.

8. Avoid trite language and have someone read the letter over to react to its tone, content, and mechanics.

9. For your own information, record the date you send out each letter and resume.

Exhibit 2.6

COVER LETTER FORMAT

Your Street Address
Your Town, State, Zip
Phone Number
Fax Number
E-mail

Date

Name
Title
Organization
Address

Dear _____:

First Paragraph. In this paragraph state the reason for the letter, name the specific position or type of work you are applying for, and indicate from which resource (career services office, website, newspaper, contact, employment service) you learned of this opening. The first paragraph can also be used to inquire about future openings.

Second Paragraph. Indicate why you are interested in this position, the company, or its products or services, and what you can do for the employer. If you are a recent graduate, explain how your academic background makes you a qualified candidate. Try not to repeat the same information found in the resume.

Third Paragraph. Refer the reader to the enclosed resume for more detailed information.

Fourth Paragraph. In this paragraph say what you will do to follow up on your letter. For example, state that you will call by a certain date to set up an interview or to find out if the company will be recruiting in your area. Finish by indicating your willingness to answer any questions they may have. Be sure you have provided your phone number.

Sincerely,

Type your name
Enclosure

Exhibit 2.7

SAMPLE COVER LETTER

143 Random Way
Shreveport, LA 71130
(318) 555-5555
Fax (318) 555-5556
rmcneal@xxx.com
March 15, 2002

Ms. Nyla Crane
Director of Human Resources
On Target Supplies
279 Main Street
Shreveport, LA 71130

Dear Ms. Crane:

In May of 2003, I will graduate from Middlesex Community College with an associate's degree in criminal justice. I read of your sales opening on the Corrections Connection website, and I am very interested in the possibilities it offers.

The job posting indicated that you are looking for knowledgeable individuals with exceptional communication skills. I believe that I possess those qualities. I've worked the past two summers at one of downtown's busiest shoe stores, and that experience has sharpened my communication skills. Providing choices, listening, satisfying customer requests, and resolving problems have demonstrated to me that I have some real skills in this area. At college, in addition to my criminal justice courses, I took a basic marketing course and another course in public speaking. I think the combination of these experiences and my education should prove valuable in the job you're hoping to fill.

As you can see by the enclosed resume, I was an admissions representative for two years at college. This was not a volunteer position but one for which I was selected by a committee through an interview process. The opportunity to present my school to different groups and prospective students and their parents allowed me to practice and refine my presentation skills.

continued

I would like to meet with you to discuss how my strengths and interests would be consistent with your needs. I will contact your office next week to discuss the possibility of an interview. In the meantime, if you have any questions or require additional information, please call me at home, (318) 555-5555.

Sincerely,

Ryan McNeal
Enclosure

CHAPTER THREE

RESEARCHING CAREERS

A common question asked of career counselors is "What can I do with my degree?" Criminal justice majors often struggle with the variety of choices they have in a field that is growing each year. Unlike their fellow students who may be pursuing narrow career goals, such as accounting or graphic design, the criminal justice major is presented with many career paths. Choices range from a behind-the-scenes legal researcher to the more in-your-face role of a drug enforcement agent. An accountant becomes an accountant. An education major becomes a teacher. But how will you choose to use your criminal justice degree?

WHAT DO THEY CALL THE JOB YOU WANT?

There is every reason to be unaware. One reason for confusion is perhaps a mistaken assumption that a college education provides job training. In most cases it does not. Of course, applied fields such as engineering, management, or education provide specific skills for the workplace, whereas most liberal arts degrees simply provide an education. A liberal arts education exposes you to numerous fields of study and teaches you quantitative reasoning, critical thinking, writing, and speaking, all of which can be successfully applied to a number of different job fields. But it still remains up to you to choose a job field and to learn how to articulate the benefits of your education in a way the employer will appreciate.

As indicated in Chapter 1 on self-assessment, your first task is to understand and value what parts of that education you enjoyed and were good at and would continue to enjoy in your life's work. Did your writing courses encourage you in your ability to express yourself in writing? Did you enjoy the research process, and did you find that your work was well received? Did you enjoy any of your required quantitative subjects such as algebra or calculus?

The answers to questions such as these provide clues to skills and interests you bring to the employment market over and above the credential of your degree. In fact, it is not an overstatement to suggest that most employers who demand a college degree immediately look beyond that degree to you as a person and your own individual expression of what you like to do and think you can do for them, regardless of your major.

Collecting Job Titles

The world of employment is a big place, and even seasoned veterans of the job hunt can be surprised about what jobs are to be found in what organizations. You need to become a bit of an explorer and adventurer and be willing to try a variety of techniques to begin a list of possible occupations that might use your talents and education. Once you have a list of possibilities that you are interested in and qualified for, you can move on to find out what kinds of organizations have these job titles.

• •

Not every organization seeking to hire a new member of its police force may be equally desirable to you. Some environments may be more attractive to you than others. A criminal justice major considering a job in law enforcement could work in a small rural town, a midsize college town, or a large metropolitan area. And the choices don't end there! There are police jobs for campus police forces, railroads, airports, port authorities, and a host of other jurisdictions. Each of these environments presents a different culture with associated norms in the pace of work, the degree of risk and types of crime, and the professionalism of your associates and senior management. Although the job title may be the same, not all these police jobs may present the same "fit" for you.

> If you majored in criminal justice and enjoyed the
> investigation classes and lab work you did as part of your
> degree and developed some good research and reporting
> skills, you may think a detective assignment would be a
> good possible goal. You're even considering graduate school
> and a law degree sometime down the road. But criminal
> justice majors with these skills also become FBI agents,
> forensic specialists, police chiefs, private investigators, and
> criminal justice consultants. Each of these job titles brings
> its own array of possible settings.

Take training, for example. Trainers write policy and procedural manuals and actively teach to assist all levels of employees in mastering various tasks and work-related systems. Trainers exist in all large corporations, banks, consumer goods manufacturers, medical diagnostic equipment firms, sales organizations, and any organization that has processes or materials that need to be presented to and learned by the staff.

In reading job descriptions or want ads for any of these positions, you would find your four-year degree a "must." However, the academic major might be less important than your own individual skills in critical thinking, analysis, report writing, public presentations, and interpersonal communication. Even more important than thinking or knowing you have certain skills are your ability to express those skills concretely and the examples you use to illustrate them to an employer.

The best beginning to a job search is to create a list of job titles you might want to pursue, learn more about the nature of the jobs behind those titles, and then discover what kinds of employers hire for those positions. In the following section we'll teach you how to build a job title directory to use in your job search.

Developing a Job Title Directory That Works for You

A job title directory is simply a complete list of all the job titles you are interested in, are intrigued by, or think you are qualified for. After combining the understanding gained through self-assessment with your own individual interests and the skills and talents you've acquired with your degree, you'll soon start to read and recognize a number of occupational titles that seem right for you. There are several resources you can use to develop your list, including computer searches, books, and want ads.

Computerized Interest Inventories. One way to begin your search is to identify a number of jobs that call for your degree and the particular skills and
interests you identified as part of the self-assessment process. There are
excellent interactive career-guidance programs on the market to help you
produce such selected lists of possible job titles. Most of these are available
at high schools and colleges and at some larger town and city libraries. Two
of the industry leaders are *CHOICES* and *DISCOVER.* Both allow you to
enter interests, values, educational background, and other information to produce lists of possible occupations and industries. Each of the resources listed
here will produce different job title lists. Some job titles will appear again
and again, while others will be unique to a particular source. Investigate all
of them!

Reference Sources. Books on the market that may be available through your
local library or career counseling office also suggest various occupations
related to specific majors. The following are only a few of the many good
books on the market: *The College Board Guide to 150 Popular College Majors,
College Majors and Careers: A Resource Guide for Effective Life Planning* both
by Paul Phifer, and *Kaplan's What to Study: 101 Fields in a Flash.* All of these
books list possible job titles within the academic major. The *Occupational
Outlook Handbook (OOH)* describes many of the job titles in the criminal
justice employment fields under broad categories such as Service, Professional
and Technical, and Managerial and Administrative Occupations and also
identifies those jobs by their *Dictionary of Occupational Titles (DOT)* code.
(See the following discussion.)

For criminal justice majors, scores of jobs are listed. Some are familiar
ones, such as police officer, private detective, and paralegal. Others are inter-
estingly different, such as inspector and compliance officer.

••

Many college and university career office Web pages offer
some great information on what you can do with specific
majors. Several of the best we've seen are from Florida
State University (www.fsu.edu/ccis/matchmajor/match
menu.html), Georgia Southern University (www2.gasou
.edu/sta/career), and the University of North Carolina at
Wilmington (www.uncwil.edu/staff/careers/majors.html).
In addition to potential job titles and/or employers, these
sites provide you with further related resources to explore,
including websites.

••

Each job title deserves your consideration. Like removing the layers of an onion, the search for job titles can go on and on! As you spend time doing this activity, you are actually learning more about the value of your degree. What's important in your search at this point is not to become critical or selective but rather to develop as long a list of possibilities as you can. Every source used will help you add new and potentially exciting jobs to your growing list.

Want Ads. It has been well publicized that newspaper want ads represent only about 10 to 15 percent of the current job market. However, with the current high state of employment as this book goes to press, the percentage of jobs advertised in the newspapers and on-line is rising dramatically, so don't ignore this source.

If you are able to be mobile in your job search, you may want to search the classified sections of newspapers in other cities. This is now possible on-line. A good source for this search is the site called www.looksmart.com. Using the keywords *newspaper classifieds* will lead you to a site where you can search by state alphabetically. It's an excellent source for want ads.

Remember, because want ads are written for what an organization *hopes* to find, you don't have to meet absolutely every criterion. However, if certain requirements are stated as absolute minimums and you cannot meet them, it's best not to waste your time.

A recent examination of the *Boston Sunday Globe* (www.boston.com) reveals the following possible occupations for a liberal arts major with some computer skills and limited work experience. (This is only a partial list of what was available.)

- Admissions representative
- Salesperson
- Compliance director
- Assistant principal gifts writer
- Public relations officer
- Technical writer
- Personnel trainee
- G.E.D. examiner
- Direct mail researcher
- Associate publicist

After performing this exercise for a few Sundays, you'll find you have collected a new library of job titles.

The Sunday want ads exercise is important because these jobs are out in the marketplace. They truly exist, and people with your qualifications are being sought to apply. What's more, many of these advertisements describe the duties and responsibilities of the job advertised and give you a beginning sense of the challenges and opportunities such a position presents. Some will indicate salary, and that will be helpful as well. This information will better define the jobs for you and provide some good material for possible interviews in that field.

Exploring Job Descriptions

Once you've arrived at a solid list of possible job titles that interest you and for which you believe you are somewhat qualified, it's a good idea to do some research on each of these jobs. The preeminent source for such job information is the *Dictionary of Occupational Titles*, or *DOT* (www.wave.net /upg/immigration/dot_index.html). This directory lists every conceivable job and provides excellent up-to-date information on duties and responsibilities, interactions with associates, and day-to-day assignments and tasks. These descriptions provide a thorough job analysis, but they do not consider the possible employers or the environments in which a job may be performed. So, although a position as public relations officer may be well defined in terms of duties and responsibilities, it does not explain the differences in doing public relations work in a college or a hospital or a factory or a bank. You will need to look somewhere else for work settings.

Learning More About Possible Work Settings

After reading some job descriptions, you may choose to edit and revise your list of job titles once again, discarding those you feel are not suitable and keeping those that continue to hold your interest. Or you may wish to keep your list intact and see where these jobs may be located. For example, if you are interested in public relations and you appear to have those skills and the requisite education, you'll want to know what organizations do public relations. How can you find that out? How much income does someone in public relations make a year and what is the employment potential for the field of public relations?

To answer these and many other questions about your list of job titles, we recommend you try any of the following resources: *Careers Encyclopedia;* a career information center site such as that provided by the American Marketing Association at www.amaboston.org/jobs.htm; *College to Career: The Guide to Job Opportunities*; and the *Occupational Outlook Handbook* (http://stats.bls.gov/ocohome.htm). Each of these resources, in a different way, will help to put the job titles you have selected into an employer context. Perhaps the most extensive discussion is found in the *Occupational Outlook Handbook*, which gives a thorough presentation of the nature of the work, the working conditions, employment statistics, training, other qualifications, and advancement possibilities as well as job outlook and earnings. Related occupations are also detailed, and a select bibliography is provided to help you find additional information.

Continuing with our public relations example, your search through these reference materials would teach you that the public relations jobs you find attractive are available in larger hospitals, financial institutions, most corporations (both consumer goods and industrial goods), media organizations, and colleges and universities.

Networking to Get the Complete Story

You now have not only a list of job titles but also, for each of these job titles, a description of the work involved and a general list of possible employment settings in which to work. You'll want to do some reading and keep talking to friends, colleagues, teachers, and others about the possibilities. Don't neglect to ask if the career office at your college maintains some kind of alumni network. Often such alumni networks will connect you with another graduate from the college who is working in the job title or industry you are seeking information about. These career networkers offer what assistance they can. For some it is a full day "shadowing" the alumnus as he or she goes about the job. Others offer partial-day visits, tours, informational interviews, resume reviews, job postings, or, if distance prevents a visit, telephone interviews. As fellow graduates, they'll be frank and informative about their own jobs and prospects in their field.

Take them up on their offer and continue to learn all you can about your own personal list of job titles, descriptions, and employment settings. You'll probably continue to edit and refine this list as you learn more about the realities of the job, the possible salary, advancement opportunities, and supply and demand statistics.

In the next section we'll describe how to find the specific organizations that represent these industries and employers so that you can begin to make contact.

WHERE ARE THESE JOBS, ANYWAY?

Having a list of job titles that you've designed around your own career interests and skills is an excellent beginning. It means you've really thought about who you are and what you are presenting to the employment market. It has caused you to think seriously about the most appealing environments to work in, and you have identified some employer types that represent these environments.

The research and the thinking that you've done thus far will be used again and again. They will be helpful in writing your resume and cover letters, in talking about yourself on the telephone to prospective employers, and in answering interview questions.

Now is a good time to begin to narrow the field of job titles and employment sites down to some specific employers to initiate the employment contact.

Finding Out Which Employers Hire People Like You

This section will provide tips, techniques, and specific resources for developing an actual list of specific employers that can be used to make contacts. It is only an outline that you must be prepared to tailor to your own particular needs and according to what you bring to the job search. Once again, it is important to communicate with others along the way exactly what you're looking for and what your goals are for the research you're doing. Librarians, employers, career counselors, friends, friends of friends, business contacts, and bookstore staff will all have helpful information on geographically specific and new resources to aid you in locating employers who'll hire you.

Identifying Information Resources

Your interview wardrobe and your new resume might have put a dent in your wallet, but the resources you'll need to pursue your job search are available for free (although you may choose to copy materials on a machine instead of taking notes by hand). The categories of information detailed here are not hard to find and are yours for the browsing.

Numerous resources described in this section will help you identify actual employers. Use all of them or any others that you identify as available in your geographic area. As you become experienced in this process, you'll quickly figure out which information sources are helpful and which are not. If you live in a rural area, a well-planned day trip to a major city that includes a college career office, a large college or city library, state and federal employment centers, a chamber of commerce office, and a well-stocked bookstore can produce valuable results.

There are many excellent resources available to help you identify actual job sites. They are categorized into employer directories (usually indexed by product lines and geographic location), geographically based directories (designed to highlight particular cities, regions, or states), career-specific directories (e.g., *Sports MarketPlace*, which lists tens of thousands of firms involved with sports), periodicals and newspapers, targeted job posting publications, and videos. This is by no means meant to be a complete treatment of resources but rather a starting point for identifying useful resources.

Working from the more general references to highly specific resources, we provide a basic list to help you begin your search. Many of these you'll find easily available. In some cases reference librarians and others will suggest even better materials for your particular situation. Start to create your own customized bibliography of job search references. Use copying services to save time and to allow you to carry away information about organizations' missions, locations, company officers, phone numbers, and addresses.

Employer Directories. Some hardcover directories can give you the information you need for your job search, but they are less current and less specific than the many fine websites posting jobs in criminal justice occupations. Some of our favorites are listed here. Be sure to ask the professionals with whom you are working to make additional suggestions.

- *Dr. Frank Schmalleger's Talk Justice: The World's Criminal Justice Forum* (www.talkjustice.com) An encyclopedic site that includes a "cybrary" of links under every possible criminal justice topic. We found twenty-six links with brief explanations under the topic of "Criminal Justice 'Zines and E-Journals." This is an incredible site.

- *Professional's Job Finder/Government Job Finder/Non-Profits Job Finder* (http://einsys.einpgh.org) A general website that will ultimately lead you to specific directories of job services, salary surveys, and periodical listings in which advertisements for jobs in the professional, government, or not-for-profit sector are found. Search under the icon "Title" for each of these directories.

- *Dr. O'Connor's Employment Mega-Links in Criminal Justice* (http://faculty.ncwc.edu/toconnor/employ.htm) This North Carolina Wesleyan College professor's site is a gold mine of job application procedures and links to criminal justice employment sites, organized by category.

- *Criminal Justice Resources Job Information* (www.lib.msu.edu/harris23/crimjust/jobs.htm) This site from the library at Michigan State University is one of the most complete listings of links to employment sites to both state and federal employers.

- *Officer.com* (www.officer.com) A classic site that will connect you to law enforcement recruiting sites. The site has many other pages of interest to the criminal justice major.

- *The Corrections Connection* (www.corrections.com) One of the authors' favorite sites with up-to-date job listings in the fields of juvenile, courts, corrections, sales, K-9, community policing, probation and parole, administration, casework, and investigations.

■ *Law Enforcement Jobs Employment Portal*
(www.lawenforcementjob.com) Employment sections for sheriff, federal positions, university and college police force work, and corrections.

■ *The Blue Line Jobs Page* (www.theblueline.com)
One aspect of this site is a jobs newsletter. The site offers an extensive sampling of current jobs and a free copy of the previous issue of the newsletter. Regular access to all job listings is by paid subscription.

■ *Crime Spider* (www.crimespider.com)
Not your traditional site. A unique informational site on almost every aspect of crime and law enforcement, including cybercrime, industrial espionage, and terrorism. Each specialized directory leads you to multiple links that include employing agencies and firms. A comprehensive resource site.

■ *About.com* (www.about.com)
Using this metasite, select "Jobs and Careers" and then choose the "Law Enforcement" link; you'll discover a wealth of potential sites with career and employment information.

Geographically Based Directories. The *Job Bank* series published by Bob Adams, Inc. (www.aip.com) contains detailed entries on each area's major employers, including business activity, address, phone number, and hiring contact name. Many listings specify educational backgrounds being sought in potential employees. Each volume contains a solid discussion of each city's or state's major employment sectors. Organizations are also indexed by industry. Job Bank volumes are available for the following places: Atlanta, Boston, Chicago, Dallas–Ft. Worth, Denver, Detroit, Florida, Houston, Los Angeles, Minneapolis, New York, Ohio, Philadelphia, San Francisco, Seattle, St. Louis, Washington, D.C., and other cities throughout the Northwest.

National Job Bank (www.careercity.com) lists employers in every state, along with contact names and commonly hired job categories. Included are many small companies often overlooked by other directories. Companies are also indexed by industry. This publication provides information on educational backgrounds sought and lists company benefits.

Periodicals and Newspapers. Several sources are available to help you locate which journals or magazines carry job advertisements in your field. Other resources help you identify opportunities in other parts of the country.

- *www.looksmart.com*
  If you want to search the classified sections of newspapers in other cities, a good source is this site. Using the keyword *newspaper classifieds* will lead you to where you can search alphabetically by state.

- *www.careerpath.com*
  Connects to classified job ads from newspapers around the country. Select the job title and then select the state or region of the state.

- *Law Enforcement Career Digest* (www.policecareers.com)
  A monthly hard-copy or Web subscription journal offering entry-level and lateral law enforcement positions nationwide.

Targeted Job Posting Publications. Although the resources that follow are national in scope, they are either targeted to one medium of contact (telephone), focused on specific types of jobs, or less comprehensive than the sources previously listed. Criminal justice majors will want to locate "omnibus" sites such as the exemplary employment opportunities links created by the University of North Texas Criminal Justice Department at www.unt.edu/cjus/employ.htm.

- *Job Hotlines USA* (www.careers.org/topic/01_002.html)
  Pinpoints more than 1,000 hard-to-find telephone numbers for companies and government agencies that use prerecorded job messages and listings. Very few of the telephone numbers listed are toll-free, and sometimes recordings are long, so—callers, beware!

- *The Job Hunter* (www.jobhunter.com)
  A national biweekly newspaper listing business, arts, media, government, human services, health, community-related, and student services job openings.

- *Current Jobs for Graduates* (www.graduatejobs.com)
  A national employment listing for liberal arts professions, including editorial positions, management opportunities, museum work, teaching, and nonprofit work.

- *Environmental Opportunities* (www.ecojobs.com)
  Serves environmental job interests nationwide by listing administrative, marketing, and human resources positions along with education-related jobs and positions directly related to a degree in an environmental field.

- *Y National Vacancy List*
  (www.ymcahrm.ns.ca/employed/jobleads.html) Shows YMCA

professional vacancies, including development, administration, programming, membership, and recreation postings.

- *ARTSearch*
  A national employment service bulletin for the arts, including administration, managerial, marketing, and financial management jobs.

- *Community Jobs*
  An employment newspaper for the nonprofit sector that provides a variety of listings, including project manager, canvas director, government relations specialist, community organizer, and program instructor.

- *College Placement Council Annual: A Guide to Employment Opportunities for College Graduates*
  An annual guide containing solid job-hunting information and, more important, displaying ads from large corporations actively seeking recent college graduates in all majors. Company profiles provide brief descriptions and available employment opportunities. Contact names and addresses are given. Profiles are indexed by organization name, geographic location, and occupation.

Videos. You may be one of the many job seekers who likes to get information via a medium other than paper. Many career libraries, public libraries, and career centers in libraries carry an assortment of videos that will help you learn new techniques and get information helpful in the job search.

Locating Information Resources

Throughout these introductory chapters, we have continually referred you to various websites for information on everything from job listings to career information. These same resources remain our best advice for your general research on criminal justice career information. Using the Web gives you a mobility at your computer that you don't enjoy if you rely solely on books or newspapers or printed journals. Moreover, material on the Web, if the site is maintained, can be up-to-date, which may be crucial if you are looking at a cutting-edge career such as cybercrime, in which technology changes almost daily. Federal government sites offer the option in some cases of downloading application materials, and many will accept your resume on-line.

You'll eventually identify the information resources that work best for you, but make certain you've covered the full range of resources before you begin to rely on a smaller list. Here's a short list of informational sites that many criminal justice job seekers find helpful:

- Public and college libraries

- College career centers

- Bookstores

- Internet

- Local and state government personnel offices

Each one of these sites offers a collection of resources that will help you get the information you need.

As you meet and talk with service professionals at all these sites, be sure to let them know what you're doing. Inform them of your job search, what you've already accomplished, and what you're looking for. The more people who know you're job seeking, the greater the possibility that someone will have information or know someone who can help you along your way.

Public and College Libraries. Large city libraries, college and university libraries, and even well-supported town library collections contain a variety of resources to help you conduct a job search. It is not uncommon for libraries to have separate "vocational choices" sections with books, tapes, computer terminals, and associated materials relating to job search and selection. Some are now even making resume-creation software available for use by patrons.

Some of the publications we name throughout this book are expensive reference items that are rarely purchased by individuals. In addition, libraries carry a wide range of newspapers and telephone yellow pages as well as the usual array of books. If resources are not immediately available, many libraries have loan arrangements with other facilities and can make information available to you relatively quickly.

Take advantage not only of the reference collections but also of the skilled and informed staff. Let them know exactly what you are looking for, and they'll have their own suggestions. You'll be visiting the library frequently, and the reference staff will soon come to know who you are and what you're working on. They'll be part of your job search network!

College Career Centers. Career libraries, which are found in career centers at colleges and universities and sometimes within large public libraries, contain a unique blend of the job search resources housed in other settings. In addition, career libraries often purchase a number of job listing publications, each of which targets a specific industry or type of job. You may find job listings specifically for entry-level positions for your major. Ask about job posting newsletters or newspapers focused on careers in the area that most interests you. Each center will be unique, but you are certain to discover some good sources of jobs.

Most college career libraries now hold growing collections of video material on specific industries and on aspects of your job search process, including dress and appearance, how to manage the luncheon or dinner interview, how to be effective at a job fair, and many other titles. Some larger corporations produce handsome video materials detailing the variety of career paths and opportunities available in their organizations.

Some career libraries also house computer-based career planning and information systems. These interactive computer programs help you to clarify your values and interests and will combine them with your education to provide possible job titles and industry locations. Some even contain extensive lists of graduate school programs.

One specific kind of service a career library will be able to direct you to is computerized job search services. These services, of which there are many, are run by private companies, individual colleges, or consortiums of colleges. They attempt to match qualified job candidates with potential employers. The candidate submits a resume (or an application) to the service. This information (which can be categorized into hundreds of separate fields of data) is entered into a computer database. Your information is then compared with the information from employers about what they desire in a prospective employee. If there is a match between what they want and what you have indicated you can offer, the job search service or the employer will contact you directly to continue the process.

Computerized job search services can complement an otherwise complete job search program. They are *not*, however, a substitute for the kinds of activities described in this book. They are essentially passive operations that are random in nature. If you have not listed skills, abilities, traits, experiences, or education *exactly* as an employer has listed its needs, there is simply no match.

Consult with the staff members at the career libraries you use. These professionals have been specifically trained to meet the unique needs you present. Often you can just drop in and receive help with general questions, or you may want to set up an appointment to speak one-on-one with a career counselor to gain special assistance.

Every career library is different in size and content, but each can provide valuable information for the job search. Some may even provide limited counseling. If you have not visited the career library at your college or alma mater, call and ask if these collections are still available for your use. Be sure to ask about other services that you can use as well.

If you are not near your own college as you work on your job search, call the career office and inquire about reciprocal agreements with other colleges that are closer to where you live. Very often, your own alma mater can arrange for you to use a limited menu of services at another school. This typically would include access to a career library and job posting information and might include limited counseling.

Bookstores. Any well-stocked bookstore will carry some job search books that are worth buying. Some major stores will even have an extensive section devoted to materials, including excellent videos, related to the job search process. You will also find copies of local newspapers and business magazines. The one advantage that is provided by resources purchased at a bookstore is that you can read and work with the information in the comfort of your own home and do not have to conform to the hours of operation of a library, which can present real difficulties if you are working full-time as you seek employment. A few minutes spent browsing in a bookstore might be a beneficial break from your job search activities and turn up valuable resources.

Internet. There's no doubt about it, the Web is a job hunter's best friend. But the Web can also be an overwhelmingly abundant source of information—so much information that it becomes difficult to identify what's important and what is not. A simple search under the phrase *law enforcement* can bring up sites that will be very meaningful for you and sites whose information is trivial and irrelevant to your job search. You need a strategy to master the Web, just as we advise a strategy to master the job search. Here are some suggestions:

1. Thoroughly utilize the websites identified throughout this guide. They've been chosen with you in mind, and many of them will be very helpful to you.

2. Begin to build your own portfolio of websites on your computer. Use the "bookmarking" function on your Web browser to build a series of bookmark folders for individual categories of good websites. You may have a folder for "entry-level job ad" sites and another folder for "professional associations," and so on. Start your folders with the sites in this book that seem most helpful to you.

3. Visit your college career center (or ask for reciprocity consideration at a local college) and your nearby local and/or state and university libraries. All of these places have staff who are skilled researchers and

can help you locate and identify more sites that are more closely targeted to your growing sense of job direction.

4. Use the E-mail function or Webmaster address that you'll find on many sites. Some sites encourage questions via E-mail. We have found that the response time to E-mail questions for website mailboxes can vary considerably, but more often than not, replies are quite prompt. Sometimes a website will list the E-mail of the "Webmaster" or "Webguru," and we have contacted those individuals with good success as well. So, if you have a question about a website, use these options to get satisfaction.

Local and State Government Personnel Offices. You'll learn that it's most efficient to establish a routine for checking job postings. Searching for a job is a full-time job (or should be!), and you don't want to waste time or feel that you're going around in circles. So, establish a routine by which each week, on the most appropriate day, you check out that day's resources. For example, if you live in a midsize city with a daily paper, you'll probably give the want ads a once-over every morning so that you can act immediately on any good job opening.

The same strategy applies to your local and state government personnel offices. Find out when and how they post jobs, and put those offices on your weekly checklist, so that you don't miss any reasonable openings. Your local municipality's personnel office may simply use a bulletin board in the town hall or a clipboard on a counter in the office. Make these stops part of your weekly routine, and you'll find that people begin to recognize you and become aware of your job search, which could prove to be very helpful. Most local governmental units are required to post jobs in public places for a stated period before the hiring process begins. It should be easy to find out where and how they do this. Keep a close eye on those sites.

State personnel offices are larger, less casual operations, but the principles are the same. State jobs are advertised, and the office can tell you what advertising mechanisms they use—which newspapers, what websites, and when jobs are posted. The personnel offices themselves are worth a visit, if you are close enough. In addition to all the current job postings, many state personnel offices have "spec sheets," which are detailed job specifications of all the positions they are apt to advertise. You could pick up a spec sheet for every job related to law enforcement or criminal justice and keep them in a file for later reference when such a job is advertised.

Many state personnel offices also publish a weekly or biweekly "open recruitment" listing of career opportunities that have not yet been filled. These listings are categorized by job title as well as by branch of government, and often by whether a test is needed to qualify for the position or not. An increasing number of state personnel or human resources offices are on-line and offer many services on the Web. A fine general website that can help you locate your state personnel office is www.piperinfo.com/state/index.cfm. While each state's site is different, you can count on access to the state human resources office and sometimes even the human resources offices of many of the state's larger cities. For example, the State of Connecticut lists an additional twenty-seven city sites that each have human resources departmental listings. So, you could search the State of Connecticut Human Resource Office and then jump to the City of Stamford and review city jobs on its site.

CHAPTER FOUR

NETWORKING

*N*etworking is the process of deliberately establishing relationships to get career-related information or to alert potential employers that you are available for work. Networking is critically important to today's job seeker for two reasons: it will help you get the information you need, and it can help you find out about *all* of the available jobs.

Getting the Information You Need

Networkers will review your resume and give you feedback on its effectiveness. They will talk about the job you are looking for and give you a candid appraisal of how they see your strengths and weaknesses. If they have a good sense of the industry or the employment sector for that job, you'll get their feelings on future trends in the industry as well. Some networkers will be very forthcoming about salaries, job-hunting techniques, and suggestions for your job search strategy. Many have been known to place calls right from the interview desk to friends and associates who might be interested in you. Each networker will make his or her own contribution, and each will be valuable.

Because organizations must evolve to adapt to current global market needs, the information provided by decision makers within various organizations will be critical to your success as a new job market entrant. For example, you might learn about the concept of virtual organizations from a networker. Virtual organizations coordinate economic activity to deliver value to customers by using resources outside the traditional boundaries of the organization. This concept is being discussed and implemented by chief executive officers of many organizations, including Ford Motor, Dell, and IBM.

Networking can help you find out about this and other trends currently affecting the industries under your consideration.

Finding Out About All of the Available Jobs

Not every job that is available at this very moment is advertised for potential applicants to see. This is called the *hidden job market*. Only 15 to 20 percent of all jobs are formally advertised, which means that 80 to 85 percent of available jobs do not appear in published channels. Networking will help you become more knowledgeable about all the employment opportunities available during your job search period.

Although someone you might talk to today doesn't know of any openings within his or her organization, tomorrow or next week or next month an opening may occur. If you've taken the time to show an interest in and knowledge of their organization, if you've shown the company representative how you can help achieve organizational goals and that you can fit into the organization, you'll be one of the first candidates considered for the position.

Networking: A Proactive Approach

Networking is a proactive rather than a reactive approach. You, as a job seeker, are expected to initiate a certain level of activity on your own behalf; you cannot afford to simply respond to jobs listed in the newspaper. Being proactive means building a network of contacts that includes informed and interested decision makers who will provide you with up-to-date knowledge of the current job market and increase your chances of finding out about employment opportunities appropriate for your interests, experience, and level of education.

An old axiom of networking says, "You are only two phone calls away from the information you need." In other words, by talking to enough people, you will quickly come across someone who can offer you help. Start with your professors. Each of them probably has a wide circle of contacts. In their work and travel they might have met someone who can help you or direct you to someone who can.

Control and the Networking Process

In deliberately establishing relationships, the process of networking begins with you in control—*you* are contacting specific individuals. As your network expands and you establish a set of professional relationships, your search for information or jobs will begin to move outside of your total control. A part of the networking process involves others assisting you by gathering information for you or recommending you as a possible job candidate. As additional people become a part of your networking system, you will have less knowledge about activities undertaken on your behalf; you will undoubtedly be contacted by individuals whom you did not initially approach. If you want to function effectively in surprise situations, you must be prepared at all times to talk with strangers about the informational or employment needs that motivated you to become involved in the networking process.

PREPARING TO NETWORK

In deliberately establishing relationships, maximize your efforts by organizing your approach. Five specific areas in which you can organize your efforts include reviewing your self-assessment, reviewing your research on job sites and organizations, deciding who it is you want to talk to, keeping track of all your efforts, and creating your self-promotion tools.

Review Your Self-Assessment

Your self-assessment is as important a tool in preparing to network as it has been in other aspects of your job search. You have carefully evaluated your personal traits, personal values, economic needs, longer-term goals, skill base, preferred skills, and underdeveloped skills. During the networking process you will be called upon to communicate what you know about yourself and relate it to the information or job you seek. Be sure to review the exercises that you completed in the self-assessment section of this book in preparation for networking. We've explained that you need to assess what skills you have acquired from your major that are of general value to an employer and to be ready to express those in ways employers can appreciate as useful in their own organizations.

Review Research on Job Sites and Organizations

In addition, individuals assisting you will expect that you'll have at least some background information on the occupation or industry of interest to you. Refer to the appropriate sections of this book and other relevant publications to acquire the background information necessary for effective networking. They'll explain how to identify not only the job titles that might be of interest to you but also what kinds of organizations employ people to do that job. You will develop some sense of working conditions and expectations about duties and responsibilities—all of which will be of help in your networking interviews.

Decide Who It Is You Want to Talk To

Networking cannot begin until you decide whom it is that you want to talk to and, in general, what type of information you hope to gain from your contacts. Once you know this, it's time to begin developing a list of contacts. Five useful sources for locating contacts are described here.

College Alumni Network. Most colleges and universities have created a formal network of alumni and friends of the institution who are particularly interested in helping currently enrolled students and graduates of their alma mater gain employment-related information.

••

One of the most encouraging things you learn from your college alumni network is the wonderful variety of talents displayed across a spectrum of employment settings. Just the diversity of employment within a list of your college's alumni who are using their criminal justice degrees should be both encouraging and informative to you. Among such a diversified group there are likely to be scores of people you would enjoy talking with and perhaps meeting.

••

It is usually a simple process to make use of an alumni network. Visit your college's website and locate the alumni office and/or your career center. Either or both sites will have information about your school's alumni network. You'll be provided with information on shadowing experiences, geographic information, or those alumni offering job referrals. If you don't find what you're looking for, don't hesitate to phone or E-mail your career center and ask what they can do to help you connect with an alum.

Alumni networkers may provide some combination of the following services: day-long shadowing experiences, telephone interviews, in-person interviews, information on relocating to given geographic areas, internship information, suggestions on graduate school study, and job vacancy notices.

••

What a valuable experience. Perhaps you are interested in working as a probation officer but are unsure if you'd enjoy the mix of paperwork and direct contact with offenders. Or, you may be uncertain about the population with which you'd prefer working—juveniles or adults.

Spending a day with an alumnus who works in probation is a good way to resolve some of those questions. Asking your alumni contacts about their own academic preparation and the role of their criminal justice education in their work, as well as observing firsthand the dynamics of a day on the job will be a better decision criterion for you than any reading on the subject could possibly provide.

···

Present and Former Supervisors. If you believe you are on good terms with present or former job supervisors, they may be an excellent resource for providing information or directing you to appropriate resources that would have information related to your current interests and needs. Additionally, these supervisors probably belong to professional organizations that they might be willing to utilize to get information for you.

···

If, for example, you are interested in working at a major correctional facility, perhaps as a correctional officer, and you are currently working part-time for your local college police force, talk with your sergeant or chief. He or she may have some contacts through friends or professional associations and may be able to connect you to professionals working in large correctional facilities. They could provide you with some contact names, telephone numbers, or E-mail addresses, and you could begin the networking process. Most professionals enjoy talking about and sharing their work and would give you a warm welcome!

···

Employers in Your Area. Although you may be interested in working in a geographic location different from the one where you currently reside, don't overlook the value of the knowledge and contacts those around you are able to provide. Use the local telephone directory and newspaper to identify the types of organizations you are thinking of working for or professionals who have the kinds of jobs you are interested in. Recently, a call made to a local hospital's financial administrator for information on working in health-care financial administration yielded more pertinent information on training seminars, regional professional organizations, and potential employment sites than a national organization was willing to provide.

Employers in Geographic Areas Where You Hope to Work. If you are think-ing about relocating, identifying prospective employers or informational con-tacts in the new location will be critical to your success. Here are some tips for on-line searching. First, use a "metasearch" engine to get the most out of your search. Metasearch engines combine several engines into one powerful tool. We frequently use www.dogpile.com and www.metasearch.com for this purpose. Try using the city and state as your keywords in a search. *New Haven, Connecticut* will bring you to the city's website with links to the cham-ber of commerce, member businesses, and other valuable resources. By using www.looksmart.com you can locate newspapers in any area, and they, too, can provide valuable insight before you relocate. Of course, both dogpile and metasearch can lead you to yellow and white page directories in areas you are considering.

Professional Associations and Organizations. Professional associations and organizations can provide valuable information in several areas: career paths that you might not have considered, qualifications relating to those career choices, publications that list current job openings, and workshops or semi-nars that will enhance your professional knowledge and skills. They can also be excellent sources for background information on given industries: their health, current problems, and future challenges.

There are several excellent resources available to help you locate profes-sional associations and organizations that would have information to meet your needs. Two especially useful publications are the *Encyclopedia of Asso-ciations* and *National Trade and Professional Associations of the United States.*

Keep Track of All Your Efforts

It can be difficult, almost impossible, to remember all the details related to each contact you make during the networking process, so you will want to develop a record-keeping system that works for you. Formalize this process by using your computer to keep a record of the people and organizations you want to contact. You can simply record the contact's name, address, and telephone number, and what information you hope to gain. Each entry might look something like this:

Contact Name	Address	Phone #	Purpose
Mr. Lee Perkins	13 Muromachi	73-8906	Local market
Osaka Branch	Osaka-shi		information

You could record this as a simple Word document and you could still use the "Find" function if you were trying to locate some data and could only recall the firm's name or the contact's name. If you're comfortable with database management and you have some database software on your computer, then you can put information at your fingertips even if you have only the zip code! The point here is not technological sophistication but good record keeping.

Once you have created this initial list, it will be helpful to keep more detailed information as you begin to actually make the contacts. Using the Network Contact Record form in Exhibit 4.1 will help you keep good information on all your network contacts. They'll appreciate your recall of details of your meetings and conversations, and the information will help you to focus your networking efforts.

Exhibit 4.1

NETWORK CONTACT RECORD

Name: (Be certain your spelling is correct.)

Title: (Pick up a business card to be certain of the correct title.)

Employing organization: (Note any parent company or subsidiaries.)

Business mailing address: (This is often different from the street address.)

Business E-mail address:

Business telephone number: (Include area code and alternative numbers.)

Business fax number:

Source for this contact: (Who referred you, and what is their relationship to the contact?)

Date of call or letter: (Use plenty of space here to record multiple phone calls or visits, other employees you may have met, names of secretaries/receptionists, and so forth.)

Content of discussion: (Keep enough notes here to remind you of the substance of your visits and telephone conversations in case some time elapses between contacts.)

Follow-up necessary to continue working with this contact: (Your contact may request

that you send him or her some materials or direct you to

contact an associate. Note any such instructions or

assignments in this space.)

Name of additional networker: (Here you would record the names and phone numbers of

Address: additional contacts met at this employer's site. Often you will

be introduced to many people, some of whom may indicate

E-mail: a willingness to help in your job search.)

Phone: _____

Fax: _____

Name of additional networker: _____

Address: _____

E-mail: _____

Phone: _____

Fax: _____

Name of additional networker: _____

Address: _____

E-mail: _____

Phone: _____

Fax: _____

Date thank-you note written: (May help to date your next contact.)

Follow-up action taken: (Phone calls, visits, additional notes.)

Other miscellaneous notes: (Record any other additional interaction you think may be

important to remember in working with this networking client.

You will want this form in front of you when telephoning or

just before and after a visit.)

Create Your Self-Promotion Tools

There are two types of promotional tools that are used in the networking process. The first is a resume and cover letter, and the second is a one-minute "infomercial," which may be given over the telephone or in person.

Techniques for writing an effective resume and cover letter are discussed in Chapter 2. Once you have reviewed that material and prepared these important documents, you will have created one of your self-promotion tools.

The one-minute infomercial will demand that you begin tying your interests, abilities, and skills to the people or organizations you want to network with. Think about your goal for making the contact to help you understand what you should say about yourself. You should be able to express yourself easily and convincingly. If, for example, you are contacting an alumnus of your institution to obtain the names of possible employment sites in a distant city, be prepared to discuss why you are interested in moving to that location, the types of jobs you are interested in, and the skills and abilities you possess that will make you a qualified candidate.

To create a meaningful one-minute infomercial, write it out, practice it as if it will be a spoken presentation, rewrite it, and practice it again if necessary until expressing yourself comes easily and is convincing.

Here's a simplified example of an infomercial for use over the telephone:

····································

Hello, Ms. Regan? My name is Jacqueline Conlon. I am a recent graduate of Assumption College, and I want to enter the law field as a paralegal. I was a criminal justice major and feel confident that I have many of the skills that are valued in paralegal work. First of all, I enjoy the challenge of research. In addition, I have strong computer skills, including familiarity with two relational database software programs. I also have had significant experience on the Web doing research, which has helped to refine my search techniques. My degree has given me a thorough background in legal issues and terminology.

Ms. Regan, I'm calling you because I still need more information about entering the paralegal field with a criminal justice degree. I'm hoping you have the time to sit down with me for about half an hour and discuss how attractive my resume might be to a law firm. I certainly am not averse to additional education, but I'm eager to begin work and I hope to acquire some good on-the-job training.

Would you be willing to talk with me? I would greatly appreciate it. I'm available most mornings, if that's convenient for you.

•••

It very well may happen that your employer contact wishes you to communicate by E-mail. The infomercial quoted above could easily be rewritten for an E-mail message. You should "cut and paste" your resume right into the E-mail text itself.

Other effective self-promotion tools include portfolios for those in the arts, writing professions, or teaching. Portfolios show examples of work, photographs of projects or classroom activities, or certificates and credentials that are job related. There may not be an opportunity to use the portfolio during an interview, and it is not something that should be left with the organization. It is designed to be explained and displayed by the creator. However, during some networking meetings, there may be an opportunity to illustrate a point or strengthen a qualification by exhibiting the portfolio.

BEGINNING THE NETWORKING PROCESS

Set the Tone for Your Communications

It can be useful to establish "tone words" for any communications you embark upon. Before making your first telephone call or writing your first letter, decide what you want the person to think of you. If you are networking to try to obtain a job, your tone words might include descriptors such as *genuine*, *informed*, and *self-knowledgeable*. When you're trying to acquire information, your tone words may have a slightly different focus, such as *courteous*, *organized*, *focused*, and *well-spoken*. Use the tone words you establish for your contacts to guide you through the networking process.

Honestly Express Your Intentions

When contacting individuals, it is important to be honest about your reasons for making the contact. Establish your purpose in your own mind and be able and ready to articulate it concisely. Determine an initial agenda, whether it be informational questioning or self-promotion, present it to your contact, and be ready to respond immediately. If you don't adequately prepare before initiating your overture, you may find yourself at a disadvantage if you're asked to immediately begin your informational interview or self-promotion during the first phone conversation or visit.

Start Networking Within Your Circle of Confidence

Once you have organized your approach—by utilizing specific researching methods, creating a system for keeping track of the people you will contact, and developing effective self-promotion tools—you are ready to begin networking. The best way to begin networking is by talking with a group of people you trust and feel comfortable with. This group is usually made up of your family, friends, and career counselors. No matter who is in this inner circle, they will have a special interest in seeing you succeed in your job search. In addition, because they will be easy to talk to, you should try taking some risks in terms of practicing your information-seeking approach. Gain confidence in talking about the strengths you bring to an organization and the underdeveloped skills you feel hinder your candidacy. Be sure to review the section on self-assessment for tips on approaching each of these areas. Ask for critical but constructive feedback from the people in your circle of confidence on the letters you write and the one-minute infomercial you have developed. Evaluate whether you want to make the changes they suggest, then practice the changes on others within this circle.

Stretch the Boundaries of Your Networking Circle of Confidence

Once you have refined the promotional tools you will use to accomplish your networking goals, you will want to make additional contacts. Because you will not know most of these people, it will be a less comfortable activity to undertake. The practice that you gained with your inner circle of trusted friends should have prepared you to now move outside of that comfort zone.

It is said that any information a person needs is only two phone calls away, but the information cannot be gained until you (1) make a reasonable guess about who might have the information you need and (2) pick up the telephone to make the call. Using your network list that includes alumni, instructors, supervisors, employers, and associations, you can begin preparing your list of questions that will allow you to get the information you need. Review the question list that follows and then develop a list of your own.

Questions You Might Want to Ask

1. In the position you now hold, what do you do on a typical day?

2. What are the most interesting aspects of your job?

3. What part of your work do you consider dull or repetitious?

4. What were the jobs you had that led to your present position?

5. How long does it usually take to move from one step to the next in this career path?

6. What is the top position to which you can aspire in this career path?

7. What is the next step in *your* career path?

8. Are there positions in this field that are similar to your position?

9. What are the required qualifications and training for entry-level positions in this field?

10. Are there specific courses a student should take to be qualified to work in this field?

11. What are the entry-level jobs in this field?

12. What types of training are provided to persons entering this field?

13. What are the salary ranges your organization typically offers to entry-level candidates for positions in this field?

14. What special advice would you give a person entering this field?

15. Do you see this field as a growing one?

16. How do you see the content of the entry-level jobs in this field changing over the next two years?

17. What can I do to prepare myself for these changes?

18. What is the best way to obtain a position that will start me on a career in this field?

19. Do you have any information on job specifications and descriptions that I may have?

20. What related occupational fields would you suggest I explore?

21. How could I improve my resume for a career in this field?

22. Who else would you suggest I talk to, both in your organization and in other organizations?

Questions You Might Have to Answer

To communicate effectively, you must anticipate questions that will be asked of you by the networkers you contact. Review the following list and see if you can easily answer each of these questions. If you cannot, it may be time to revisit the self-assessment process.

1. Where did you get my name, or how did you find out about this organization?

2. What are your career goals?

3. What kind of job are you interested in?

4. What do you know about this organization and this industry?

5. How do you know you're prepared to undertake an entry-level position in this industry?

6. What course work have you done that is related to your career interests?

7. What are your short-term career goals?

8. What are your long-term career goals?

9. Do you plan to obtain additional formal education?

10. What contributions have you made to previous employers?

11. Which of your previous jobs have you enjoyed the most and why?

12. What are you particularly good at doing?

13. What shortcomings have you had to face in previous employment?

14. What are your three greatest strengths?

15. Describe how comfortable you feel with your communication style.

General Networking Tips

Make Every Contact Count. Setting the tone for each interaction is critical. Approaches that will help you communicate in an effective way include politeness, being appreciative of time provided to you, and being prepared and thorough. Remember, *everyone* within an organization has a circle of influence, so be prepared to interact effectively with each person you encounter in the networking process, including secretarial and support staff. Many information or job seekers have thwarted their own efforts by being rude to some individuals they encountered as they networked because they made the incorrect assumption that certain persons were unimportant.

Sometimes your contacts may be surprised at their ability to help you. After meeting and talking with you, they might think they have not offered much in the way of help. A day or two later, however, they may make a contact that would be useful to you and refer you to that person.

With Each Contact, Widen Your Circle of Networkers. Always leave an informational interview with the names of at least two more people who can help you get the information or job that you are seeking. Don't be shy about asking for additional contacts; networking is all about increasing the number of people you can interact with to achieve your goals.

Make Your Own Decisions. As you talk with different people and get answers to the questions you pose, you may hear conflicting information or get conflicting suggestions. Your job is to listen to these "experts" and decide what information and which suggestions will help you achieve *your* goals. Only implement those suggestions that you believe will work for you.

SHUTTING DOWN YOUR NETWORK

As you achieve the goals that motivated your networking activity—getting the information you need or the job you want—the time will come to inactivate all or parts of your network. As you do, be sure to tell your primary supporters about your change in status. Call or write to each one of them and give them as many details about your new status as you feel is necessary to maintain a positive relationship.

Because a network takes on a life of its own, activity undertaken on your behalf will continue even after you cease your efforts. As you get calls or are contacted in some fashion, be sure to inform these networkers about your change in status, and thank them for assistance they have provided.

Information on the latest employment trends indicates that workers will change jobs or careers several times in their lifetime. Networking, then, will be a critical aspect in the span of your professional life. If you carefully and thoughtfully conduct your networking activities during your job search, you will have a solid foundation of experience when you need to network the next time around.

CHAPTER FIVE

INTERVIEWING

*C*ertainly, there can be no one part of the job search process more fraught with anxiety and worry than the interview. Yet seasoned job seekers welcome the interview and will often say, "Just get me an interview and I'm on my way!" They understand that the interview is crucial to the hiring process and equally crucial for them, as job candidates, to have the opportunity of a personal dialogue to add to what the employer may already have learned from the resume, cover letter, and telephone conversations.

Believe it or not, the interview is to be welcomed, and even enjoyed! It is a perfect opportunity for you, the candidate, to sit down with an employer and express yourself and display who you are and what you want. Of course, it takes thought and planning and a little strategy; after all, it *is* a job interview! But it can be a positive, if not pleasant, experience and one you can look back on and feel confident about your performance and effort.

For many new job seekers, a job, any job, seems a wonderful thing. But seasoned interview veterans know that the job interview is an important step for both sides—the employer and the candidate—to see what each has to offer and whether there is going to be a "fit" of personalities, work styles, and attitudes. And it is this concept of balance in the interview, that both sides have important parts to play, that holds the key to success in mastering this aspect of the job search strategy.

Try to think of the interview as a conversation between two interested and equal partners. You both have important, even vital, information to deliver and to learn. Of course, there's no denying the employer has some leverage, especially in the initial interview for recruitment or any interview scheduled by the candidate and not the recruiter. That should not prevent the interviewee from seeking to play an equal part in what should be a fair exchange of information. Too often the untutored candidate allows the interview to become one-sided. The employer asks all the questions and the candidate simply responds. The ideal would be for two mutually interested parties to sit down and discuss possibilities for each. This is a conversation of significance, and it requires preparation, thought about the tone of the interview, and planning of the nature and details of the information to be exchanged.

PREPARING FOR THE INTERVIEW

The length of most initial interviews is about thirty minutes. Given the brevity, the information that is exchanged ought to be important. The candidate should be delivering material that the employer cannot discover on the resume, and in turn, the candidate should be learning things about the employer that he or she could not otherwise find out. After all, if you have only thirty minutes, why waste time on information that is already published? The information exchanged is more than just factual, and both sides will learn much from what they see of each other, as well. How the candidate looks, speaks, and acts are important to the employer. The employer's attention to the interview and awareness of the candidate's resume, the setting, and the quality of information presented are important to the candidate.

Just as the employer has every right to be disappointed when a prospect is late for the interview, looks unkempt, and seems ill-prepared to answer fairly standard questions, the candidate may be disappointed with an interviewer who isn't ready for the meeting, hasn't learned the basic resume facts, and is constantly interrupted by telephone calls. In either situation there's good reason to feel let down.

There are many elements to a successful interview, and some of them are not easy to describe or prepare for. Sometimes there is just a chemistry between interviewer and interviewee that brings out the best in both, and a good exchange takes place. But there is much the candidate can do to pave the way for success in terms of his or her resume, personal appearance, goals, and interview strategy—each of which we will discuss. However, none of this preparation is as important as the time and thought the candidate gives to personal self-assessment.

Self-Assessment

Neither a stunning resume nor an expensive, well-tailored suit can compensate for candidates who do not know what they want, where they are going, or why they are interviewing with a particular employer. Self-assessment, the process by which we begin to know and acknowledge our own particular blend of education, experiences, needs, and goals, is not something that can be sorted out the weekend before a major interview. Of all the elements of interview preparation, this one requires the longest lead time and cannot be faked.

Because the time allotted for most interviews is brief, it is all the more important for job candidates to understand and express succinctly why they are there and what they have to offer. This is not a time for undue modesty (or for braggadocio either); it is a time for a compelling, reasoned statement of why you feel that you and this employer might make a good match. It means you have to have thought about your skills, interests, and attributes; related those to your life experiences and your own history of challenges and opportunities; and determined what that indicates about your strengths, preferences, values, and areas needing further development.

A common complaint of employers is that many candidates didn't take advantage of the interview time; they didn't seem to know why they were there or what they wanted. When candidates are asked to talk about themselves and their work-related skills and attributes, employers don't want to be faced with shyness or embarrassed laughter; they need to know about you so they can make a fair determination of you and your competition. If you don't take advantage of the opportunity to make a case for your employability, you can be certain the person ahead of you has or the person after you will, and it will be on the strength of those impressions that the employer will hire.

If you need some assistance with self-assessment issues, refer to Chapter 1. Included are suggested exercises that can be done as needed, such as making up an experiential diary and extracting obvious strengths and weaknesses from past experiences. These simple assignments will help you look at past activities as collections of tasks with accompanying skills and responsibilities. Don't overlook your high school or college career office. Many offer personal counseling on self-assessment issues and may provide testing instruments such as the *Myers-Briggs Type Indicator* (*MBTI*), the *Harrington-O'Shea Career Decision-Making System* (*CDM*), the *Strong Interest Inventory* (*SII*), or any other of a wide selection of assessment tools that can help you clarify some of these issues prior to the interview stage of your job search.

The Resume

Resume preparation has been discussed in detail, and some basic examples of various types were provided. In this section we want to concentrate on how best to use your resume in the interview. In most cases the employer will have seen the resume prior to the interview, and, in fact, it may well have been the quality of that resume that secured the interview opportunity.

An interview is a conversation, however, and not an exercise in reading. So, if the employer hasn't seen your resume and you have brought it along to the interview, wait until asked or until the end of the interview to offer it. Otherwise, you may find yourself staring at the back of your resume and simply answering "yes" and "no" to a series of questions drawn from that document.

Sometimes an interviewer is not prepared and does not know or recall the contents of the resume and may use the resume to a greater or lesser degree as a "prompt" during the interview. It is for you to judge what that may indicate about the individual performing the interview or the employer. If your interviewer seems surprised by the scheduled meeting, relies on the resume to an inordinate degree, and seems otherwise unfamiliar with your background, this lack of preparation for the hiring process could well be a symptom of general management disorganization or may simply be the result of poor planning on the part of one individual. It is your responsibility as a potential employee to be aware of these signals and make your decisions accordingly.

••••••••••••••••••••••••••••••••••••

> In any event, it is perfectly acceptable for you to get the conversation back to a more interpersonal style by saying something such as, "Ms. Dwyer, you may be interested in some recent counseling experience I gained in a volunteer position at a women's shelter that is not detailed on my resume. May I tell you about it?" This can return the interview to two people talking to each other, not one reading and the other responding.

••••••••••••••••••••••••••••••••••••

By all means, bring at least one copy of your resume to the interview. Occasionally, at the close of an interview, an interviewer will express an interest in circulating a resume to several departments, and you could then offer the copy you brought. Sometimes, an interview appointment provides an opportunity to meet others in the organization who may express an interest in you and your background, and it may be helpful to follow up with a copy of your resume. Our best advice, however, is to keep it out of sight until needed or requested.

Appearance

Although many of the absolute rules that once dominated the advice offered to job candidates about appearance have now been moderated significantly, conservative is still the watchword unless you are interviewing in a fashion-related industry. For men, conservative translates into a well-cut dark suit with appropriate tie, hosiery, and dress shirt. A wise strategy for the male job seeker looking for a good but not expensive suit would be to try the men's department of a major department store. They usually carry a good range of sizes, fabrics, and prices; offer professional sales help; provide free tailoring; and have associated departments for putting together a professional look.

For women, there is more latitude. Business suits are still popular, but they have become more feminine in color and styling with a variety of jacket and skirt lengths. In addition to suits, better-quality dresses are now worn in many environments and, with the correct accessories, can be most appropriate. Company literature, professional magazines, the business section of major newspapers, and television interviews can all give clues about what is being worn in different employer environments.

Both men and women need to pay attention to issues such as hair, jewelry, and makeup; these are often what separates the candidate in appearance from the professional workforce. It seems particularly difficult for the young job seeker to give up certain hairstyles, eyeglass fashions, and jewelry habits, yet those can be important to the employer who is concerned with your ability to successfully make the transition into the organization. Candidates often find the best strategy is to dress conservatively until they find employment. Once employed and familiar with the norms within your organization, you can begin to determine a look that you enjoy, works for you, and fits your organization.

Choose clothes that suit your body type, fit well, and flatter you. Feel good about the way you look! The interview day is not the best time for a new hairdo, a new pair of shoes, or any other change that will distract you or cause you to be self-conscious. Arrive a bit early to avoid being rushed, and ask the receptionist to direct you to a restroom for any last-minute adjustments of hair and clothes.

Employer Information

Whether your interview is for graduate school admission, an overseas corporate position, or a reporter position with a local newspaper, it is important to know something about the employer or the organization. Keeping in mind that the interview is relatively brief and that you will hopefully have other interviews with other organizations, it is important to keep your research in proportion. If secondary interviews are called for, you will have additional time to do further research. For the first interview, it is helpful to know the organization's mission, goals, size, scope of operations, and so forth. Your research may uncover recent areas of challenge or particular successes that may help to fuel the interview. Use the "What Do They Call the Job You Want?" section of Chapter 3, your library, and your career or guidance office to help you locate this information in the most efficient way possible. Don't be shy in asking advice of these counseling and guidance professionals on how best to spend your preparation time. With some practice, you'll soon learn how much information is enough and which kinds of information are most useful to you.

INTERVIEW CONTENT

We've already discussed how it can help to think of the interview as an important conversation—one that, as with any conversation, you want to find pleasant and interesting and to leave you with a good feeling. But because this conversation is especially important, the information that's exchanged is critical to its success. What do you want them to know about you? What do you need to know about them? What interview technique do you need to particularly pay attention to? How do you want to manage the close of the interview? What steps will follow in the hiring process?

Except for the professional interviewer, most of us find interviewing stressful and anxiety-provoking. Developing a strategy before you begin interviewing will help you relieve some stress and anxiety. One particular strategy that has worked for many and may work for you is interviewing by objective. Before you interview, write down three to five goals you would like to achieve for that interview. They may be technique goals: smile a little more, have a firmer handshake, be sure to ask about the next stage in the interview process before leaving. They may be content-oriented goals: find out about the company's current challenges and opportunities; be sure to speak of your recent research, writing experiences, or foreign travel. Whatever your goals, jot down a few of them as goals for each interview.

Most people find that in trying to achieve these few goals, their interviewing technique becomes more organized and focused. After the interview, the most common question friends and family ask is "How did it go?" With this technique, you have an indication of whether you met *your* goals for the meeting, not just some vague idea of how it went. Chances are, if you accomplished what you wanted to, it improved the quality of the entire interview. As you continue to interview, you will want to revise your goals to continue improving your interview skills.

Now, add to the concept of the significant conversation the idea of a beginning, a middle, and a closing and you will have two thoughts that will give your interview a distinctive character. Be sure to make your introduction warm and cordial. Say your full name (and if it's a difficult-to-pronounce name, help the interviewer to pronounce it) and make certain you know your interviewer's name and how to pronounce it. Most interviews begin with some "soft talk" about the weather, chat about the candidate's trip to the interview site, or national events. This is done as a courtesy to relax both you and the interviewer, to get you talking, and to generally try to defuse the atmosphere of excessive tension. Try to be yourself, engage in the conversation, and don't try to second-guess the interviewer. This is simply what it appears to be—casual conversation.

Once you and the interviewer move on to exchange more serious information in the middle part of the interview, the two most important concerns become your ability to handle challenging questions and your success at asking meaningful ones. Interviewer questions will probably fall into one of three categories: personal assessment and career direction, academic assessment, and knowledge of the employer. The following are some examples of questions in each category:

Personal Assessment and Career Direction

1. How would you describe yourself?

2. What motivates you to put forth your best effort?

3. In what kind of work environment are you most comfortable?

4. What do you consider to be your greatest strengths and weaknesses?

5. How well do you work under pressure?

6. What qualifications do you have that make you think you will be successful in this career?

7. Will you relocate? What do you feel would be the most difficult aspect of relocating?

8. Are you willing to travel?

9. Why should I hire you?

Academic Assessment

1. Why did you select your college or university?

2. What changes would you make at your alma mater?

3. What led you to choose your major?

4. What subjects did you like best and least? Why?

5. If you could, how would you plan your academic study differently? Why?

6. Describe your most rewarding college experience.

7. How has your college experience prepared you for this career?

8. Do you think that your grades are a good indication of your ability to succeed with this organization?

9. Do you have plans for continued study?

Knowledge of the Employer

1. If you were hiring a graduate of your school for this position, what qualities would you look for?

2. What do you think it takes to be successful in an organization like ours?

3. In what ways do you think you can make a contribution to our organization?

4. Why did you choose to seek a position with this organization?

The interviewer wants a response to each question but is also gauging your enthusiasm, preparedness, and willingness to communicate. In each response you should provide some information about yourself that can be related to the employer's needs. A common mistake is to give too much information. Answer each question completely, but be careful not to run on too long with extensive details or examples.

Questions About Underdeveloped Skills

Most employers interview people who have met some minimum criteria of education and experience. They interview candidates to see who they are, to learn what kind of personality they exhibit, and to get some sense of how this person might fit into the existing organization. It may be that you are asked about skills the employer hopes to find and that you have not documented. Maybe it's grant-writing experience, knowledge of the European political system, or a knowledge of the film world.

To questions about skills and experiences you don't have, answer honestly and forthrightly and try to offer some additional information about skills you do have. For example, perhaps the employer is disappointed you have no grant-writing experience. An honest answer may be as follows:

> No, unfortunately, I was never in a position to acquire those skills. I do understand something of the complexities of the grant-writing process and feel confident that my attention to detail, careful reading skills, and strong writing would make grants a wonderful challenge in a new job. I think I could get up on the learning curve quickly.

The employer hears an honest admission of lack of experience but is reassured by some specific skill details that do relate to grant writing and a confident manner that suggests enthusiasm and interest in a challenge.

For many students, questions about their possible contribution to an employer's organization can prove challenging. Because your education has probably not included specific training for a job, you need to review your academic record and select capabilities you have developed in your major that an employer can appreciate. For example, perhaps you read well and can analyze and condense what you've read into smaller, more focused pieces. That could be valuable. Or maybe you did some serious research and you know you have valuable investigative skills. Your public speaking might be highly developed and you might use visual aids appropriately and effectively. Or maybe your skill at correspondence, memos, and messages is effective. Whatever it is, you must take it out of the academic context and put it into a new, employer-friendly context so your interviewer can best judge how you could help the organization.

Exhibiting knowledge of the organization will, without a doubt, show the interviewer that you are interested enough in the available position to have done some legwork in preparation for the interview. Remember, it is not necessary to know every detail of the organization's history but rather to have a general knowledge about why it is in business and how the industry is faring.

Sometime during the interview, generally after the midway point, you'll be asked if you have any questions for the interviewer. Your questions will tell the employer much about your attitude and your desire to understand the organization's expectations so you can compare it to your own strengths. The following are some selected questions you might want to ask:

1. What are the main responsibilities of the position?

2. What are the opportunities and challenges associated with this position?

3. Could you outline some possible career paths beginning with this position?

4. How regularly do performance evaluations occur?

5. What is the communication style of the organization? (meetings, memos, and so forth)

6. What would a typical day in this position be like for me?

7. What kinds of opportunities might exist for me to improve my professional skills within the organization?

8. What have been some of the interesting challenges and opportunities your organization has recently faced?

Most interviews draw to a natural closing point, so be careful not to prolong the discussion. At a signal from the interviewer, wind up your presentation, express your appreciation for the opportunity, and be sure to ask what the next stage in the process will be. When can you expect to hear from them? Will they be conducting second-tier interviews? If you are interested and haven't heard, would they mind a phone call? Be sure to collect a business card with the name and phone number of your interviewer. On your way out, you might have an opportunity to pick up organizational literature you haven't seen before.

With the right preparation—a thorough self-assessment, professional clothing, and employer information—you'll be able to set and achieve the goals you have established for the interview process.

CHAPTER SIX

NETWORKING OR INTERVIEW FOLLOW-UP

 uite often there is a considerable time lag between interviewing for a position and being hired or, in the case of the networker, between your phone call or letter to a possible contact and the opportunity of a meeting. This can be frustrating. "Why aren't they contacting me?" "I thought I'd get another interview, but no one has telephoned." "Am I out of the running?" You don't know what is happening.

CONSIDER THE DIFFERING PERSPECTIVES

Of course, there is another perspective—that of the networker or hiring organization. Organizations are complex, with multiple tasks that need to be accomplished each day. Hiring is a discrete activity that does not occur as frequently as other job assignments. The hiring process might have to take second place to other, more immediate organizational needs. Although it may be very important to you, and it is certainly ultimately significant to the employer, other issues such as fiscal management, planning and product development, employer vacation periods, or financial constraints may prevent an organization or individual within that organization from acting on your employment or your request for information as quickly as you or they would prefer.

USE YOUR COMMUNICATION SKILLS

Good communication is essential here to resolve any anxieties, and the responsibility is on you, the job or information seeker. Too many job seekers and networkers offer as an excuse that they don't want to "bother" the organization by writing letters or calling. Let us assure you here and now, once and for all, that if you are troubling an organization by over-communicating, someone will indicate that situation to you quite clearly. If not, you can only assume you are a worthwhile prospect and the employer appreciates being reminded of your availability and interest. Let's look at follow-up practices in the job interview process and the networking situation separately.

FOLLOWING UP ON THE EMPLOYMENT INTERVIEW

A brief thank-you note following an interview is an excellent and polite way to begin a series of follow-up communications with a potential employer with whom you have interviewed and want to remain in touch. It should be just that—a thank-you for a good meeting. If you failed to mention some fact or experience during your interview that you think might add to your candidacy, you may use this note to do that. However, this should be essentially a note whose overall tone is appreciative and, if appropriate, indicative of a continuing interest in pursuing any opportunity that may exist with that organization. It is one of the few pieces of business correspondence that may be handwritten, but always use plain, good-quality, standard-size paper.

If, however, at this point you are no longer interested in the employer, the thank-you note is an appropriate time to indicate that. You are under no obligation to identify any reason for not continuing to pursue employment with that organization, but if you are so inclined to indicate your professional reasons (pursuing other employers more akin to your interests, looking for greater income production than this employer can provide, a different geographic location), you certainly may. It should not be written with an eye to negotiation, for it will not be interpreted as such.

As part of your interview closing, you should have taken the initiative to establish lines of communication for continuing information about your candidacy. If you asked permission to telephone, wait a week following your thank-you note, then telephone your contact simply to inquire how things are progressing on your employment status. The feedback you receive here should be taken at face value. If your interviewer simply has no information, he or she will tell you so and indicate whether you should call again and when. Don't be discouraged if this should continue over some period of time.

If during this time something occurs that you think improves or changes your candidacy (some new qualification or experience you may have had), including any offers from other organizations, by all means telephone or write to inform the employer about this. In the case of an offer from a competing but less desirable or equally desirable organization, telephone your contact, explain what has happened, express your real interest in the organization, and inquire whether some determination on your employment might be made before you must respond to this other offer. An organization that is truly interested in you may be moved to make a decision about your candidacy. Equally possible is the scenario in which they are not yet ready to make a decision and so advise you to take the offer that has been presented. Again, you have no ethical alternative but to deal with the information presented in a straightforward manner.

When accepting other employment, be sure to contact any employers still actively considering you and inform them of your new job. Thank them graciously for their consideration. There are many other job seekers out there just like you who will benefit from having their candidacy improved when others bow out of the race. Who knows, you might at some future time have occasion to interact professionally with one of the organizations with which you sought employment. How embarrassing it would be to have someone remember you as the candidate who failed to notify them that you were taking a job elsewhere!

In all of your follow-up communications, keep good notes of whom you spoke with, when you called, and any instructions that were given about return communications. This will prevent any misunderstandings and provide you with good records of what has transpired.

FOLLOWING UP ON THE NETWORK CONTACT

Far more common than the forgotten follow-up after an interview is the situation where a good network contact is allowed to lapse. Good communications are the essence of a network, and follow-up is not so much a matter of courtesy here as it is a necessity. In networking for job information and contacts, you are the active network link. Without you, and without continual contact from you, there is no network. You and your need for employment are often the only shared elements among members of the network. Because network contacts were made regardless of the availability of any particular employment, it is incumbent upon the job seeker, if not simple common sense, to stay in regular communication with the network if you want to be considered for any future job opportunities.

This brings up the issue of responsibility, which is likewise very clear. The job seeker initiates network contacts and is responsible for maintaining those contacts; therefore, the entire responsibility for the network belongs with him or her. This becomes patently obvious if the network is left unattended. It very shortly falls out of existence because it cannot survive without careful attention by the networker.

You have many ways to keep the lines of communication open and to attempt to interest the network in you as a possible employee. You are limited only by your own enthusiasm for members of the network and your creativity. However, you as a networker are well advised to keep good records of whom you have met and contacted in each organization. Be sure to send thank-you notes to anyone who has spent any time with you, whether it was an E-mail message containing information or advice, a quick tour of a department, or a sit-down informational interview. All of these thank-you notes should, in addition to their ostensible reason, add some information about you and your particular combination of strengths and attributes.

You can contact your network at any time to convey continued interest, to comment on some recent article you came across concerning an organization, to add information about your training or changes in your qualifications, to ask advice or seek guidance in your job search, or to request referrals to other possible network opportunities. Sometimes just a simple note to network members reminding them of your job search, indicating that you have been using their advice, and noting that you are still actively pursuing leads and hope to continue to interact with them is enough to keep communications alive.

The Internet has opened up the world of networking. You may be able to find networkers who graduated from your high school or from the college you're attending, who live in a geographic region where you hope to work, or who are employed in a given industry. The Internet makes it easy to reach out to many people, but don't let this perceived ease lull you into complacency. Internet networking demands the same level of preparation as the more traditional forms of networking.

Because networks have been abused in the past, it's important that your conduct be above reproach. Networks are exploratory options; they are not backdoor access to employers. The network works best for someone who is exploring a new industry or making a transition into a new area of employment and who needs to find information or to alert people to his or her search activity. Always be candid and direct with contacts in expressing the purpose of your E-mail, call, or letter and your interest in their help or information about their organization. In follow-up contacts keep the tone professional and direct. Your honesty will be appreciated, and people will respond as best they can if your qualifications appear to meet their forthcoming needs. The network does not owe you anything, and that tone should be clear to each person you meet.

FEEDBACK FROM FOLLOW-UPS

A network contact may prove to be miscalculated. Perhaps you were referred to someone and it became clear that your goals and his or her particular needs did not make a good match. Or the network contact may simply not be in a position to provide you with the information you are seeking. Or in some unfortunate situations, the party may become annoyed by being contacted for this purpose. In such a situation, many job seekers simply say "Thank you" and move on.

If the contact is simply not the right connection, but the individual you are speaking with is not annoyed by the call, it might be a better tactic to express regret that the contact was misplaced and then tell the person what you are seeking and ask for his or her advice or possible suggestions as to a next step. The more people who are aware that you are seeking employment, the better your chances of connecting, and that is the purpose of a network. Most people in a profession have excellent knowledge of their field and varying amounts of expertise in areas tangent to their own. Use their expertise and seek some guidance before you dissolve the contact. You may be pleasantly surprised.

Occasionally, networkers will express the feeling that they have done as much as they can or provided all the information that is available to them. This may be a cue that they would like to be released from your network. Be alert to such attempts to terminate, graciously thank the individual by letter, and move on in your network development. A network is always changing, adding, and losing members, and you want the network to be composed only of those who are actively interested in supporting you.

A FINAL POINT ON NETWORKING FOR CRIMINAL JUSTICE MAJORS

In any of the fields that a criminal justice major may hope to enter, networkers as well as interviewers will be evaluating your interpersonal and communications skills. This fact should not come as news, given the emphasis on these skills in your course work. So, always keep in mind the importance of the quality of your presentations to people in a position to help you in your job search.

CHAPTER SEVEN

JOB OFFER CONSIDERATIONS

for many recent college graduates, the thrill of their first job and, for some, the most substantial regular income they have ever earned seems an excess of good fortune coming at once. To question that first income or to be critical in any way of the conditions of employment at the time of the initial offer seems like looking a gift horse in the mouth. It doesn't seem to occur to many new hires even to attempt to negotiate any aspect of their first job. And, as many employers who deal with entry-level jobs for recent college graduates will readily confirm, the reality is that there simply isn't much movement in salary available to these new college recruits. The entry-level hire generally does not have an employment track record on a professional level to provide any leverage for negotiation. Real negotiations on salary, benefits, retirement provisions, and so forth come to those with significant employment records at higher income levels.

Of course, the job offer is more than just money. It can be composed of geographic assignment, duties and responsibilities, training, benefits, health and medical insurance, educational assistance, car allowance or company vehicle, and a host of other items. All of this is generally detailed in the formal letter that presents the final job offer. In most cases this is a follow-up to a personal phone call from the employer representative who has been principally responsible for your hiring process.

That initial telephone offer is certainly binding as a verbal agreement, but most firms follow up with a detailed letter outlining the most significant parts of your employment contract. You may, of course, choose to respond immediately at the time of the telephone offer (which would be considered a binding oral contract), but you will also be required to formally answer the letter of offer with a letter of acceptance, restating the salient elements of the employer's description of your position, salary, and benefits. This ensures that both parties are clear on the terms and conditions of employment and remuneration and any other outstanding aspects of the job offer.

IS THIS THE JOB YOU WANT?

Most new employees will respond affirmatively in writing, glad to be in the position to accept employment. If you've worked hard to get the offer and the job market is tight, other offers may not be in sight, so you will say, "Yes, I accept!" What is important here is that the job offer you accept be one that does fit your particular needs, values, and interests as you've outlined them in your self-assessment process. Moreover, it should be a job that will not only use your skills and education but also challenge you to develop new skills and talents.

Jobs are sometimes accepted too hastily, for the wrong reasons, and without proper scrutiny by the applicant. For example, an individual might readily accept a sales job only to find the continual rejection by potential clients unendurable. An office worker might realize within weeks the constraints of a desk job and yearn for more activity. Employment is an important part of our lives. It is, for most of our adult lives, our most continuous productive activity. We want to make good choices based on the right criteria.

If you have a low tolerance for risk, a job based on commission will certainly be very anxiety-provoking. If being near your family is important, issues of relocation could present a decision crisis for you. If you're an adventurous person, a job with frequent travel would provide needed excitement and be very desirable. The importance of income, the need to continue your education, your personal health situation—all of these have an impact on whether the job you are considering will ultimately meet your needs. Unless you've spent some time understanding and thinking about these issues, it will be difficult to evaluate offers you do receive.

More important, if you make a decision that you cannot tolerate and feel you must leave that job, you will then have both unemployment and self-esteem issues to contend with. These will combine to make the next job search tough going, indeed. So make your acceptance a carefully considered decision.

NEGOTIATING YOUR OFFER

It may be that there is some aspect of your job offer that is not particularly attractive to you. Perhaps there is no relocation allotment to help you move your possessions, and this presents some financial hardship for you. It may be that the health insurance is less than you had hoped. Your initial assignment may be different from what you expected, either in its location or in the duties and responsibilities that comprise it. Or it may simply be that the salary is less than you anticipated. Other considerations may be your official starting date of employment, vacation time, evening hours, dates of training programs or schools, and other concerns.

If you are considering not accepting the job because of some item or items in the job offer "package" that do not meet your needs, you should know that most employers emphatically wish that you would bring that issue to their attention. It may be that the employer can alter it to make the offer more agreeable for you. In some cases it cannot be changed. In any event the employer would generally like to have the opportunity to try to remedy a difficulty rather than risk losing a good potential employee over an issue that might have been resolved. After all, they have spent time and funds in securing your services, and they certainly deserve an opportunity to resolve any possible differences.

Honesty is the best approach in discussing any objections or uneasiness you might have over the employer's offer. Having received your formal offer in writing, contact your employer representative and indicate your particular dissatisfaction in a straightforward manner. For example, you might explain that while you are very interested in being employed by this organization, the salary (or any other benefit) is less than you have determined you require. State the terms you need, and listen to the response. You may be asked to put this in writing, or you may be asked to hold off until the firm can decide on a response. If you are dealing with a senior representative of the organization, one who has been involved in hiring for some time, you may get an immediate response or a solid indication of possible outcomes.

Perhaps the issue is one of relocation. Your initial assignment is in the Midwest, and because you had indicated a strong West Coast preference, you are surprised at the actual assignment. You might simply indicate that while you understand the need for the company to assign you based on its needs, you are disappointed and had hoped to be placed on the West Coast. You could inquire if that were still possible and, if not, would it be reasonable to expect a West Coast relocation in the future.

If your request is presented in a reasonable way, most employers will not see this as jeopardizing your offer. If they can agree to your proposal, they will. If not, they will simply tell you so, and you may choose to continue your candidacy with them or remove yourself from consideration. The choice will be up to you.

Some firms will adjust benefits within their parameters to meet the candidate's need if at all possible. If a candidate requires a relocation cost allowance, he or she may be asked to forego tuition benefits for the first year to accomplish this adjustment. An increase in life insurance may be adjusted by some other benefit trade-off; perhaps a family dental plan is not needed. In these decisions you are called upon, sometimes under time pressure, to know how you value these issues and how important each is to you.

Many employers find they are more comfortable negotiating for candidates who have unique qualifications or who bring especially needed expertise to the organization. Employers hiring large numbers of entry-level college graduates may be far more reluctant to accommodate any changes in offer conditions. They are well supplied with candidates with similar education and experience so that if rejected by one candidate, they can draw new candidates from an ample labor pool.

COMPARING OFFERS

The condition of the economy, the job seekers' academic major and particular geographic job market, and individual needs and demands for certain employment conditions may not provide more than one job offer at a time. Some job seekers may feel that no reasonable offer should go unaccepted for the simple fear there won't be another.

In a tough job market, or if the job you seek is not widely available, or when your job search goes on too long and becomes difficult to sustain financially and emotionally, it may be necessary to accept an inferior offer. The alternative is continued unemployment. Even here, when you feel you don't have a choice, you can at least understand that in accepting this particular offer, there may be limitations and conditions you don't appreciate. At the time of acceptance, there were no other alternatives, but you can begin to use that position to gain the experience and talent to move toward a more attractive position.

Sometimes, however, more than one offer is received, and the candidate has the luxury of choice. If the job seeker knows what he or she wants and has done the necessary self-assessment honestly and thoroughly, it may be clear that one of the offers conforms more closely to those expressed wants and needs.

However, if, as so often happens, the offers are similar in terms of conditions and salary, the question then becomes which organization might provide the necessary climate, opportunities, and advantages for your professional development and growth. This is the time when solid employer research and astute questioning during the interviews really pays off. How much did you learn about the employer through your own research and skillful questioning? When the interviewer asked during the interview "Do you have any questions?" did you ask the kinds of questions that would help resolve a choice between one organization and another? Just as an employer must decide among numerous applicants, so must the applicant learn to assess the potential employer. Both are partners in the job search.

RENEGING ON AN OFFER

An especially disturbing occurrence for employers and career counseling professionals is when a job seeker formally (either orally or by written contract) accepts employment with one organization and later reneges on the agreement and goes with another employer.

There are all kinds of rationalizations offered for this unethical behavior. None of them satisfies. The sad irony is that what the job seeker is willing to do to the employer—make a promise and then break it—he or she would be outraged to have done to him- or herself: have the job offer pulled. It is a very bad way to begin a career. It suggests the individual has not taken the time to do the necessary self-assessment and self-awareness exercises to think and judge critically. The new offer taken may, in fact, be no better or worse than the one refused. You should be aware that there have been incidents of legal action following job candidates' reneging on an offer. This adds a very sour note to what should be a harmonious beginning of a lifelong adventure.

CHAPTER EIGHT

THE GRADUATE SCHOOL CHOICE

The reasons for furthering one's education in graduate school can be as varied and unique as the individuals electing this course of action. Many continue their studies at an advanced level because they simply find it difficult to end the educational process. They love what they are learning and want to learn more and broaden their academic exploration.

··

Maybe an experience you had in a practicum or internship in your criminal justice program intrigued you about the possibilities of becoming a lawyer. Conducting intake interviews in a legal services clinic, you saw firsthand the difference that legal expertise made in these people's lives. You were impressed and felt strongly that you'd like to make a similar contribution. Accompanying staff attorneys to court, you gained an even deeper appreciation for the complexities of the judicial process and the various roles played by judicial workers. The courtroom arena opened up further possibilities that you had not known existed. You became excited about the role of law in people's lives and want to learn more and at a more sophisticated level of study. Law school and the degree of Juris Doctor (J.D.) can offer that.

Others attend graduate school for purely practical reasons; they have examined employment prospects in the field of study, and all indications are that a graduate degree is requisite. A law degree is required, for example, for major promotional advancement in some federal employment, in senior-level corrections work, and in court administration. Teaching on the college level is also possible with a law degree. A J.D. degree is still considered a terminal degree (no higher degree necessary to teach in this field) at some colleges, particularly at many community, technical, and smaller public and private colleges.

Whether you're considering law school to further your education in criminal justice or to sit out a tough job market, the wonderful thing about this graduate school choice is that it doesn't narrow your job opportunities but instead explodes them. Often, taking advanced graduate studies means fewer jobs and a narrow job market. You become "overqualified" for many positions that are still attractive to you. But, in this case, it's not unusual for a state trooper to hold a J.D. degree. Having the degree provides the trooper with significant opportunities for increased responsibility and salary on the job but does not preclude a private practice in law. You won't find this situation with many other graduate fields.

CONSIDER YOUR MOTIVES

The answer to the question of "Why graduate school?" is a personal one for each applicant. Nevertheless, it is important to consider your motives carefully. Graduate school involves additional time out of the employment market, a high level of critical evaluation, significant autonomy as you pursue your studies, and considerable financial expenditure. For some students in doctoral programs, there may be additional life choice issues, such as relationships, marriage, and parenthood, that may present real challenges while in a program of study. You would be well advised to consider the following questions as you think about your decision to continue your studies.

Are You Postponing Some Tough Decisions by Going to School?
Graduate school is not a place to go to avoid life's problems. There is intense competition for graduate school slots and for the fellowships, scholarships, and financial aid available. This competition means extensive interviewing,

resume submission, and essay writing that rivals corporate recruitment. Likewise, the graduate school process is a mentored one in which faculty stay aware of and involved in the academic progress of their students and continually challenge the quality of their work. Many graduate students are called upon to participate in teaching and professional writing and research as well.

In other words, this is no place to hide from the spotlight. Graduate students work very hard and much is demanded of them individually. If you elect to go to graduate school to avoid the stresses and strains of the "real world," you will find no safe place in higher academics. Vivid accounts, both fictional and nonfictional, have depicted quite accurately the personal and professional demands of graduate school work.

The selection of graduate studies as a career option should be a positive choice—something you *want* to do. It shouldn't be selected as an escape from other, less attractive or more challenging options, nor should it be selected as the option of last resort (i.e., "I can't do anything else; I'd better just stay in school."). If you're in some doubt about the strength of your reasoning about continuing in school, discuss the issues with a career counselor. Together you can clarify your reasoning, and you'll get some sound feedback on what you're about to undertake.

On the other hand, staying on in graduate school because of a particularly poor employment market and a lack of jobs at entry-level positions has proven to be an effective "stalling" strategy. If you can afford it, pursuing a graduate degree immediately after your undergraduate education gives you a year or two to "wait out" a difficult economic climate, while at the same time acquiring a potentially valuable credential.

Have You Done Some "Hands-On" Reality Testing?

There are experiential options available to give some reality to your decision-making process about graduate school. Internships or work in the field can give you a good idea about employment demands, conditions, and atmosphere.

∙∙

Perhaps as a justice administration major, you're considering a graduate program in business administration, with an eye to a career as a senior court administrator. You realize you'll need the graduate work in systems administration, accounting, and management that the business degree will deliver. A summer job or internship that puts you in contact with professionals who are working in court administration will help you to further define your grad uate school objectives. Even with the experience of only one employment setting, you'll have a stronger concept of the pace of the job, interaction with colleagues, legal and operational procedures, opportunities for personal development, and amount of paperwork involved. Talking to people and asking questions are invaluable exercises in helping you better understand the objective of your graduate study.

For justice administration majors, this kind of reality testing demonstrates far more authoritatively than any other method what real-world skills are necessary, how they are used, and what aspects of your anticipated graduate preparation will prove valuable. It's evident in today's employment market that undergraduate degrees in the criminal justice area are highly marketable, and a graduate degree will only enhance your attractiveness to an employer. Experiencing internships, practicums, and/or co-op experiences enables you to explore and clarify your graduate school decision.

....

Do You Need an Advanced Degree to Work in Your Field?

Certainly there are fields such as law, psychiatry, medicine, and college teaching that demand advanced degrees. Is the field of employment you're considering one that also puts a premium on an advanced degree? You may be surprised. Read job ads on the Internet and in a number of major Sunday newspapers for positions you would enjoy. How many of those require an advanced degree?

Retailing, for example, has always put a premium on what people can do rather than how much education they have had. Successful people in retailing come from all academic preparations. A Ph.D. in your field may bring more prestige to a job, but it may not bring a more senior position or better pay. In fact, it may disqualify you for some jobs because an employer might believe you will be unhappy to be overqualified for a particular position. Or your motives in applying for the work may be misconstrued, and the employer might think you will only be working at this level until something better comes along. None of this may be true for you, but it comes about because you are working outside of the usual territory for that degree level.

When economic times are especially difficult, we tend to see stories featured about individuals with advanced degrees doing what is considered unsuitable work, such as the Ph.D. in French driving a cab or the Ph.D. in chemistry waiting tables. Actually, this is not particularly surprising when you consider that as your degree level advances, the job market narrows appreciably. At any one time, regardless of economic circumstances, there are only so many jobs for your particular level of expertise. If you cannot find employment for your advanced degree level, chances are you will be considered suspect for many other kinds of employment and may be forced into temporary work far removed from your original intention.

Before making an important decision such as graduate study, learn your options and carefully consider what you want to do with your advanced degree. Ask yourself whether it is reasonable to think you can achieve your goals. Will there be jobs when you graduate? Where will they be? What will they pay? How competitive will the market be at that time, based on current predictions?

If you're uncertain about the degree requirements for the fields you're interested in, you should check a publication such as the U.S. Department of Labor's *Occupational Outlook Handbook* (www.bls.gov). Each entry on the *OOH* includes a section on training and other qualifications that will indicate clearly what the minimum educational requirement is for employment, what degree is the standard, and what employment may be possible without the required credential.

For example, for physicists and astronomers a doctoral degree in physics or a closely related field is essential. Certainly this is the degree of choice in academic institutions. However, the *Occupational Outlook Handbook* also indicates what kinds of employment may be available to individuals holding a master's or even a bachelor's degree in physics.

Have You Compared Your Expectations of What Graduate School Will Do for You with What It Has Done for Alumni of the Program You're Considering?

Most colleges and universities perform some kind of postgraduate survey of their students to ascertain where they are employed, what additional education they have received, and what levels of salary they are enjoying. Ask to see this information either from the university you are considering applying to or from your own alma mater, especially if it has a similar graduate program. Such surveys often reveal surprises about occupational decisions, salaries, and work satisfaction. This information may affect your decision.

The value of self-assessment (the process of examining and making decisions about your own hierarchy of values and goals) is especially important in analyzing the desirability of possible career paths involving graduate education. Sometimes a job requiring advanced education seems to hold real promise but is disappointing in salary potential or number of opportunities available. Certainly it is better to research this information before embarking on a program of graduate studies. It may not change your mind about your decision, but by becoming better informed about your choice, you become better prepared for your future.

Have You Talked with People in Your Field to Explore What You Might Be Doing After Graduate School?

In pursuing your undergraduate degree, you will have come into contact with many individuals trained in the field you are considering. You might also have the opportunity to attend professional conferences, workshops, seminars, and job fairs where you can expand your network of contacts. Talk to them all! Find out about their individual career paths, discuss your own plans and hopes, get their feedback on the reality of your expectations, and heed their advice about your prospects. Each will have a unique tale to tell, and each will bring a different perspective on the current marketplace for the credentials you are seeking. Talking to enough people will make you an expert on what's out there.

Are You Excited by the Idea of Studying the Particular Field You Have in Mind?

This question may be the most important one of all. If you are going to spend several years in advanced study, perhaps engendering some debt or postponing some lifestyle decisions for an advanced degree, you simply ought to enjoy what you're doing. Examine your work in the discipline so far. Has it been fun? Have you found yourself exploring various paths of thought? Do you read in your area for fun? Do you enjoy talking about it, thinking about it, and sharing it with others? Advanced degrees often are the beginning of a lifetime's involvement with a particular subject. Choose carefully a field that will hold your interest and your enthusiasm.

If nothing else, do the following:

- Talk and question (remember to listen!)

- Reality test

- Soul-search by yourself or with a person you trust

FINDING THE RIGHT PROGRAM FOR YOU: SOME CONSIDERATIONS

There are several important factors in coming to a sound decision about the right graduate program for you. You'll want to begin by locating institutions that offer appropriate programs, examining each of these programs and their requirements, undertaking the application process by reviewing catalogs and obtaining application materials, visiting campuses if possible, arranging for letters of recommendation, writing your application statement, and, finally, following up on your applications.

Locate Institutions with Appropriate Programs

Once you decide on a particular advanced degree, it's important to develop a list of schools offering such a degree program. Perhaps the best source of graduate program information is Peterson's. The website (www.petersons .com) and the printed *Guides to Graduate Study* allow you to search for information by institution name, location, or academic area. The website also allows you to do a keyword search. Use the website and guides to build your list. In addition, you may want to consult the College Board's *Index of Majors and Graduate Degrees*, which will help you find graduate programs offering the degree you seek. It is indexed by academic major and then categorized by state.

Now, this may be a considerable list. You may want to narrow the choices down further by a number of criteria: tuition, availability of financial aid, public versus private institutions, United States versus international institutions, size of student body, size of faculty, application fee, and geographic location. This is only a partial list; you will have your own important considerations. Perhaps you are an avid scuba diver and you find it unrealistic to think you could pursue graduate study for a number of years without being able to ocean dive from time to time. Good! That's a decision and it's honest. Now, how far from the ocean is too far, and what schools meet your other needs? In any case, and according to your own criteria, begin to put together a reasonable list of graduate schools that you are willing to spend time investigating.

Examine the Degree Programs and Their Requirements

Once you've determined the criteria by which you want to develop a list of graduate schools, you can begin to examine the degree program requirements, faculty composition, and institutional research orientation. Again, using resources such as Peterson's website or guides can reveal an amazingly rich level of material by which to judge your possible selections.

In addition to degree programs and degree requirements, entries will include information about application fees, entrance test requirements, tuition, percentage of applicants accepted, numbers of applicants receiving financial aid, gender breakdown of students, numbers of full- and part-time faculty, and often gender breakdown of faculty as well. Numbers graduating in each program and research orientations of departments are also included in some entries. There is information on graduate housing; student services; and library, research, and computer facilities. A contact person, phone number, and address are also standard information in these listings.

It can be helpful to draw up a chart and enter relevant information about each school you are considering in order to have a ready reference on points of information that are important to you.

Undertake the Application Process

Program Information. Once you've decided on a selection of schools, obtain program information and applications. Nearly every school has a website that contains most of the detailed information you need to narrow your choices. In addition, applications can be printed from the site. If, however, you don't want to print out lots of information, you can request that a copy of the catalog and application materials be sent to you.

When you have your information in hand, give it all a careful reading and make notes of issues you might want to discuss via E-mail, on the telephone, or in a personal interview.

....

If you are interested in graduate work in criminology, for example, in addition to courses in research methods, criminological theory, psychology, and criminal justice, are there courses in forensic psychology, public policy, organizational behavior, criminology and deviance, and others?

....

What is the ratio of faculty to the required number of courses for your degree? How often will you encounter the same faculty member as an instructor?

If the program offers a practicum or off-campus experience, who arranges this? Does the graduate school select a site and place you there, or is it your responsibility? What are the professional affiliations of the faculty? Does the program merit any outside professional endorsement or accreditation?

Critically evaluate the catalogs of each of the programs you are considering. List any questions you have and ask current or former teachers and colleagues for their impressions as well.

The Application. Preview each application thoroughly to determine what you need to provide in the way of letters of recommendation, transcripts from undergraduate schools or any previous graduate work, and personal essays.

Make a notation for each application of what you will need to complete that document.

Additionally, you'll want to determine entrance testing requirements for each institution and immediately arrange to register for appropriate tests. Information can be obtained from associated websites, including www.ets.org (GRE, GMAT, TOEFL, PRAXIS, SLS, Higher Education Assessment), www.lsat.org (LSAT), and www.tpcweb.com/mat (MAT). Your college career office should also be able to provide you with advice and additional information.

Visit the Campus if Possible

If time and finances allow, a visit, interview, and tour can help make your decision easier. You can develop a sense of the student body, meet some of the faculty, and hear up-to-date information on resources and the curriculum. You will have a brief opportunity to "try out" the surroundings to see if they fit your needs. After all, it will be home for a while. If a visit is not possible but you have questions, don't hesitate to call and speak with the dean of the graduate school. Most are more than happy to talk to candidates and want them to have the answers they seek. Graduate school admission is a very personal and individual process.

Arrange for Letters of Recommendation

This is also the time to begin to assemble a group of individuals who will support your candidacy as a graduate student by writing letters of recommendation or completing recommendation forms. Some schools will ask you to provide letters of recommendation to be included with your application or sent directly to the school by the recommender. Other graduate programs will provide a recommendation form that must be completed by the recommender. These graduate school forms vary greatly in the amount of space provided for a written recommendation. So that you can use letters as you need to, ask your recommenders to address their letters "To Whom It May Concern," unless one of your recommenders has a particular connection to one of your graduate schools or knows an official at the school.

Choose recommenders who can speak authoritatively about the criteria important to selection officials at your graduate school. In other words, choose recommenders who can write about your grasp of the literature in your field of study, your ability to write and speak effectively, your class performance, and your demonstrated interest in the field outside of class. Other characteristics that graduate schools are interested in assessing include your emotional maturity, leadership ability, breadth of general knowledge, intellectual ability, motivation, perseverance, and ability to engage in independent inquiry.

When requesting recommendations, it's especially helpful to put the request in writing. Explain your graduate school intentions and express some of your thoughts about graduate school and your appreciation for their support. Don't be shy about "prompting" your recommenders with some suggestions of what you would appreciate being included in their comments. Most recommenders will find this direction helpful and will want to produce a statement of support that you can both stand behind. Consequently, if your interaction with one recommender was especially focused on research projects, he or she might be best able to speak of those skills and your critical thinking ability. Another recommender may have good comments to make about your public presentation skills.

Give your recommenders plenty of lead time in which to complete your recommendation, and set a date by which they should respond. If they fail to meet your deadline, be prepared to make a polite call or visit to inquire if they need more information or if there is anything you can do to move the process along.

Whether or not you are providing a graduate school form or asking for an original letter to be mailed, be sure to provide an envelope and postage if the recommender must mail the form or letter directly to the graduate school.

Each recommendation you request should provide a different piece of information about you for the selection committee. It might be pleasant for letters of recommendation to say that you are a fine, upstanding individual, but a selection committee for graduate school will require specific information. Each recommender has had a unique relationship with you, and his or her letter should reflect that. Think of each letter as helping to build a more complete portrait of you as a potential graduate student.

Write Your Application Statement

For a criminal justice major, this should be an exciting and challenging assignment and one you are able to complete successfully. You can assume that any required essays on a graduate application for criminal justice will weigh heavily in the decision process of the admissions committee.

An excellent source to help in writing this essay is *How to Write a Winning Personal Statement for Graduate and Professional School,* by Richard J. Stelzer. It has been written from the perspective of what graduate school selection committees are looking for when they read these essays. It provides helpful tips to keep your essay targeted on the kinds of issues and criteria that are important to selection committees and that provide them with the kind of information they can best utilize in making their decision.

Follow Up on Your Applications

After you have finished each application and mailed it along with your transcript requests and letters of recommendation, be sure to follow up on the progress of your file. For example, call the graduate school administrative staff to see whether your transcripts have arrived. If the school required your recommenders to fill out a specific recommendation form that had to be mailed directly to the school, you will want to ensure that they have all arrived in good time for the processing of your application. It is your responsibility to make certain that all required information is received by the institution.

RESEARCHING FINANCIAL AID SOURCES, SCHOLARSHIPS, AND FELLOWSHIPS

Financial aid information is available from each graduate school. You may be eligible for federal, state, and/or institutional support. There are lengthy forms to complete, and some of these will vary by school, type of school (public versus private), and state. Be sure to note the deadline dates on each form.

There are many excellent resources available to help you explore all of your financial aid options. Visit your college career office or local public library to find out about the range of materials available. Two excellent resources are Peterson's website (www.petersons.com) and its book *Peterson's Grants for Graduate and Post Doctoral Study*. Another good reference is the Foundation Center's *Foundation Grants to Individuals*. These types of resources generally contain information that can be accessed by indexes including field of study, specific eligibility requirements, administering agency, and geographic focus.

EVALUATING ACCEPTANCES

If you apply to and are accepted at more than one school, it is time to return to your initial research and self-assessment to evaluate your options and select the program that will best help you achieve the goals you set for pursuing graduate study. You'll want to choose a program that will allow you to complete your studies in a timely and cost-effective way. This may be a good time to get additional feedback from professors and career professionals who are familiar with your interests and plans. Ultimately, the decision is yours, so be sure you get answers to all the questions you can think of.

SOME NOTES ABOUT REJECTION

Each graduate school is searching for applicants who appear to have the qualifications necessary to succeed in its program. Applications are evaluated on a combination of undergraduate grade point average, strength of letters of recommendation, standardized test scores, and personal statements written for the application.

A carelessly completed application is one reason many applicants are denied admission to a graduate program. To avoid this type of needless rejection, be sure to carefully and completely answer all appropriate questions on the application form, focus your personal statement given the instructions provided, and submit your materials well in advance of the deadline. Remember that your test scores and recommendations are considered a part of your application, so they must also be received by the deadline.

If you are rejected by a school that especially interests you, you may want to contact the dean of graduate studies to discuss the strengths and weaknesses of your application. Information provided by the dean will be useful in reapplying to the program later or applying to other, similar programs.

PART TWO

THE CAREER PATHS

CHAPTER NINE

CRIMINAL JUSTICE: A DEGREE IN DEMAND

o many opportunities abound for people with formal education in criminal justice that the list of possible jobs is truly endless. More jobs are becoming available each year, with new positions being created in public safety, private protective services, and the growing field of Internet security. Though you'll see statistics quoted, it is impossible to delineate all the available positions and vacancies in criminal justice that exist on the federal, state, and local levels.

Along with strong employment prospects overall and in the variety of job titles, *Great Jobs for Criminal Justice Majors* highlights the dramatic shift in criminal justice–related jobs from semiprofessional status to professional status. In both the fieldwork and research involved in producing this career guide, we saw an increasing emphasis on the educational preparation of job applicants and growing number of advanced degrees among established criminal justice workers. As the supply of more highly educated workers has increased, the education standards for entry-level jobs have correspondingly been raised. The job market begins to demand what the market can deliver!

Criminal justice jobs cannot be encompassed in one prototypical job or assignment. The occupations in this field span a broad spectrum of responsibilities, functions, and stressors. Higher entry-level education requirements, training, professional development, and additional postsecondary education are molding the modern criminal justice professional. This second half of the book gives you a close-up encounter with five career categories, or paths, that are open to you.

The safety and well-being of our nation's citizens greatly depend on the police officers, sheriffs, state troopers, highway patrol officers, federal agents, and others in **law enforcement** responsible for enforcing statutes, laws, and regulations. Those in the field of **corrections** are responsible for overseeing individuals who have been arrested, are awaiting trial or some other hearing, or who have been convicted of a crime and sentenced to serve time in jail, prison, or community service. **Juvenile justice** professionals work with the courts, social service agencies, caregivers, and the community to provide, where possible, alternatives to the criminal court system as they attempt to rehabilitate young people who have broken the law. The **courts** offer positions in security, administration, research, and legal affairs that can provide a stimulating and engrossing viewpoint on the criminal justice system as it is played out in the courtroom. The **business** sector was once chiefly the alternative for retired criminal justice professionals, who would go on to serve as consultants on criminal proceedings, security, and the prevention of theft, fire, vandalism, and illegal entry. Now, with the growth, complexity, emphasis on professionalism and training, and technological sophistication of the criminal justice field, business opportunities have expanded beyond those bounds. Claims investigation, property loss management, private security, and protection specialists are all viable career areas.

Each of these exciting areas is surveyed in the chapters that follow. As you read about the five career paths you'll probably be pleased to see how often employers ask specifically for your major. In writing this book, we drew upon job ads we see every day in our work as career counselors. Employers want criminal justice majors for these jobs in law enforcement, juvenile justice, court-related occupations, and corrections. Sure, they may go on to list other acceptable educational backgrounds in the social sciences, but the criminal justice major involves a distinctly different academic preparation.

For employers, the important difference in the background of criminal justice majors is the combination of a liberal arts education with the specialized knowledge of policing, the courts, corrections, and the justice system. Most criminal justice curricula provide students with a theoretical foundation of the discipline along with a solid grounding in the social science methodologies as they apply to criminal justice. Criminal justice majors have had special work in social interactions and the related forces that contribute to social order, conflict, and societal change. Employers realize that other curricula in the social sciences offer some of the same background but that it is not targeted as in the criminal justice curriculum and does not include the practical applications.

Perhaps you have added to your college preparation with an internship or practicum experience, either as part of your formal studies or on your own during summer or winter break. If you are reading this book *before* you graduate, now's the time to maximize the value of an internship or other hands-on experience in criminal justice. The opportunity to work alongside seasoned professionals, to observe the pace and nature of their day-to-day activities and routines, brings a new awareness and reality to your appreciation of law enforcement work. If your experience is a formal internship, you'll have an opportunity to make your own contribution to the efforts of your employer, and that experience is likely to be a deeply satisfying one. You'll begin to see that others treat you as a colleague, that you are able to do the work, and then you can assess whether you like it or not and whether the job holds promise for you as a career field. That's the whole point of internships. Even if they end up teaching you that a particular field is not the right one for you, they are immensely valuable because they give you the insight that helps you make better choices after you graduate—whatever those choices are.

Because criminal justice confronts societal issues as they are happening right now, the people who work in criminal justice comprise a microcosm of society. Being able to choose from inner-city, rural, or urban settings for a variety of career interests, including policing, juvenile probation, correctional security, counseling, arson investigation, and local, state, and federal law enforcement, means that you can aim for the type of criminal justice career and the particular environment that best fits your needs. Criminal justice is so dynamic and is growing so rapidly that it's difficult to confidently predict what the future holds for the field. As we discuss in Chapter 14, among the current issues surrounding the Internet are concerns about privacy, security of information (especially credit card data), and the legitimacy of electronic signatures.

You'll be working with people from a wide variety of cultural, religious, socioeconomic, racial, ethnic, and gender orientations. That's important to conscientious criminal justice majors because, as a group, they are inquisitive about people and what makes them "tick." Police on the street need this curiosity and so do correctional officers and counseling professionals. Sensitivity to diversity, strong interpersonal skills, and healthy attitudes combined with solid critical thinking skills and high ethical standards are the prerequisites across the board in all the jobs described in Part Two. Another common denominator underlying all the career paths presented is the need to be proactive in crime prevention.

However, the appreciation of diversity that is a strength in the workforce of criminal justice is not without some attendant problems. It would be naive to ignore the challenges that race, ethnicity, and gender bring to the workplace. Not a week goes by that the popular press does not carry a story reflecting one of these themes. It may be contested opportunities for women in law enforcement management, inadequate promotional rates for African Americans in the FBI, or any of numerous possible accusations of discriminatory practices by the public against the police. But, as you read and examine these stories, you'll frequently find corresponding "sidebar" articles detailing improved opportunities, less discrimination, and more equity in hiring and promotion. Because of the strong public scrutiny, employment areas in criminal justice come in for some significant attention by various interested publics, and because of that attention, they just get better and better.

A FULL PLATE OF CHOICES

This is an exciting professional field to be considering for your life's work, and this book presents many wonderful career options. Because of that, in reading these chapters you may become overwhelmed by the number and variety of jobs and by your own enthusiasm and interest *in every one of them*! It's kind of like moving your tray along the line of a particularly wonderful buffet. It gets increasingly frustrating as you proceed because the choices get tougher. You want a bit of everything.

Well, here's the good news! Most of the jobs profiled here are entry-level positions; in the first few years of your career, you'll still be exploring your options, and nothing you do now is cast in stone. Your employers know that as well. Sometimes they know better than you do that after a year or two, you may decide to try your hand in some other aspect of the profession. And that's OK! In the criminal justice field, your degree gives you wonderful flexibility, and most of these entry-level jobs would be considered highly desirable work experiences for the next advanced position in any of the other fields.

So, enjoy the variety presented in this book, and don't get frustrated over "the decision." You can make changes as your career develops. One thing you must do: listen to yourself; listen to your heart. You know who you are, and you know the decisions you've made in the past and what's worked and what hasn't. Even the self-assessment exercises in Chapter 1 are more about confirming what you already knew intuitively. After all, given your twenty years or so of experience, you should be an expert on you! So, as you learn about the possibilities for the beginning of your career in criminal justice, hold each job up to what you know about yourself and your interests and enthusiasms, and go with your personal preferences and your strong intuition about who you are and what you want. You won't go wrong!

CHAPTER 10

PATH 1: LAW ENFORCEMENT: PATROL YOUR POSSIBILITIES

P olicing is the front line of law enforcement. Almost three-quarters of a million men and women serve in police positions in the United States. It's a big job, and it's an important one. Police work has a long and proud tradition: police officers are part of our social and cultural landscape and have been ever since we were old enough to answer the question "What do you want to be when you grow up?" Like doctor, firefighter, and teacher, "policeman" was a common childhood aspiration. These were the idealized jobs of our youth because they were important, they were helpful, and—though maybe we couldn't articulate it—they were noble, too.

While we hope this book will serve to strengthen your belief in and esteem for the policing profession, along with that respect you should have a realistic and grounded view of the career path as it stands today. Policing and law enforcement in general are changing and evolving. It's an exciting field that's responding positively and with dramatic new initiatives to a dynamic society. How exciting to be part of that! But with those changes and new initiatives come new demands on anyone who wants to work in law enforcement at the local, state, or federal level.

In our field research for this volume of the *Great Jobs* series, we would frequently come away from an interview with law enforcement officials feeling grateful that these high-quality people had elected to devote their lives to law enforcement. But our gratitude was almost overtaken by our surprise at the range of concerns and demands placed on those whose job it is to enforce the law. In this chapter, we hope to give you an accurate picture of what you need to succeed as a law enforcement officer today.

First and foremost, the new mandate for recent graduates thinking about careers in law enforcement is a need to be intelligent, open, and curious. You must have a positive outlook about people and a sincere appreciation that your role in law enforcement is most successfully fulfilled if it is preventative and anticipatory, not reactive and punitive. At one meeting we had in a midsize city police department, the captain told us that he wants his officers to be in the community "like a fish among the reeds." He wants them and the public to be comfortable with police mixing into the community—causing few, if any, ripples in the social fabric. While sensitively and poetically expressed, this officer's view of policing today is not unusual. As the pool of qualified applicants has become increasingly talented, educated, and prepared for the larger scope of law enforcement today, the individuals doing the hiring have raised the hurdles accordingly.

For all the policing jobs described in this path, a group interview is almost always part of the final stages of the job search. Even for small city police departments, it is not uncommon for the candidate to appear before an interview "board" made up of police representatives, city officials, and other interested parties. The question "Why did you decide to enter law enforcement?" (or some variation on that phrasing) is sure to be asked. Before facing that question, you need to ask *yourself* if you are ready for the law enforcement jobs of today. You'll need to sort through your motives, thinking clearly about your role as a law enforcement official. These examining and interviewing boards are not interested in swagger or bullying. They want sensitive, intelligent, thoughtful police officers who can react first with their minds and resolve problems to avoid having situations escalate into trouble. It's clear, then, that law enforcement today is a more demanding and challenging job than ever before. It also follows that the interviewing and screening processes to enter the field have become correspondingly sophisticated.

DEFINITION OF THE CAREER PATH

Most people think they have a pretty good idea of what police officers do on the job. What they may discover is that the common view of law enforcement jobs has been distorted by images from television, films, and literature. These portrayals do not always provide an accurate and complete depiction of a police officer's job. There are many varieties of police work, and each has its own demands and rewards. State troopers, detectives, police officers on the "beat," and many other types of law enforcement officials (sheriffs, liquor commission officials, etc.) keep public order and protect lives and property by enforcing the statutes, laws, and regulations decided upon by local, regional, state, and federal legislatures. The functions of each of these officials can vary widely. Differences occur because of the size and type of the organization, the specific job description, and sometimes the impact of being "on" or "off duty." Generally, however, these officials are required in most cases to exercise the authority they have been given whenever that action is necessary.

Let's look at the possible positions and their mission in local and county, state, and federal law enforcement jobs:

Exhibit 10.1

POSSIBLE POSITIONS AND THEIR MISSIONS

LOCAL AND COUNTY LAW ENFORCEMENT

Position	Basic Mission
Police Officer	On patrol. A "generalist" who maintains law and order and arrests violators.
Sheriff	Similar to police officer, with the added responsibility of maintaining the county jail.

STATE LAW ENFORCEMENT

Position	Basic Mission
State Trooper	Statewide patrol; maintains law and order.
Highway Patrol Officer	Patrols state highways, conducts traffic, and performs general law enforcement duties.
University Police Officer College Public Safety	Maintains law and order on state university or college campuses or properties.
Conservation and Wildlife Officer	Patrols the outdoors for violations of laws regarding wildlife and natural resources.
Park Police	Patrols state parks and reservations.
Corrections Officer	Maintains the custody, security, and well-being of inmates in a state correctional facility.
Parole Officer	Provides supervision and guidance to an assigned caseload of releasees from state and local correctional facilities.

FEDERAL LAW ENFORCEMENT

Position	Basic Mission
Border Patrol Agent	Protects U.S. borders from illegal entry.
Federal Police Officer	Maintains protection of employees and property of designated federal agencies.
Federal Corrections Officer	Maintains safekeeping, care, and protection of federal inmates.
Federal Parole Officer	Maintains supervision and guidance of federal releasees.
Federal Protection Officer	Maintains protection of federal buildings nationwide.
Postal Inspector	Conducts investigations of postal crimes.
DEA Special Agent	Enforces laws and regulations involving narcotics and controlled substances.
Deputy U.S. Marshal	Provides protection for U.S. courts and judges; apprehends federal fugitives; transports federal prisoners.
IRS Agent	Conducts criminal investigations involving tax laws.
Customs Inspector	Enforces laws governing the importation of merchandise, including the inspection of persons and carriers.
Immigration Inspector	Prevents ineligible people from entering the United States.
FBI Agent	Investigates violations of federal criminal law; protects the United States from foreign intelligence activities.
Secret Service Agent	Protects the president and other dignitaries and investigates threats against them; investigates counterfeiting crimes.
U.S. Park Ranger	Patrols and protects United States parks and reservations.

ATF Special Agent	Investigates criminal use of firearms and explosives; enforces federal alcohol and tobacco regulations.

These lists do not enumerate all the possible law enforcement positions available. Not included here, for example, are the many law enforcement agencies to be found in the military, nor all the "special" police forces formed to protect airports, harbors, transit systems, railroads, and other authorities.

Police Officers

Some new entrants into local law enforcement will start as police officers and begin their careers as patrol officers (discussed at length in the following section, "Working Conditions"). Other police officers specialize and become proficient in a variety of law enforcement areas, such as chemical and microscopic analysis, firearms identification, or handwriting and/or fingerprint analysis. Others want to work with specialized units, such as K-9, horse-mounted, or motorcycle patrol units. You could also pursue work, depending on your location, with harbor patrols or with special weapon or emergency response teams, including bomb detection and disposal units. Beyond these assignments, many specific units are assembled to combat certain types of crime, including Internet felonies.

You may be interested in the work of detectives or special agents. These jobs are plainclothes positions whose task it is to collect and assemble evidence for criminal cases. They do a lot of interviewing, researching of records, observing of suspects, and participating in raids or arrests. Curiosity, patience, judgment, discernment, and good research skills, including Web search skills, are essential.

Entry-level positions in law enforcement vary with the hiring agency. For example, most police officers begin with basic patrol duties for a specific area. As you rise in the ranks, duties become more specific, and you become eligible for candidacy in other types of police work. Federal positions, such as in the FBI, usually pair new entrants into the force with a more experienced agent and rotate them through a variety of cases so that they receive a solid grounding in surveillance, report writing, and investigative procedures. Not very glamorous, perhaps, but important for gaining competence to achieve more sophisticated assignments.

State Troopers and Sheriffs

Some graduates will be attracted to state trooper jobs or sheriff's departments. Sheriffs and state troopers maintain order in bigger areas than those of local police: large, thinly populated areas and, of course, our nation's highways.

Roles of sheriffs can vary greatly in scope and variety from one end of the country to the other. Think of sheriff's duties as those of local or county police chiefs with far smaller departments, and you'll have a sense of the role. Generally, the position is analogous to the commanding officer of a county's law enforcement provider. In states where counties play a larger part in state governance, sheriffs' roles tend to be larger. In some states, regular police fulfill the county law enforcement job, and in other states, both sheriffs and regular police provide services for the county. In larger cities, the sheriff's department may maintain the jail or serve legal papers. In many counties, they are assigned principally to court and prison tasks. In most situations in the United States, sheriffs are elected and have significant administrative workloads, so computer skills, writing, management, and some accounting background could come in handy.

State police officers (which you may know as state troopers or the highway patrol, depending on where you live) patrol our nation's highways and enforce motor vehicle laws and regulations. If an accident occurs, they reroute traffic, give first aid, summon appropriate emergency equipment and personnel, and, most important, write up the report of the accident to determine cause. State police have another role as well, and that is to assist officers of other law enforcement agencies in enforcing criminal laws. In some very rural or underpopulated areas with poor local police coverage, the state police may take over even some of the routine primary law enforcement activities, such as the investigation of burglaries and assaults.

Federal Law Enforcers

Employment upon graduation by the federal government presents a host of law enforcement possibilities. While many of them are addressed in this chapter, for a fine guide to accessing federal law enforcement jobs and how to apply, you should visit the website of Dr. Tom O'Connor of North Carolina Wesleyan College, Department of Justice Studies, where he has assembled a federal jobs "employment mega-site" at http://faculty.ncwc.edu/toconnor/employ.htm. The Federal Bureau of Investigation remains the principal federal agency charged with investigating violations of most federal statutes. Agents of the FBI use surveillance techniques (observation as well as sophisticated electronic surveillance, including court-ordered wiretaps, phone taps, and powerful distance microphones), examine records (a large area of FBI investigative effort is "white-collar crime"), participate in undercover activities involving sensitivity and high risk, and track the interstate movement of property and individuals for criminal purposes.

Special agents employed by the U.S. Department of the Treasury work for the Bureau of Alcohol, Tobacco, and Firearms (ATF) investigating violations of federal firearms and explosives laws. You may be familiar with this agency for its involvement in the raids on the Branch Davidian compound in Waco, Texas.

The Drug Enforcement Agency (DEA) is also well known for its work in enforcing our federal drug laws. The investigations carried out by this agency can be intensive and complex, as drug activity is highly secretive and drug rings can involve numerous people and business entities to disguise their illegal activities.

Jobs in the federal arena include work with the U.S. Border Patrol (protecting our land and water boundaries), U.S. Marshals (transporting prisoners, witnesses, juries, and judges and providing court security), the Internal Revenue Service (special agents in this department collect evidence against those defrauding the federal government by nonpayment or underpayment of taxes), and, of course, the U.S. Secret Service, protecting our president and vice president and their families. The Secret Service also investigates counterfeiting and fraudulent check and credit card use.

Other possibilities in the federal government include:

- Federal Air Marshals

- General Service Administration's Federal Protective Service

WORKING CONDITIONS

One of the marvelous things about a career in law enforcement is that unlike some other professions, police officers are located everywhere, from the smallest, most rural areas to the great cities of our country and everywhere in between. Because of that flexibility, we encourage you to spend some time in your self-assessment work in Chapter 1 thinking about the advantages and disadvantages of various locales and how you'd "fit" into various environments. For example, you may prefer a very rural area that in addition to its natural beauty may also provide lower housing costs and even the future opportunity to build or buy a home on a generous piece of land. Thinking further ahead, however, you may also plan to raise a family and may find that having proximity to good schools, neighbors and friends for the children, services, and medical care for all means striking a compromise in a somewhat more densely populated area to begin your career.

Police Officers

Your classroom work, your textbooks, law enforcement guests on campus, job fairs, and other activities, including your own work and internship experience, have probably given you some sense of the reality of the police officer's job—especially at the entry level. General law enforcement duties and responsibilities are the name of the game in your first job as a police officer. Directing traffic, frequently at the scene of a fire or accident (or parade!), is a common activity. Investigating a burglary or even administering first aid likewise are parts of a "normal" day's activity, if there is such a thing for a police officer.

If you work in a larger police department, your duties will be less generalized. In larger departments, new recruits are often assigned to a specific type of duty, such as patrolling a designated business district or residential community to prevent crime. Patrol work can be immensely satisfying on many counts. You may be working with a regular partner—or a series of regular partners—and often strong friendships develop as you learn to appreciate each other's special skills and talents and realize the synergy that can occur in a team situation.

Best of all, you become deeply acquainted with an area and its residents and realize that your active presence is a deterrent to criminal activities. Even in larger cities, you will know your patrol area well and be able to recognize suspicious circumstances easily as the rhythm of your "beat" becomes familiar to you. Even such mundane events as an open door, unusual activity in a building, or a missing manhole cover will be readily noted and corrected.

TRAINING AND QUALIFICATIONS

To join a police force, from the smallest community on up to state and federal criminal justice positions, applicants must meet an ever increasing ladder of strict criteria to be considered competitive for these jobs. While it may seem that it's easier to secure a local police position than a state trooper or federal law enforcement job, the reality is a bit more complicated. Although standards do become increasingly tougher for state and federal positions, you may be unprepared for the scrutiny involved for candidates in local police jobs. Successful completion of a formal police academy program; extensive interviewing, both one-on-one and before commissions or panels; physical and psychological testing; fitness evaluations; and subjection to a wide variety of evaluative tools mean that anyone entering policing today is going to have his or her candidacy scrutinized for fitness, suitability, motive, and potential to succeed.

Civil service regulations govern police and other criminal justice positions in almost every state. Candidates must be U.S. citizens, be at least twenty years of age, and meet rigorous personal and physical qualifications. There will be written examinations and physicals that include vision, hearing, strength, and agility. You will also undergo a formal personal interview, frequently before a board made up of police and other interested parties.

A word about education: criminal justice programs abound in both two- and four-year colleges. It has been and is, without doubt, a popular major. While the major is increasingly available at four-year colleges and universities, we found many honest hiring officials who were not clear on the advantages of a bachelor's degree over an associate's degree. Some went so far as to say that law enforcement on the local level has yet to convincingly validate the importance of any formal criminal justice education per se. What officials did agree on is that there is an ample supply of bachelor-degreed applicants. The result is that most hiring officials, regardless of their view of the value of the degree, interview only bachelor-degreed graduates because the market has abundantly supplied them. Their philosophy can be summarized as "While we don't necessarily agree that a bachelor's degree means a better law enforcement officer than an associate's degree graduate, if there are plenty of four-year applicants, wouldn't we want those candidates with more education?"

The implications of this are clear: students with associate's degrees may find that their opportunities are better in areas that are less well supplied with candidates, and they should consider enrolling in some courses toward a bachelor's degree to better qualify for promotions. In fact, many observers predict that because of the growing numbers of bachelor-degree graduates in criminal justice, in five years' time a bachelor's degree will become the standard educational requirement for most police positions.

When your candidacy advances and you become a finalist for the position you seek, most employers (even in small towns) will institute a background check. Since these background checks are expensive, they are often reserved for finalists or even selected candidates for whom the job offer is pending on the results of the background examination. Because your ethics, honesty, judgment, and sense of maturity bear directly on your profession, it's important that hiring officials have detailed knowledge of how others perceive you and of your personal record.

Local and State Police

During an interview that we conducted with a police chief in a small rural town, we asked who got patrol officer jobs in his department. He said, "People I know. I only hire people I know." When we asked why they would opt to work in his town when only thirty minutes away law enforcement salaries average $8,000 to $9,000 more, he said, "The people who apply here might have worked in other towns and not been rehired or even been fired. I'm their last chance to stay in law enforcement." But even in making such an honest statement about the employee pool, the chief maintained that in a small town such as his, he wouldn't hire anyone he didn't know. So, if you live in a small town and think you want to someday police in that town, make yourself known to the police department. Volunteer your time, do an internship, or make an appointment for an informational interview. Let them know who you are and what your career goals are.

Ten to fourteen weeks of training at the state police academy is standard for all new recruits before they receive any assignments and frequently even before the hiring process is complete. The program includes intensive training in legal issues, civil rights, constitutional law, and state laws and ordinances, as well as technique training in reporting accidents, directing traffic, use of weapons, self-defense, first aid, and how to respond to a variety of emergency situations. While police academy standards of education vary from state to state, the Texas Commission on Law Enforcement 560-Hour Basic Peace Officer Course can be used as a guide. It can be found on the Web at www.geocities.com/capitolhill/lobby/5715/97index.html. The general subject areas include:

- Fitness and Wellness

- History of Policing

- State Laws

- The Criminal Justice System

- Arrest, Search, and Seizure

- Penal Code

- Traffic

- Alcohol and Drugs

- Juvenile Issues

- Field Note-Taking

- Interpersonal Communications

- Use of Force

- Strategies of Defense

- Emergency Medical Assistance

- Emergency Communications

- Problem Solving and Critical Thinking

- Police Driving

- Professional Policing

- Patrol

- Victims of Crime

- Family Violence and Related Offenses

- Recognizing and Interacting with Persons with Mental Illness and Mental Retardation

- Crowd Management

- Hazardous Materials Awareness

- Criminal Investigation

Federal Police Work

Using the example of the Federal Bureau of Investigation as a possible choice for entering the U.S. government in a law enforcement career, you will need to be between twenty-three and thirty-seven years of age. That restriction may present some problems for students graduating at twenty-two or even twenty-one years old, and it may be best for those candidates to consider entering the police academy and pursuing a job at the local or state level until they qualify in age or to be prepared to enter the FBI in a non-agent position. Beyond physical requirements, which are strict, a bachelor's degree is the *minimum* required educational attainment, and candidates with master's or law degrees are not uncommon. The FBI has five entry programs: Law, Accounting, Science, Language, and Diversified. Each of these programs has its own specific academic requirements.

The application process is legendary for its thoroughness. Screening includes background checks on character and history; credit checks, including criminal checks; and interviews with neighbors, friends, and roommates. Drug tests, a physical exam, and often a polygraph test are also part of the qualifying process. If you make it through this intensive selection procedure, you will spend four months at the FBI Academy in Virginia studying investigative techniques, personal defense, and a variety of firearms. Even during this training, you are under scrutiny, and candidates are disqualified if they display any physical, emotional, or mental handicaps that would impair their performance of the potentially dangerous duties of the FBI agent.

More on the Background Investigation

The subject of background investigations raises a very serious point. Though you may be well along in your degree progress or even have already graduated, it may not be too late to benefit from a strict admonishment heard frequently in criminal justice circles: if you want to be selected for a law enforcement position, keep your record clean! In addition to frequently required drug testing or lie detector tests, applicants' criminal records (if any) will be researched, and candidates with no record or minimal violations stand a much stronger chance of being hired. During our research for this book, we heard stories of arrests made during college dorm parties that resulted in an applicant's disqualification from candidacy for a law enforcement position. While that is not always the case with an arrest, a felony conviction would, in almost every instance, prevent you from being considered for a law enforcement job.

Job candidates must also have a responsible financial history and a pattern of respect and honesty in dealings with individuals and organizations. Improper conduct, a poor employment and/or military record, and a poor driving history record can all affect a candidate's suitability for consideration in law enforcement work.

REQUIREMENTS FOR PROMOTION

Local and State Police

Promotions allow people to move into specialized fields. Line promotion (going up in rank within a police force) requires a high passing score on a written exam and favorable performance evaluations. Your seniority and place on the list of those eligible for promotion are equally significant determinants.

Generally speaking, you must serve on the force for five years before you are eligible to sit for the lieutenant's exam, and after two years as a lieutenant, you can take the captain's test. Each advancement also requires additional education, and as degree levels in the profession continue to rise, it is expected that these requirements for additional educational attainment will become correspondingly more demanding.

After starting your law enforcement job, in most cases, you'll be eligible for promotion after these periods, which may vary depending on the size and complexity of your employer. Almost all police begin with a period of six months' probation. Generally these probationary periods have a great deal to do with the kind of training and grooming you are receiving as a new officer. Organizations whose probationary periods are longer than three months do more training and cross training, more professional development, and more mentoring of new officers, so your career is hardly on hold during that time.

Federal

Again using the example of the FBI, agents begin their careers paired with more experienced agents in a specific division. They learn the tools of their trade (report writing, surveillance, investigation, etc.) and rotate through assignments over the first few years to gain exposure to a range of divisions.

At about five years, agents can apply for a variety of other positions, including senior status in the field as well as more deskbound administrative positions. Continued promotion to managerial level and assistant director-ship (and above) positions occur at about ten years and beyond into your career. These promotions go to those agents who continue to develop their skills, build a track record of performance, participate in lifelong learning, and stay motivated and energized about their jobs. Often at this point in their careers, successful FBI agents return to the training school at Quantico, Virginia, to serve as instructors, trainers, and educators for new recruits.

Stories from the Field: So Near and Yet So Far

Two accounts we heard as we researched this book demonstrate that no matter how successful someone is in all the testing, training, and preemployment screening, employment is never guaranteed. In the first instance, a candidate was hired for a midsize city police job after graduating from the police academy in the state, passing all the physical and psychological exams, successfully completing his board interview, and passing his background investigation. During the background examination, several former employers and contacts commented on the candidate's pronounced ability to follow orders. According to the detective recounting this story, those comments proved to be prophetic. Once hired, the young patrolman did nothing without being told. "Get out of the car!" or "Finish your paperwork before you sign off." It didn't matter what the task, this young man had to be directed. As you can imagine, it became a burden to his colleagues and he was fired.

In another instance, a candidate who also had passed all prerequisites with flying colors caused his prospective employer concern when he continually called the station to double-check his next scheduled meeting (he had forgotten the time and date) or to confirm information that he had already received. This behavior led them to question how organized and mature he was, and he was not hired.

Law enforcement continues to raise the hurdles in the employment race. Most hiring officials want only the very best, and this chapter should give you a sense of the many dimensions on which you'll be evaluated. The following list highlights some of the skills and aptitudes that employers consider desirable in this career path.

- Computer skills
- Interpersonal communication
- Presentation skills
- Critical thinking
- Problem solving
- Sensitivity to issues and culture

- Teamwork
- Written communication
- Initiative
- Listening
- Investigative skills
- Foreign language

Any related training or certifications you can pick up along the way such as CPR, first aid, EMT, lifesaving, mediation skills, and/or grant writing will further enhance your value as a job candidate.

EARNINGS

Salaries can be very different, depending on what part of the country you are looking at. Even at the local level of law enforcement, you will find varying salary ranges within each state and even between communities that border on one another. We found a good example right in our local area. The entry-level salary for a police officer in a small rural community was $20,800, while literally down the road in a small city the starting salary for a police officer was $29,000.

Local Law Enforcement

According to the latest data provided by the 2000–2001 *Occupational Outlook Handbook*, on-line at http://stats.bls.gov.ocohome.htm, the median salary for police patrol officers in 1998 was $37,710. Most earned between $28,840 and $47,890. Keep in mind that these figures represent the "base" salary, which does not include a uniform allowance provided by most departments, holiday pay, hazard pay, overtime, educational incentives, shift differential, or special-detail assignments. Such additional payments can be significant and can, in some cases, nearly double your salary. The size of the department and the community help determine how much additional income you can anticipate. It stands to reason that in a small town with a correspondingly small police force, the opportunity for special-detail assignments, such as directing traffic around road construction crews, will be more limited than those you would find in a large metropolitan area.

In many communities, a college degree automatically qualifies you for a higher salary. Then, as you continue to move up the ladder to sergeant, captain, and so on, you will garner a steady increase. Police chiefs may earn a base salary of between $56,300 and $69,600. The median salary for detectives and criminal investigators is $46,180, with most earning between $35,540 and $62,520.

In other law enforcement positions at the local level, such as health and code inspector, you can expect to earn, on average, $31,800. Once again, this will vary with geographic location, size, and even the community's budget.

County and State Law Enforcement

According to the most recently released data from the U.S. Department of Justice Bureau of Justice Statistics, in a 1997 study of state police agencies employing 100 officers or more, base salaries for entry-level officers ranged from $19,190 in Alabama to $42,275 in Alaska. After one year on the job, those same officers were earning $22,820 and $51,943, respectively. As you can see, geographic location can make quite a difference!

Law enforcement officials employed by state governments outside of the state police, such as state park rangers and bank examiners, earned a median salary of $33,700 according to the *Occupational Outlook Handbook*.

At the county level, most recent (1998) data show that the majority of sheriffs and deputy sheriffs earned between $23,310 and $36,090 per year.

Federal Law Enforcement

All federal employees are paid according to a government pay scale, and a special salary rate table applies for federal employees working in law enforcement. FBI agents, for example, enter government service at the GS-10 grade level, which, in 2000, translated to an annual salary of $36,847. By comparison, other government employees hired at the GS-10 level earn $35,658 per year. Further, the government has designated thirty-two "locality pay areas" in the country, which have a slightly higher salary table, in line with the prevailing local pay level in those areas. This means, for instance, that a newly hired FBI agent in Boston or New York City will enter service at the GS-10 level but earn $42,743. Additionally, in recognition of the huge amount of overtime required of federal special agents and inspectors, they qualify for law enforcement availability pay (LEAP), which amounts to 25 percent of their grade and step. So, at the end of the first year of work, that same Boston FBI agent will have earned a total of $53,429!

Most entry-level professional positions in federal law enforcement start at the GS-5 through GS-7 level, which generally translates to an annual salary of $26,354 to $29,998. For complete salary rate information, visit the website of the U.S. Office of Personnel Management at www.opm.gov/oca/payrates/index.

For those who choose to work in government law enforcement, be it local, state, or federal, most agencies offer liberal pension plans that include early-retirement benefits. Often you are eligible to retire after twenty to twenty-five years of service. This means that if you enter the field in your early twenties, you may be eligible to retire in your forties. At that point, you could receive a pension (and benefits) and still work full- or part-time in another career!

CAREER OUTLOOK

Ours is a very security-conscious society. As a result, employment of police officers, detectives, and criminal investigators is expected to grow faster than the average for all occupations through 2008. In a 1999 survey on crime and public safety commissioned by the National Association of Police Organizations, voters expressed concern over drug-related crimes, violent crimes such as murder and rape, gang violence, and child abuse. The results of the survey also demonstrated overwhelming support for increases in government funding to address and prevent such crimes, the most popular solution being to hire more police officers. As the public demands more police services, particularly at the local and state levels, you can expect to see more government spending targeted toward law enforcement.

According to the Bureau of Labor Statistics, employment of police patrol officers is expected to increase by 31.6 percent between 1998 and 2008, with most of the increase expected to be at the local and state levels. Similarly, the projected employment increase for sheriffs and deputy sheriffs is 34.2 percent, while, for the same period, employment of detectives and criminal investigators will rise by 21 percent. Turnover in police and detective positions is among the lowest of all occupations. Most openings will develop as a result of increased local and state law enforcement budgets in response to concerns about crime in local communities, along with the replacement of retirees and of employees who transfer to other occupations or stop working altogether. Projected increases in employment at the federal level are not quite as strong, due to tighter budgetary constraints.

People interested in positions as inspectors and compliance officers can also expect to see an increase (although less pronounced) in job openings. It is estimated that four out of five of these jobs are in local, state, and federal government agencies that enforce regulations and laws on health (e.g., environmental health inspectors), safety (e.g., aviation safety inspectors), food quality (e.g., food inspectors), licensing (e.g., alcohol beverage control officers), and finance (e.g., bank examiners). Employment in these areas is expected to show an average growth of 10.5 percent between 1998 and 2008.

While the career outlook for law enforcement jobs is promising, keep in mind that the competition is keen. The jobs are appealing for many reasons: they are challenging and sometimes exciting, they satisfy one's need to serve and protect other members of society, and they enjoy the public's respect and admiration. Salaries and benefit packages are attractive, and opportunities for advancement are widely available. Also, job security is considerable, and layoffs are rare. Therefore, the number of qualified candidates exceeds the number of openings not only in federal agencies but also in most local and state departments. According to the *Occupational Outlook Handbook*, however, "applicants with college training in police science, military police experience, or both should have the best opportunities."

STRATEGY FOR FINDING THE JOBS

As you probably know by now, virtually all law enforcement positions are with local, county, state, or federal government agencies. This knowledge will enable you to focus or target your job search more narrowly. It's a fact that the application process can be more challenging than the private-sector equivalent, as it may include detailed application forms, extensive job announcements, and specific hiring rules. As you pursue this course, try to remember that the government at all levels is made up of people just like you. They are interested in your application and are looking for you to be a good fit for the position. So, if the going gets tough, and it may, ask for help.

GENERAL WORDS OF ADVICE

Personalize Your Search. Successful government job seekers say that one way to break through the bureaucracy is to personalize your efforts. Call the agencies and departments with which you are seeking employment, and speak to a representative. Tell him or her what you're doing, and ask for assistance and guidance. This will put a voice and a name to the employer, and he or she will likely have valuable advice about the job specifications and application and hiring procedures.

Follow Up as You Would with Any Other Employer. Following up on your federal, state, or local government application is just as important as it is in the private sector. You can verify that your materials were received and that your application is complete. You'll show the hiring official that you are committed to your job search and remind him or her that you are qualified and available for employment.

Because of the highly structured classification of employees in these sectors, most applicants believe that once you submit your application, there is little you can do but wait out the process. However, in many important ways government employers are no different from any other employers. When faced with a hiring decision, they want to employ the best person for the job and one who will be a good fit with the existing organization. So, while the application processes and hiring conditions are definitely more codified than in the private sector, that does not mean you cannot put a face to your application or a voice to your name with a visit or a phone call. If you are near enough to visit a potential employment site, by all means do so. You may get a tour and an opportunity to meet some staff. Remember to be on your best behavior and respectful to every person you meet. Don't believe that your professional behavior and attitude are to be saved for the hiring officer. Everyone with whom you interact has the potential to influence the decision to hire you.

Before trying to find where the jobs are, you have to decide in which level of government or area of law enforcement you are most interested. Once that has been determined, you can take advantage of some specific tips for finding jobs in each category.

Local and State

Civil service exams, which are administered by individual states, are required of almost all police and detectives at this level. You can find out about upcoming test dates through your local civil service commission, which is usually located in your town or city hall personnel office. You can also visit your state's website, where you should find civil service exam information listed on the human resources or personnel page. To prepare for this exam, it's a good idea to study and take practice exams so that you're familiar with the subject matter and types of questions that will be asked. While exams will vary by state, you can expect questions about judgment, memory, picture identification, face matches, grammar, reading comprehension, and mathematics. Don't worry, there are guides that can help you, such as Barron's *How to Prepare for the Police Officer Examination*. In addition, some states have produced guides to help you prepare for their specific exams. You can purchase many of these at your local bookstore or at on-line bookstores such as amazon.com or barnesandnoble.com.

When it comes to locating law enforcement jobs in your city or town, here is one place where the Internet may not be of much help since many smaller communities do not have extensive websites, if they have one at all. Once again, visit your town or city hall personnel office for information on available openings. Don't just visit once; establish a routine in which you visit every couple of weeks, depending on when the job boards are updated. While you're there, you may want to request an informational meeting with the chief of police or a representative. Introduce yourself, and let these people get to know you and witness your motivation, enthusiasm, knowledge, and commitment to the field of local law enforcement. Find out about upcoming opportunities that may not be posted yet, and learn what you can do to position yourself as a top candidate.

Job openings at the state level are usually advertised on each state's human resources page on the Internet, or you can visit the office in person. Lots of good websites provide job vacancy announcements in state law enforcement (see Chapter 3). A particularly good one is The Official Directory of State Patrol and State Police Sites at www.sover.net/~tmartin/state.htm. This site links you to individual state police/highway patrol Web pages as well as to each state's overall website. In many cases, you will also find specific recruiting information for state police and links to special police units such as forensics, K-9, and criminal investigation.

Most local and state openings will also be posted in your local newspaper, so get into the habit of checking these once a week, preferably on Sundays, when the classified section is largest. If you're interested in working in local or state law enforcement outside of where you're living now, you may want to visit www.careerpath.com, where you will be connected to newspaper classifieds from around the country.

Federal

Within the federal government there are approximately sixty police agencies, and each is responsible for enforcing different kinds of laws. So, your first step is to investigate the various individual agencies, the area of enforcement for which they are responsible, and the types of employment they have to offer. Most of the agencies with which you are likely to be familiar fall under either the Department of Justice, which includes the FBI, or the Department of the Treasury, which includes the Secret Service. These agencies have created their own websites at which you will discover comprehensive information on the mission of the agency, types of employment, qualifications, and application procedures. Here's a list of some in which you may be interested:

U.S. Department of Justice   www.usdoj.gov

- Drug Enforcement Administration   www.usdoj.dea
- FBI   www.fbi.gov

- Immigration and Naturalization   www.ins.usdoj.gov
  Service (Border Patrol and
  Interior Enforcement)

- U.S. Marshals Service   www.usdoj.gov/marshals

U.S. Department of the Treasury   www.treas.gov

- Bureau of Alcohol, Tobacco,   www.atf.treas.gov
  and Firearms

- Internal Revenue Service   www.irstreas.gov/irs

- U.S. Customs Service   www.customs.ustreas.gov

- U.S. Secret Service   www.treas.gov/usss

Other Federal Agencies

- Bureau of Diplomatic Security   www.ds.state.gov
  /index_n.html

- Central Intelligence Agency   www.odci.gov

- Federal Aviation Administration   www.faa.gov

- Federal Trade Commission   www.ftc.gov

- National Park Service   www.nps.gov

- National Security Agency   www.nsa.gov

- Securities and Exchange Com-   www.sec.gov/enforce.htm
  mission (Enforcement Division)

- U.S. Environmental Protection   www.epa.gov
  Agency

- U.S. Fish and Wildlife Service   www.fws.gov

- U.S. Park Police   www.doi.gov/usparkpolice

- U.S. Postal Inspection Service   www.usps.gov/websites
  /depart/inspect

You will also find a listing of U.S. military police departments at www.pima.edu/dps/mil.htm.

The federal government lists its current openings on its website at www.usajobs.opm.gov. While you will not find agency background information here as you will in the agency-specific sites, this site is valuable because it centrally locates job listings available at all of the government agencies. It may be worth reviewing some of these job vacancy announcements to get a sense of the variety and scope of opportunities available. The announcements are somewhat lengthy, but they contain a wealth of information and are all presented in the following format, which makes them easier to track:

- Salary range and promotion potential.

- Specific duties. Carefully review this section to see if you would like this particular kind of work.

- Qualifications. If you find that you're not qualified for a position in which you're interested, how can you become qualified? Do you need a year of graduate course work? A year of law enforcement experience? It may at first seem frustrating to not qualify, but at least you'll have a plan of action if you want to pursue this option.

- Knowledge, skills, and abilities required. Pay particular attention to this section, and match the requirements against the results of your self-assessment from Chapter 1.

- Conditions of employment. This section tells you whether drug testing or a physical examination is required, whether you will be expected to qualify for and carry firearms, how much overtime can be anticipated, if a uniform is required, and so forth.

- Application procedures. Applying used to be a much more difficult (and dreaded) process than it is now. For most federal positions, you can apply with either a resume or the Optional Application for Federal Employment (OF 612). The more traditional (and extensive) application, the SF 171, is still used and may be preferred by some agencies. A word of caution here: as you will see, the job descriptions are quite detailed and specific. When you apply, be sure to indicate all of the experience and skills you have that qualify you for the job. In most cases, your resume does not reflect everything you've done or are capable of doing. Therefore, it may behoove you to fill out the more detailed application form instead of, or in addition to, using your resume. It is often worth checking with the agency to see which format is preferred. The usajobs website (www.usajobs.opm.gov) provides convenient on-line and downloadable application formats. If you decide to use one of the applications, be sure to complete it carefully and with no errors.

POSSIBLE EMPLOYERS

As noted previously, virtually all law enforcement jobs are in local, state, and federal government agencies. At the local level, the town or city police department is the primary employer, accounting for approximately 82 percent of police patrol officers in the country and 64 percent of detectives and criminal investigators. Local county sheriff's departments employ more than 99 percent of all sheriffs and deputy sheriffs.

Among the fifty states, there are twenty-six highway patrol agencies, twenty-three state police agencies, and one department of public safety (in Hawaii). They account for approximately 15 percent of the police officers hired in this country and more than 11 percent of detectives and criminal investigators. In addition to police, other state agencies that employ law enforcement personnel include:

College and University Campuses

Department of Agriculture

Department of Alcohol Beverage Control

Department of Environmental Resources

Department of Finance

Department of Industrial Relations, including:

- Division of Labor Law Enforcement and Fair Employment Practices

Department of Insurance

Department of Investments

Department of Justice, including:

- Bureau of Criminal Investigation

- Bureau of Narcotics

Department of Motor Vehicles

Department of Public Health, including:

- Bureau of Food and Drug Inspection

Department of Social Services

Parks and Recreation

Port Authority

According to the most recent report from the Bureau of Justice Statistics, as of 1998, federal agencies employed about 83,000 full-time federal officers. The majority of those, 46,818, were employed in investigation/enforcement, followed by police response and patrol with 16,186. The largest employers of federal officers, in order, were the Immigration and Naturalization Service, Bureau of Prisons, FBI, and U.S. Customs Service. Geographic location is a significant factor in these numbers. About half of these officers were employed in California, Texas, the District of Columbia, New York, and Florida. By comparison, fewer than 100 federal officers were employed in either New Hampshire or Delaware.

POSSIBLE JOB TITLES

The list that follows is purposely extensive to demonstrate the variety and scope of positions available to you in using your education and interest in criminal justice within the specific path of law enforcement. As you can see, the possibilities extend well beyond "police officer" and "special agent."

Local/State

Public Safety

Airport Security Officer	Mounted Police Officer
Booking Officer	Park Ranger
Communications Specialist	Park Security Officer
Community Policing Officer	Patrol Cadet
Community Service Officer	Peace Officer
Constable	Police Cadet
Crossing Guard	Police Dispatcher
Deputy Sheriff	Police Inspector
Emergency Dispatcher/911 Call Taker	Police Manager
K-9 Officer	Police Officer
Law Enforcement Officer	Public Safety Officer

School Resource Officer

Sheriff

State Trooper

Water Patrol Officer

Traffic Safety Officer

University/Campus Police Officer

Investigative

Animal Treatment Investigator

Arson Investigator

Detective

Investigator

Narcotics Investigator

Police Detective

Compliance

Bank Examiner

Compliance Manager

Discrimination Investigator

Environmental Conservation Officer

Fish and Game Warden

Gaming Enforcement Officer

Safety Inspector

Specialist

Ballistics Expert

Crime Intelligence Analyst

Criminalist

Criminologist

Document Examiner

Fingerprint Examiner

Forensic Chemist

Forensic Pathologist

Polygraph Examiner

Serology Specialist

Toolmark Specialist

Technical

Crime Lab Analyst

Crime Lab Technician

Crime Scene Investigation Technician

Federal

Federal Agents

Air Force Special Agent

Alcohol, Tobacco, and Firearms Agent

Army Special Agent

Border Patrol Agent

CIA Agent

Customs Agent

Drug Enforcement Agent

FBI Agent

Foreign Service Officer

Fish and Wildlife Service Special Agent

Secret Service Agent

Compliance

Adjudication Officer

Bank Examiner

Compliance Manager

Customs Canine Enforcement Officer

Customs Inspector

Consumer Safety Inspector

Consumer Safety Officer

Deportation Officer

Discrimination Investigator

Environmental Health Inspector

FAA Aviation Safety Inspector

Fish and Game Warden

Food Inspector

Immigration and Naturalization Inspector

Investigative

Federal Investigations Investigator

Inspector General Investigator

Internal Revenue Internal Security Investigator

Internet Crime Investigator

Narcotics Investigator

Naval Investigator

Postal Service Investigator

Revenue Officer

Securities Investigator

Protective

Capitol Police Officer

Federal Protective Service Officer

Military Officer

National Park Ranger

Secret Service Uniformed Officer

U.S. Marshal

RELATED OCCUPATIONS

Still other occupations could tap into your interest in the enforcement of laws and regulations in settings within and outside of the government. They include:

Contracts Administrator   Real Estate Portfolio Manager

Employment Agency Recruiter   Records Manager

Housing/Tenant Representative   Research Analyst/Statistician

Photographer   Sanitation Officer

Public Relations Officer   Sexual Assault Prevention Educator

PROFESSIONAL ASSOCIATIONS

Listed in this section are some of the associations that relate to careers in law enforcement. For more information about these professional associations, either check the websites listed or consult the *Encyclopedia of Associations,* published by the Gale Group. Review the Members/Purpose notes for each organization to determine if it pertains to your interests. Membership in one or more of these organizations may gain you access to job listings, networking opportunities, and employment search services. Some provide information at no charge, but if you want to receive specific publications that list job opportunities, you may need to join. If you're still in college, check for student member rates.

American Academy of Forensic Sciences
P.O. Box 669
Colorado Springs, CO 80901-0669
www.aafs.org
Members/Purpose: A professional society dedicated to the application of science to the law. Membership includes physicians, criminalists, toxicologists, attorneys, dentists, physical anthropologists, document examiners, engineers, psychiatrists, educators, and others who practice and perform research in the many diverse fields relating to forensic science. Members reside in all fifty states, Canada, and fifty other countries throughout the world.
Publications: *Show Your Pride.*

Training: AAFS annual meeting, held every February, at which time more than 500 scientific papers, breakfast seminars, workshops, and other special events are presented.

American Association of State Troopers
National Lodge
1949 Raymond Diehl Rd.
Tallahassee, FL 32308
www.statetroopers.org
Members/Purpose: This association was formed for the purpose of improving conditions of law enforcement officers by solidifying their strength and promoting their mutual welfare.
Publications: *Trooper Connection*, a quarterly newsletter.

American Federation of Police and Concerned Citizens
3801 Biscayne Blvd.
Miami, FL 33137
www.aphf.org
Members/Purpose: Governmental and private law enforcement officers united for the prevention of crime and the apprehension of criminals.
Publications: Newsletter; *Police Times* magazine, quarterly.
Training: Biennial conference.

American Police Academy
1000 Connecticut Ave. NW, Suite 9
Washington, DC 20036
Members/Purpose: Establishes professional certification standards for career officers. Conducts workshops and home-study programs.
Publications: *Police Times* magazine; *Who's Who in Law Enforcement*.

Association of National Park Rangers
P.O. Box 108
Larned, KS 67550-0108
www.anpr.org
Members/Purpose: An organization created to communicate for, about, and with park rangers and to promote and enhance the park ranger profession and its spirit.
Publications: Quarterly magazine.
Training: Facilitated mentoring program; annual meeting.

Association of Public-Safety Communications Officials International, Inc.
2040 S. Ridgewood Ave.
South Daytona, FL 32119-8437
www.apcointl.org
Members/Purpose: Dedicated to the enhancement of public safety communications. Membership comprises employees of public safety organizations, including 911 emergency call centers; municipal, state, county, and federal public safety agencies; emergency medical services; emergency management centers; transportation agencies and facilities; highway maintenance; forestry services; and manufacturers of public safety communication products.
Publications: *APCO Monthly Bulletin*; jobs listing.
Training: Annual international conference and exposition, plus three regional conferences in the United States and one in Canada; APCO Institute provides customized education and training programs, technical and operations publications, and information services for members.

Federal Criminal Investigators Association
P.O. Box 23400
Washington, DC 20026
www.fedcia.org
Members/Purpose: Dedicated to promoting professional excellence through training and communication, enhancing the image of federal law enforcement officers, fostering cooperation among all law enforcement professionals, and providing a fraternal environment for the advancement of the membership and the community.
Publications: None available.
Training: National conference; training seminars.

Federal Law Enforcement Officers Association
P.O. Box 1306
Grand Central Station
New York, NY 10163-1306
www.fleoa.org
Members/Purpose: Provides access to legal advice and representation, and gives voice to the concerns of more than 600,000 enforcement officers on matters critical to working federal agents.
Publications: *1811*, a bimonthly newsletter.

High Technology Crime Investigation Association
1471 Freeman Dr.
Amissville, VA 20106
http://htcia.org
Members/Purpose: Designed to encourage, promote, aid, and effect the voluntary interchange of data, information, experience, ideas, and knowledge about methods, processes, and techniques relating to investigations and security in advanced technologies among members.
Publications: None available.
Training: International conference; regional seminars.

International Association of Campus Law Enforcement Administrators
342 N. Main St.
West Hartford, CT 06117-2507
www.iaclea.org
Members/Purpose: Advances public safety for educational institutions by providing educational resources, advocacy, and professional development to its members.
Publications: Variety of publications, including *The Standards for Campus Law Enforcement*, a training guide for public safety and security agencies; *Campus Law Enforcement Journal*; crime reports; and monographs.
Training: Annual conferences and meetings. Professional training and development is a high priority for IACLEA. The annual conference, regional meetings, and state workshops provide a variety of training opportunities in all phases of campus security, public safety, and law enforcement administration.

International Association of Crime Analysts
PMB 352
1001-A E. Harmony Rd.
Ft. Collins, CO 80525-3309
www.iaca.net
Members/Purpose: Organized to enhance effectiveness and consistency in the fields of crime and intelligence analysis.
Publications: None available.
Training: Annual conference.

International Association of Financial Crimes Investigators
385 Bel Marin Keys, Suite H
Novato, CA 94949
www.iafci.org
Members/Purpose: This nonprofit international organization provides services and an environment within which information about financial

fraud, fraud investigation, and fraud prevention methods can be collected, exchanged, and taught for the common good of the financial payment industry and our global society.

Publications: Membership directory; quarterly newsletter.

Training: Annual training seminar.

International Association of Women Police
R.R. #1 Box 149
Deer Isle, ME 04627
www.iawp.org

Members/Purpose: Strives to ensure equity for women in the criminal justice field by utilizing, investing, and celebrating the individual strengths, talents, and skills of its members.

Publications: *Women Police* magazine.

Training: Annual conference; regional training events.

International Crime Scene Investigators Association
PMB 385
15774 S. LaGrange Rd.
Orland Park, IL 60462
www.icsia.com

Members/Purpose: To encourage the exchange of information useful in crime-scene-related matters. To improve the level of expertise in the field by providing timely answers through membership participation.

Publications: *The Examiner*, the ICSIA newsletter.

Training: Training classes through a host agency; Web-based on-line training courses.

International Footprint Association
1095 Market St., Room 206
San Francisco, CA 94103

Members/Purpose: Brings together, on a social basis, conscientious law enforcement personnel and citizens of all professions interested in improving knowledge of law enforcement problems.

Publications: None available.

Training: None available.

National Association of Blacks in Criminal Justice
North Carolina Central University
P.O. Box 19788
Durham, NC 27707
www.nabcj.org

Members/Purpose: Established to examine and act upon the needs, concerns, and contributions of African Americans and other minorities as they relate to the administration of equal justice. The National Association of Blacks in Criminal Justice seeks to focus attention on relevant legislation, law enforcement, prosecution, and defense-related needs and practices, with emphasis on the courts, corrections, and the prevention of crime. Among its chief concerns are the general welfare and increased influence of African Americans in and on the administration of justice. It also coordinates the efforts of any and all organizations that are concerned with the elimination of injustice within the justice system.
Publications: *Commitment*, official newsletter.
Training: Annual conference and training institute.

National Association of Police Organizations Inc.
750 First St. NE, Suite 920
Washington, DC 20002
www.napo.org
Members/Purpose: A coalition of police unions and associations from across the United States that serves to advance the interests of America's law enforcement officers through legislative and legal advocacy, political action, and education.
Publications: *The Washington Report*, newsletter.
Training: Seminars throughout the year; annual convention.

National Association of School Resource Officers
P.O. Box 40
Boynton Beach, FL 33425-0040
www.nasro.org
Members/Purpose: NASRO is dedicated to the children of America; its mission is to break down the barriers between law enforcement and youth by establishing better communication about the legal system.
Publications: Lesson plans for members to use in classrooms.
Training: School resource training classes; annual conference.

National Black Police Association
3251 Mt. Pleasant St. NW, Second Floor
Washington, DC 20010-2103
www.blackpolice.org
Members/Purpose: A nationwide organization of African American police associations dedicated to the promotion of justice, fairness, and effectiveness in law enforcement.

Publications: *What to Do When Stopped by the Police*; *Sergeant Assessment Center*, Volumes I and II.
Training: The NBPA hosts an annual education and training conference for its members and others interested in law enforcement, as well as regional training conferences.

National Constables Association
16 Stonybrook Dr.
Levittown, PA 19055
www.angelfire.com/la/nationalconstable/
Members/Purpose: This association's purpose is to unite the constables of America; to help preserve and clearly define the role of the constable in the delivery of the justice system; and to train, educate, and upgrade the quality of performance.
Publications: Newsletter.
Training: National Convention of Constables.

National Criminal Justice Association
444 N. Capitol St. NW, Suite 618
Washington, DC 20001
www.sso.org/ncja/
Members/Purpose: A special-interest group that represents states on crime control and public safety matters. The NCJA's work focuses primarily on helping develop and implement national policy in the criminal justice field and on helping states address related problems.
Publications: Monthly *Justice Bulletin*; *Policy and Practice*, a quarterly publication for criminal justice policy makers and practitioners.
Training: National forum; internships available; regional training seminars.

National Drug Enforcement Officers Association
2020 Pennsylvania Ave. NW, Suite 299
Washington, DC 20006-1846
www.ndeoa.org
Members/Purpose: The objective of this association is to promote cooperation, education, and exchange of information among all law enforcement agencies involved in the enforcement of controlled substance laws.
Publications: None available.
Training: Annual training conference; numerous training sessions throughout the year on a variety of topics, including surveillance, gangs, investigations, computers and the Internet, and more.

National Police Canine Association
P.O. Box 1143
Loxahatchee, FL 33470
www.npca.net
Members/Purpose: Established to promote and assist in the utilization of police service dogs in prevention and detection of crime; promote educational programs in the use of police service dogs in law enforcement; provide assistance to law enforcement agencies in the implementation of police service dogs; and promote a task-related, minimum standard of certification of police service dogs.
Publications: Training articles.
Training: National training seminar.

National Sheriffs' Association
1450 Duke St.
Alexandria, VA 22314-3490
www.sheriffs.org
Members/Purpose: A nonprofit organization dedicated to raising the level of professionalism in the criminal justice field. Through the years, the NSA has been involved in numerous programs to enable sheriffs, their deputies, chiefs of police, and others in the field of criminal justice to perform their jobs in the best possible manner and to better serve the people of their cities/counties or jurisdictions.
Publications: *International Bulletin for Court Security and Services, Inc.*; *Community Policing Exchange*; *Sheriff Times*; *Triad News*; NSA's annual report.
Training: Seminars and training on topics such as school violence and jail privatization; annual conference and exhibition.

National United Law Enforcement Officers
256 E. McLemore Ave.
Memphis, TN 38106
Members/Purpose: Membership includes law enforcement officers from all departments, as well as interested persons from the community. Develops community-based programs designed to improve the relationship between law enforcement officers and the community, with an emphasis on the black community.
Publications: *Law Enforcement Association News*; annual report.
Training: Annual training conference (with exhibits); also holds an annual community forum.

North American Police Work Dog Association
4222 Manchester Ave.
Perry, OH 44081
www.napwda.com
Members/Purpose: The NAPWDA is composed of law enforcement officers throughout the United States and several other countries who are dedicated to assisting police work dog teams throughout the world.
Publications: None available.
Training: National and state workshops.

CHAPTER 11

PATH 2: THE COURTS: THE CASE FOR GREAT CAREERS

*O*ne reason criminal justice is such an exciting college major and a rewarding career field is the diversity of occupational areas possible. Our second career path, "The Courts," highlights a large number of jobs surrounding the legal system and court proceedings, including probation and parole officers, attorneys, victim advocates, bailiffs, court reporters, paralegals, and legal researchers. Juvenile justice occupations are covered separately in Path 4, Chapter 13.

Of the five career paths presented in Chapters 10 through 14, the courts present the greatest number of open and varied occupations. Students exploring careers in the court system will find that all of these occupations are strongly interpersonal. In addition to working with people, you'll be helping to ensure that our court system functions the way it was meant to: that people are presumed innocent, that the trial process is fair and orderly, and that sanctions meted out to those convicted are appropriate within the law. Criminal justice majors working in the court system help in the same way that law enforcement officials do—by preventing crime and protecting the public. Their part in the effective operation of our court system can serve not only as a corrective but also as a deterrent to criminal activity.

Something else the court system shares with law enforcement careers is that the area of work has been glamorized by the media. The courtroom is almost always depicted as "high drama," fast-paced and full of action. The truth is that working in the court system is demanding, and there is often an expectation to produce high-quality work under pressure of time. The real excitement of working in the courts comes from skillful teamwork, daily exercise of your growing interpersonal skills, and opportunities to employ your analytical mind and to make decisions. But as with most other jobs, the court system is not nonstop excitement. It is a blend of tasks including desk duty and paperwork that provide variety, stimulation, and a never-ending stream of new situations for those committed to the job.

As with any of the criminal justice career paths, if you are interested in working in the courts, it behooves you to plan ahead. Talk to your professors and your career counselor in college about hooking up with a local judge, bailiff, or parole officer. Meet with these professionals for an informational interview. Prepare some good questions (see Chapter 4 on networking), and begin to build your understanding of court-related criminal justice occupations. Courts vary from state to state, between state and federal levels, and sometimes even from community to community. Talking to people who work in the courts and perhaps volunteering or doing a recognized internship will give you the insight you need to make a good decision about your future in this important area of criminal justice.

THE COURTS

How Courts Work

All courts are part of the judicial branch of government and are authorized to decide the cases brought before them. Courts (and those who administer them) decide cases based on laws of the state and/or the U.S. Constitution. They try to be fair, consistent, and efficient in administering justice to all. In thinking about employment in the court system, it's important to remember there are more than sixteen thousand federal and state courts in the United States. Each has its own *jurisdiction*—the limited area in which it can make decisions. When this authority to make decisions is challenged by participants in the legal process, we have trial courts, appellate courts, and courts of last resort at both the state and federal levels, including the U.S. Supreme Court.

An individual's arrest is generally the first step in a case moving into the court system. Trial courts rule based on the verbal testimony and physical evidence presented, and they can hear both civil and criminal cases. Civil cases have to do with injustices of one person against another, while criminal cases are about injustices that affect the rights of all of us.

Above trial courts in the hierarchy of the court system are the appellate courts. *Appellate* means just what it sounds and looks like—"appeal." These courts review the decisions of trial courts and how the law was interpreted and determine whether the decision was well founded in the law.

Supreme courts (both state and federal) handle appeals from courts under them, and their decisions are binding on all lower courts.

The U.S. Information Agency publishes an electronic journal entitled *Issues of Democracy*. At the website for this journal, you will find one entire issue devoted to "How U.S. Courts Work," with noted articles on the functions of the court system, key players in the judicial process, and common law and civil law systems. You can find all this at http://usinfo.state.gov/journals/itdhr/0999/ijde/ijde0999.htm.

The Courtroom Process

The court process begins with a preliminary hearing. During this initial court appearance, police often turn over their evidence to a prosecutor because they believe the evidence justifies arrest. A judge or magistrate then decides if the case warrants the court's attention.

If the case is deemed sufficiently sound for the suspect's arrest, then the suspect is arraigned. If a judge or magistrate does not feel the evidence is sufficient, then the suspect is released. *Arraignment* is the formal charge of the crime. This is the point at which the person charged pleads guilty or not guilty. Once the *plea* is entered, the court must decide how to handle the person charged. Some people are released to their homes and families on their own *recognizance* because the court feels they pose no threat to society and they are considered good risks for future court appearances. If, however, the judge or magistrate believes there is a possibility of nonappearance or any risk associated with releasing the suspect back into society, the judge may ask for *bail* to be posted. The amount of bail is related to the seriousness of the offense and the risk posed by not incarcerating the suspect. For dangerous crimes or highly suspect individuals, bail is not allowed, and the individual is jailed until the date of the court case.

Sometimes, when the suspect pleads guilty, the court (the judge, the suspect and his or her attorneys, and the prosecutor) will work out a *plea bargain*, which generally results in a less severe sentence than could have been imposed had the case gone to trial. The plea bargain decides the sentence and ends the trial process. The reduction in the severity of punishment is a recognition of saving the court's time and money in bringing the judicial process to a quicker, yet still judicially sound, close. Of course, if the suspect does not plead guilty, then the case must go to court.

Not very many cases actually reach the trial stage, and not all trials involve a jury of one's peers. Some cases are conducted as "bench trials" in front of the judge, who decides the sentence after hearing all the evidence and arguments. In either type of trial, if the decision is *not guilty*, the defendant is released.

Of course, if the defendant is found guilty, by either the judge or the jury, a *sentencing* follows. The sentence could be a fine, probation, or jail time.

Conditions of the sentence include stipulations of time and/or money or probation. Once sentenced, the defendant and his or her lawyers may appeal the conviction to a higher court.

Once part of a sentence has been served, the individual serving the sentence may become eligible for *revocation* of the sentence or some form of conditional release (*probation* or *parole*). Probation and parole involve strict conditions that are designed to help the convicted individual safely transition back into mainstream society. Violation of these conditions can result in further punishment. Once the probation or parole period is successfully completed, the parolee is discharged, and the case is closed.

DEFINITION OF THE CAREER PATH

Probation and Parole Officers

The probation officer enters the court process before a criminal is sentenced. The officer writes a report recommending the types and conditions of sentencing. If that sentence is to include probation, then the probation officer will supervise that probationer. The officer often works with the offender's family and even the person's employer to help everyone understand the conditions surrounding the probation. The probation officer enforces the conditions of probation and helps to guide and encourage the offender in making the necessary social adjustments. The probationer and the probation officer meet regularly to record and discuss the offender's progress.

The parole officer's job is remarkably similar except that the client has been jailed and his or her release is conditional. The parole officer helps the client to readjust to life in the community and observe the parole conditions to avoid returning to jail.

This is a great field with fair employment prospects because we, as a nation, are concerned about the overcrowding of our prisons. These positions are part of the solution of avoiding prison and also reducing prison populations. Both positions serve to enhance the efficiency of the criminal justice system. With experience on the job and continued education, including a master's degree, you can be eligible for promotion to a district or regional administrator.

WORKING CONDITIONS

You'll walk a delicate line between social worker and rules enforcer. It's a constant balancing act between caring and discipline—firm yet fair. This is definitely challenging work, but it can be deeply rewarding, as you may be a catalyst in turning someone's life around.

While you may be confronted with some of the starkest realities of negative human behavior, your job is to provide the stability and structure to allow people to regain their freedom and dignity. You will find the frustrations and challenges of this job very difficult to handle unless you come to your own personal philosophy of what your role should be vis-à-vis your clients. Parole and probation officers develop their own individual styles for working with their clientele, and most of these ways of doing business are a combination of that individual's personality and understanding of the job.

Personal counseling, referrals to community resources, home visits, interviews and briefings of families, extensive telephone work, and detailed record keeping are the day-to-day activities that will occupy most of your time.

TRAINING AND QUALIFICATIONS

Probation and parole officers are required to have a bachelor's degree. Frequently the degree is in criminal justice or other social sciences such as human behavior, psychology, anthropology, or sociology. Probation and parole jobs are often filled on the basis of the results of civil service testing. Talk to your college career office or local civil service office for specific eligibility requirements and test dates.

DEFINITION OF THE CAREER PATH

Victim Advocate

Victim services, or victim advocacy, represents an exciting new development in the court system and a job field that is still defining itself, still setting professional standards, and growing by leaps and bounds. You can enter this field on the ground floor and become part of its history.

Victim advocacy provides an opportunity to better serve crime victims by focusing on the important job of notifications of probation and parole of crime perpetrators and offering a unique and important overview of our legal system from the standpoint not of the offender but of the victim.

To receive services from a victim advocate, crime victims must register with the state office of victim advocacy (which may be called victim services or a similar name). In most situations, they are alerted to their rights as victims by the state's attorney general sometime before sentencing of the offender. Following this registration, the office of victim services provides the victim with notifications of probation or parole of the offender as well as of the right to comment to the parole or probation boards on these decisions. Victims also are afforded the right to be notified if an offender has escaped or been transferred to another facility.

Advocates represent victims' interests in other ways as well. During the trial, they provide victims with information and support that may affect their decision to testify. Advocates know full well that a victim may suffer, rather than benefit, from the prosecutorial process. For example, in a domestic violence case, the offender could be the sole financial support of the family. The victim advocate may reluctantly support intensive mediation and supervision rather than incarceration, as incarceration may mean that the victim and any children become penniless and further victimized.

WORKING CONDITIONS

This is obviously a job with considerable pressure. Serious crimes and social problems, including rape and domestic violence, drug and alcohol abuse, incest, child abuse, and a host of other heinous offenses, are the daily work of victim advocates. You will be exposed frequently to disturbing crisis situations. It takes strength and moral courage to be able to support and inform victims day after day in the face of such egregious events.

As with any other direct service dealing with human problems, building trust, being empathetic, reducing client stress, supporting your client, and presenting options without making decisions for your client are essential skills. In addition to your personal skills as a counselor and advocate, you will need to have in-depth knowledge of legal policy as it relates to victim services in your state and to develop a network of community resources that can provide support.

TRAINING AND QUALIFICATIONS

Because the field of victim advocacy is in its infancy, there are many ways to access these jobs. First, you may simply use your desire to work for victims' rights and your criminal justice degree to enter the field. Many victims' rights offices will provide extensive in-service training in specific issues and techniques. To stay competitive as an employee, you'll want to continue your self-development with additional course work on your own time.

Job seekers with either an associate's or a bachelor's degree in criminal justice may want to consider one of the new certificate programs in victim services offered by some two- and four-year colleges. These certificate programs (often an offshoot of a fully developed two-year degree program) offer courses in victimology, social problems, psychology, diversity issues, the grieving process, and criminal law. Many include fieldwork or a practicum that you can accomplish "on the job." A good example of the variety of programs offered can be seen at the website of the Kansas City Kansas Community College Victim Services Program at www.kckcc.cc.ks.us/ss/ssp victi.htm. This program, the first in the Midwest, is one of the more extensive programs offered and a good benchmark for your consideration.

DEFINITION OF THE CAREER PATH

Bailiff

Bailiff is a position you might not have thought of during your criminal justice studies. It's worth your consideration, especially as an entry-level position, if you're eager to start your career in criminal justice and are interested in the courts as your arena of work. Remember that the United States has more than sixteen thousand courts of various types, and more than a quarter of them utilize the position of bailiff. There may be an opening for you!

The bailiff is an interesting position from a historical perspective. It dates from the thirteenth century in England, where bailiffs were used as night watchmen to patrol the streets and protect against fire. "Nine o'clock and all's well" was the bailiff's cry, and the populace could then sleep worry-free. In the event of a crime, a fire, or some other incident, the bailiff would rouse the public with his alarm.

The bailiff in the courtroom today still serves as an alert watchman over the proceedings, charged with keeping order. Bailiffs accompany defendants into and out of the courtroom and serve to prevent their escape. Likewise, they are responsible for the safety of juries; they escort jurors into and out of the courtroom and remain while the jury is sequestered. They also protect jurors from the public and the media, if need be. It is the bailiff who announces the entry of the judge into the courtroom and calls each witness to the stand. The opening words "Oyez, Oyez" are Middle English and are a living reminder of the heritage of our legal system.

WORKING CONDITIONS

While most bailiffs would say that day to day they are comfortable and relaxed in their jobs, new entrants to the field must weigh the realities and possible worst-case scenarios of any prospective career. You do carry a gun in this position, and that weapon is not just an ornament. Courtrooms are places of extremely heightened emotions, and outbursts often occur. That's why physical fitness and alertness are stressed. While you hope nothing happens, you need to be ready and have a plan if something does. In this job, standard procedures and a fairly orderly and static workplace always contain the threat of some untoward action or event for which you must be ready. Anticipation is everything!

TRAINING AND QUALIFICATIONS

In many instances, you will find that the qualifications for this position are similar to those of an entry-level law enforcement officer, including graduation from a police academy and passing physical and written examinations. In fact, bailiffs serving in federal courtrooms are U.S. marshals; they have the same jobs as bailiffs in other courts but their prisoners, juries, and judges are all federal.

Bailiffs must remain alert and must be well schooled in the use of a handgun. While at one time a high school degree was sufficient, competition and increasingly higher educational attainment among law enforcement professionals have raised the hurdle on minimum qualifications.

DEFINITION OF THE CAREER PATH

Court Reporter

You've seen court reporters, often located between the attorneys' tables and the judge's bench, using a stenotype machine to record court proceedings. The stenotype machine is an unusual typewriter that allows court reporters to press multiple keys at a time to record combinations of letters that represent sounds, words, or phrases. These symbols are recorded on computer discs or CD-ROMs, which are then translated and displayed as text using computer-aided transcription. Sometimes the stenotype machine is linked directly to a computer for real-time transcription so that the text being recorded is instantly available to television, hearing-impaired audiences, courts, classrooms, or meetings. Of course, accuracy is imperative, as one person is responsible for the official transcript. You have to be good at what you do when what you do is court reporting!

Because the accuracy of your transcription is the measure of your competence as a reporter, it takes only one or two incidents of carelessness to lose any possibility of future job referrals. The best court reporters speak of attaining an almost trancelike state, in which words enter their ears and move through their fingers onto the keyboard effortlessly. Most say that this sense of "flow" is one of the most attractive parts of their job.

While it's common to see the court reporter on television and in the movies as well as in television news of actual trials, we seldom see the majority of court reporters who work outside the court. Many work as freelancers, taking depositions in attorneys' offices and recording meetings and procedures from government agencies. Some specialists in the field, called *stenocaptioners*, work for television and caption live sporting events, news broadcasts, or emergency newscasts.

WORKING CONDITIONS

This is indoor work in nice surroundings—generally climate controlled. One concern worth noting is that of any job that requires you to maintain a certain body position for long periods. Strains to the back, neck, or eyes may result, and there is always the possibility of some repetitive-motion syndrome (such as carpal tunnel). This can be a serious hazard since your entire career depends on your ability to type. Whereas most of us who type as part of our jobs could compensate and work around a repetitive-motion injury, for a court reporter, such an injury means no work.

On the positive side, the workplace is becoming more ergonomically astute, and furniture and computer placement design are increasingly able to minimize these risks.

The workweek is a standard forty hours, with possibilities for overtime frequent, especially during busy court periods. Approximately one in four court reporters works part-time, and many are self-employed, which may result in irregular but self-determined hours.

Because your work involves no emotional commitment (in fact, objectivity is a requirement), most court reporters find their lives sharply divided between work and nonwork activities. Likewise, since there is no promotional ladder (other than professional certifications), you'll note an absence of politics.

TRAINING AND QUALIFICATIONS

More than 300 postsecondary vocational and technical colleges offer the court reporter training program. Of these, approximately 110 are approved by the National Court Reporters Association (NCRA), and those programs offer training in computer-aided transcription and real-time reporting. NCRA-sanctioned programs require students to be able to capture at least 225 words per minute; court reporters in the federal government employment system must be able to capture 205 words a minute as their minimum.

Court reporters need at least an associate's degree and more commonly, a bachelor's degree. Some states require that a court reporter be a notary public or a certified court reporter (CCR). To earn the certified court reporter designation, you must pass a state certification test administered by a board of examiners. The NCRA also offers other professional certifications such as registered professional reporter (RPR) and certified real-time reporter (CRR).

Learning the skill of court reporting requires lots of study and practice, practice, practice. You need superb grammatical skills and lots of patience. The work, in addition to its physical demands, requires intense concentration since your performance directly influences the decision rendered and you must certify that your transcript is an accurate and faithful copy of what took place in the proceedings you transcribed.

DEFINITION OF THE CAREER PATH

Clerks of Court

Sometimes called the court clerk, this position is frequently an elected or appointed court officer. Clerks of court are visible during a trial, but much of their real work occurs before and after. Tasks performed by the clerk of court include summoning potential jurors and subpoenaing witnesses for both the prosecution and the defense. In some larger courts, the clerk's office is a full department with assistants. In certain jurisdictions, clerks of court have the power to issue warrants. In smaller courts, clerk of court positions wield considerable influence, as magistrates may be itinerant and part-time and the clerk's position may be the only constant. When there is no contest involved, the clerk of court can exercise all of the power and authority of a probate judge.

During the trial, it is the clerk of court who swears in witnesses and identifies and marks physical evidence as it is entered into the record of the court proceedings. The clerk of court is also responsible for the physical storage and security of evidence during a trial. Some clerks collect fees, fines, costs, and bail payments. In some states they issue marriage licenses, administer oaths, take depositions, and act as county recorders.

WORKING CONDITIONS

This is a busy and responsible job that requires you to be in constant contact with other court personnel as you coordinate courtroom activity and judges' schedules. You'll have an office, but your work is varied; you appear in the courtroom when you are not behind the scenes managing the operations of the court. Telephone work, much one-on-one contact, and writing memos and many internal communications, including some protocol and procedural documents, mean a busy and varied day.

As in any other management-type position that is salaried, your day may not have a crisp definition as to its beginning or end. Each day will be different, and you'll need to remain poised and ready to handle a variety of situations. For people who enjoy change, a varied work setting, and constant challenges, this is an exciting opportunity.

TRAINING AND QUALIFICATIONS

A bachelor's degree in criminal justice is a strong qualification, although you may still find smaller court jurisdictions that will accept less than a bachelor's degree. In some larger courts, you may find the position of clerk of court restricted to individuals with a law degree.

DEFINITION OF THE CAREER PATH

Court Administrator

You've discussed the overcrowding of courts in your criminal justice classes, and you've probably become more sensitized to hearing news and television reports about time-to-trial lags, case backlogs, and delays for sentencing. Up till now, courts have managed with judges and clerks of court handling the increasingly demanding administrative workload. But as our criminal justice system grows and changes, the courts have had to change as well. To alleviate the backlog and bottlenecks in the judicial process, a new level of administration has been added, and that is represented by the job of court administrator.

The court administrator works closely with the judge or magistrate to create the court's *docket*, or calendar. Since the object of the court administrator is to streamline operations, the position places strong emphasis on the budget—monitoring existing budget allocations and planning for future fiscal years.

All of the court administrator's functions may be reduced to analysis and problem solving. With a systems approach, the court administrator seeks to refine and improve the court system to reduce backlogs, speed the process, and eliminate inefficiencies and redundancies in procedures.

WORKING CONDITIONS

Of the many jobs detailed in this chapter, it would be easy to make the case that court administrators have the most demanding and most entailed job description. Because this position was created to alleviate bottlenecks, you will find it in the larger court systems. Consequently, the conditions of the job are multidimensional, ranging from complex scheduling issues to personnel and staffing concerns. Court administrators are involved in every aspect of the court's functioning, from cleaning services to climate control.

This is a hands-on management position that requires you to be "out and about," anticipating problems before they occur and quickly deciding on solutions for a wide range of situations. Working conditions vary in proportion to the size of the court that employs you. You will need energy, patience, creativity, and good judgment to meet the surprises that will, without fail, arise.

TRAINING AND QUALIFICATIONS

Organizational skills are paramount in this job. Managing court dockets, personnel schedules, staff supervision, case monitoring, and a host of other duties and responsibilities calls for someone who is truly comfortable with multitasking and who can develop viable systems to manage time and work flow.

Since efficiency is also a prime responsibility of this position and the impact it should have on the court's proceedings, you need to be a decision maker, comfortable with bringing closure to a situation.

It's not surprising, then, that an increasing number of court administrators have master's degrees in business administration; likewise, many applicants have law degrees. However, if you can present solid administrative experience and documented skills along with your bachelor's degree in criminal justice, you may be in a good competitive position. Nevertheless, even with your strong background, it's advisable to seek out additional training in accounting practices and the various software programs available for calendar and budget management.

DEFINITION OF THE CAREER PATH

Paralegal

Paralegals are part of a growing trend of professionals (including nurse practitioners and religious lay leaders) who are assuming a larger range of tasks in their professions. While lawyers assume responsibility for their legal work, they often assign many of their tasks to paralegals. Paralegals thus perform many of the same tasks as lawyers, but they cannot perform any duties that could be perceived as the practice of law, such as setting fees, representing clients in legal proceedings, rendering legal advice, or presenting cases in court. Paralegals are crucial to lawyering today, and the numbers entering the profession and the numbers being hired prove it!

Paralegals are found in law firms, corporate legal departments, and various levels of government. They work in all areas of the law, including litigation, personal injury, corporate law, criminal law, employee benefits, intellectual property, labor law, and real estate. Within specialties, functions may be broken down so that paralegals deal with a specific area. For example, a paralegal specializing in labor law may deal only with employee benefits.

If work in the courts is not immediately available to you or you desire a change, it should be encouraging to know that paralegals are found in corporate work settings, where they often assist attorneys with employee contracts, shareholder agreements, stock option plans, and employee benefit plans. They may help prepare and file annual financial reports, maintain minutes of corporate meetings and resolutions, and help with the paperwork to secure loans for the corporation. They may be asked to review government regulations to ensure that the corporation is in compliance.

If you choose to work in the public sector, your job will be determined largely by the kind of agency that employs you. Researching for attorneys and collecting and analyzing evidence for agency hearings will be important tasks. You may prepare material for agency staff on relevant laws and regulations or policy for use by the agency itself or by the general public. Your constituency may include poor people, senior citizens, or other disadvantaged groups in need of legal assistance. You may help these individuals file forms, conduct research, or prepare documents, and, where authorized, you may even represent these clients at administrative (nonlegal) hearings.

If you work in a small or midsize law firm, you may research judicial opinions or help prepare contracts. Your work will probably range over a variety of tasks demanding a comprehensive general knowledge of the law. In the largest firms, you will probably specialize in one aspect of the law.

WORKING CONDITIONS

Generally, the workweek is a standard forty hours, although that depends on your employer. Some law firms may require significant overtime during big cases or busy seasons. Rewards include overtime pay or additional vacation and/or end-of-year bonuses. Initial assignments usually are routine and repetitive until you gain content knowledge and begin to demonstrate your experience.

While some paralegals have jobs that involve travel or time out of the office, most have jobs that keep them close to their desks and computers or law libraries.

TRAINING AND QUALIFICATIONS

For job seekers who have either an associate's or bachelor's degree in criminal justice, the best route to a paralegal career is to add a certification program in paralegal training. The combination of your criminal justice academic training and paralegal certification will make you a viable candidate. Many firms still prefer to train their paralegals themselves, hiring college graduates whose academic backgrounds (such as criminal justice or other social science degrees) are complementary.

Computer use, especially of specific software packages, has become commonplace, and you will use a variety of CD-ROM research databases in your work as well. Database management, software familiarity, imaging technology (many documents will be scanned into computer files), and billing programs all require a high level of computer literacy.

In addition to being computer literate, paralegals need to be good readers since reading the law is a major activity in the profession. Writing is another required skill, as you distill the results of your research and present your findings to attorneys; a sizable portion of your work will be writing reports and drafting documents for litigation. Solid research skills are also paramount.

Although professional certification is not a requirement of most employers, gaining some credentials may not only help your job search but also prolong your career. The National Association of Legal Assistants offers a certified legal assistant (CLA) certification. Also, the National Federation of Paralegal Associations offers the Paralegal Competency Exam; passing the exam allows you to use the designation registered paralegal (RP).

DEFINITION OF THE CAREER PATH

Legal Researcher

Perhaps your criminal justice degree program left you with a real interest in the law and how it works. Maybe you found that you enjoyed your reading assignments about case law, the courts, and the history of jurisprudence in the United States. Completing the self-assessment exercises in Chapter 1 may confirm that your preference is to work with data rather than people and you enjoy wrestling with and solving problems. If this description applies, a legal research position in the court system may be for you!

Legal precedence for a particular argument, contract research, case histories, average times to trial, analyses of sentences handed down, demographics of crime statistics—your days will be filled with fascinating assignments, and many people will come to depend on you as "the person with all the answers." Your corresponding responsibility for all that praise is to be consistent, accurate, and thorough in all of your research and to present that information (which may involve considerable editing on your part) in a manner that is clear and concise and yet faithful to the facts.

WORKING CONDITIONS

The working conditions are those of professional offices. Your workweek in most cases will be a standard forty hours. Some circumstances may require extra hours, and those would be compensated by overtime pay (if you are hourly) or compensatory time off (for salaried positions). Because the bulk of your work will be on the computer, you'll want to ensure that you have an ergonomically appropriate workstation to minimize body stress.

Some legal researchers occasionally leave the work site to travel to specialized law libraries and other research facilities. Others work independently, frequently from home, on a part-time or case-by-case basis. Of course, independent freelancers must support their own benefits package and must invest in sometimes costly CD-ROM packages of legal research databases. Given the high demands in this position for access to information, good advice for entry-level people is to first take a staff position with ample support services and gain some expertise before assuming the risk of becoming an independent contractor.

TRAINING AND QUALIFICATIONS

Legal research is a support position in the court system, and your criminal justice degree is a strong qualifier. However, your degree isn't training enough. Since much of your work will be computer-based and in libraries (although even those resources are increasingly available on database search engines), you need to be a skilled researcher.

In addition to strong research skills, you'll need a working familiarity with computers. Good legal researchers don't waste time doing the same search more than once. To avoid that, they frequently build their own databases to help them find materials they've used before. Strong word-processing skills, database management skills, and knowledge of relational databases will be especially helpful in securing and staying competitive in your job.

If your position also includes managing statistics for the court, you must have the appropriate quantitative background. It is not unusual for job descriptions for research analyst/statistician positions to cite a bachelor's degree as a minimum requirement, with a preference for a master's degree and demonstrated familiarity with descriptive and qualitative statistics.

Many of your assignments will present investigative challenges. You need to be a person who enjoys a problem and figuring out all the possible ways to solve it. Especially in legal research, patience is a virtue! If you are easily frustrated or need a high level of variety and change in a working day, legal research may prove to be too static for you. It is largely a mental process, requiring persistence, logic, a good memory, and creativity.

Interpersonal skills are also important in these positions. Yes, you'll have many hours of uninterrupted work (although you need to be comfortable with last-minute "emergency" requests for data), but you'll be interacting with attorneys, magistrates, judges, court administrators, and a host of other judicial workers. Your interpersonal skills help you clarify what people need. You must master questioning and probing skills so that you have a firm grasp of the research assignment ahead of you and be willing to approach colleagues and receive feedback along the way so that you don't get too far into an assignment and discover you're barking up the wrong tree!

DEFINITION OF THE CAREER PATH

Lawyer

Great Jobs for Criminal Justice Majors was written to explore the wonderful opportunities available to you now with your degree in criminal justice studies. Obviously, the job of attorney requires additional education: specifically, a degree from a law school. Notwithstanding, we feature attorneys as one of the jobs in our career path on the courts for three reasons. First, many criminal justice majors go on to complete a law degree at some point in their careers. It's a logical extension of their undergraduate studies and can be a smart and satisfying career move. In fact, many law enforcement officers have or are working on a J.D. (Juris Doctor) degree to advance up the career ladders.

Second, positions in this career path are often supervised by lawyers. Paralegals and legal researchers, for instance, get most of their direction and work at the behest of lawyers. Many paralegals, researchers, and others working under the supervision of a lawyer naturally begin to think about the advantages of having a law degree themselves. If you are entering the courts as a career path, you may come to this decision at some point on your own.

Third, and most pertinent to this chapter, lawyers are principal operatives of the court system. They are the active agents of the courtroom process and are often seen as the ones who "get things done" and can effect real change as they seek to either prosecute or exonerate in their pursuit of justice. The media have also done their part to glamorize the profession, and while it is true that there are many wealthy lawyers, a very small percentage of lawyers accounts for the highest income strata, and that income is achieved after years and years of professional experience. Perhaps a more instructive statistic is the $46,000 average median salary of lawyers six months into their profession (reported by the U.S. Bureau of Labor Statistics). Bear in mind also that the J.D. is a graduate degree; in comparison, undergraduate professional and technical majors may well have starting salaries that exceed the $46,000 median salary for lawyers in their first year. So, if guaranteed huge income production is your primary aim, you may want to do more investigation.

Keep in mind, too, that many men and women entering the legal profession have been disappointed with the career. More than 30 percent of people with law degrees are not practicing law. Maybe those people not practicing the profession for which they prepared were disappointed in the long hours, or perhaps law school corridor gossip had inflated income projections. Or, maybe they did realize some good income potential, but it took a toll on their personal lives that they weren't willing to sustain. Speculations aside, you, at least, can enter this profession with your eyes wide open to both its potential rewards and its great demands and can weigh those against your personal needs.

WORKING CONDITIONS

Working conditions for lawyers depend on the setting. If you go into public-interest law, you won't earn much money and you'll work long hours, but you'll also gain valuable experience and the knowledge that you have made a significant contribution to the welfare of people less fortunate. Many lawyers who choose to pursue private work after a time in public service find the contacts they made over that period to be valuable during the transition. If you work in a busy private law firm, you may also find your hours long, of course, but your paycheck may be compensation enough for the job demands!

Most lawyers work hard, despite the public's often jaded perception. Eighteen-hour days are not uncommon, so it's important that you like what you do. In the first few years, you may begin to clarify your preferences. Maybe you like the crisp definition of transactional law (contracts and real estate, etc.), or you may be drawn to litigation (criminal or civil work). It is an intellectually challenging job that puts equal emphasis on the details and the "big picture."

TRAINING AND QUALIFICATIONS

To qualify for the bar exam in most states, lawyers must have a law degree from a law school accredited by the American Bar Association (ABA), www.abanet.org. In addition to criminal justice majors moving on to earn law degrees, many other people come to law school with backgrounds in the liberal arts. Everyone must take the Law School Admission Test (LSAT) (www.lsac.org). Currently there are only 175 accredited law schools in the United States, so competition for entrance is stiff.

Most law students work in one or more legal settings during their law school days (usually during the summer) as they explore what area of law they want to practice. Even law schools themselves focus on specific areas. For example, Franklin Pierce Law School in Concord, New Hampshire, is known for its expertise in intellectual property, while Vermont Law School in Royalton, Vermont, attracts students interested in environmental law.

To practice law in a particular state, you must pass that state's bar exam. The bar exam is a two-day written test of the specific laws of that state. Some states have formed multistate pacts that admit you to practice in several states by passing one exam. Once you have passed that examination, some states require an oral examination to determine your character and fitness to practice in that state.

Simply put, the best qualifications for anyone considering becoming a lawyer are strong work habits (the job can be demanding, requiring long hours), excellent oral and written skills, curiosity, and a pronounced ability to work with, and for, others.

EARNINGS

Jobs in the court system are available at local/county, state, and federal levels. As is true of other career fields that fit these criteria, salaries vary, sometimes significantly, from one level of government to the next and from one part of the country to the next. Generally, the higher the level of government, the greater the salary. Also keep in mind that the same job title can sometimes carry very different responsibilities (and salary levels). For example, the position of court clerk in some courts is an administrative or managerial position charged with overseeing all of the court's operations. Such a position commands a relatively high salary. In other courts, a court clerk is an office-support position focused on providing mostly clerical services and, as you would guess, earning a relatively low salary. Always read job descriptions carefully to be certain the job is the type and level of sophistication you seek.

Probation and Parole Officers

According to *The Corrections Yearbook 1998*, the most recent salary study published by the Criminal Justice Institute, Inc., the average starting salary for probation officers nationwide was $26,014. The entry-level salary for parole officers was slightly higher at $27,888. Some states employ a combination probation/parole officer, and these employees earned slightly less at $24,410. The state of New York paid the highest starting salary, $40,631, for a parole officer, while, at the other end, Kentucky paid entry-level probation/parole officers $17,964. That's quite a difference!

Average salaries (which take into account everyone working in these occupations, entry-level and experienced alike) were about the same for probation and parole officers at just over $34,000, although the combined probation/parole officer again had slightly lower average earnings of just over $32,000. The highest average salaries were earned by probation officers, averaging $46,325, followed by the combined probation/parole officer salaries of $43,066 and finally $42,441 by parole officers.

With significantly increased experience and a master's degree or, for some, a law degree (J.D.), you can advance to chief probation officer and into district or regional administration. The average probation administrator earned $79,293, the average parole administrator earned $71,810, and the average combined probation/parole administrator earned $68,504. As noted at the outset of this section, you may find that salaries increase with the level of government. One recent vacancy announcement for a deputy chief probation officer at a U.S. district court stated a salary range of $70,655 to $122,607.

Victim Advocate

Victim advocates are often viewed as human service workers and not as criminal justice team members, and this status is reflected in a reduced earning potential as well. A recent sampling of actual job openings around the country turned up salaries as low as $18,000 to $20,000 for entry-level positions and as high as $35,000 for more experienced staff positions or for those requiring additional education or training, such as licensed social workers. The majority of the salaries fell within the mid-$20s range. As you gain experience in victim advocacy services, and perhaps complete an advanced degree in either a human service field or business if your ultimate goal is administration or management, you will find salaries in the $40,000-to-$50,000 range.

Bailiff

Bailiffs earned an average annual salary of $28,000 in 1998, with half earning $22,000 to $37,800. At the high end of the scale, bailiffs in the state of Washington earned an average salary of $47,000, while those in South Carolina earned $18,000.

As mentioned previously, bailiffs in U.S. federal courts are U.S. marshals. Their entry-level salaries range from $25,235 to $31,376. Also as discussed in the previous chapter, federal law enforcement officers qualify for law enforcement availability pay (LEAP) amounting to 25 percent of their annual salary. This raises the entry-level salary range to $31,544 to $39,220. If you're working in an area where the prevailing wage rate is higher than the average in the country, you may receive an additional 3 percent to 16 percent of your base salary.

Court Reporter

In court reporting, income depends on the type of reporting jobs, the experience of the reporter, certification, and how much time the reporter is willing to devote to the job, as many court reporters choose to work on a part-time basis. Many also work as independent contractors, and some even own their own agencies and hire other court reporters.

The Bureau of Labor Statistics (BLS) indicates that on average court reporters can expect to earn $25,400. Since many work part-time, it may be helpful to know that most court reporters earned between $10.13 and $15.13 an hour. According to the National Court Reporters Association (NCRA), however, citing a February 1999 study, the average annual income for court reporters participating in the study was $61,830. You may wonder how the difference in average salaries reported by the BLS and the NCRA can be so great. Several points should help to clarify the divergence. First, the Bureau of Labor Statistics combines court reporters with stenographers; since stenographers usually earn lower salaries than court reporters, combining them brings the overall average down somewhat. Also, the NCRA figure does not include all court reporters, just those who participated in the study. It is likely that the survey participants were more senior or experienced and therefore earning the highest salaries, and/or they were freelance court reporters who worked for themselves and possibly owned a court reporting firm.

In any event, salaries for court reporters are considered relatively high and, in view of the number of hours worked, may in fact be some of the highest within the legal field.

Clerk of Court

Clerks of court basically oversee much of the court processes aside from trials: they call cases, maintain the records, formulate policies and administrative procedures, supervise office personnel, and often even hear traffic ticket cases (a "clerk's hearing"). These positions can range from high-level managerial posts with salary levels of $90,000 to $100,000 to lower-level, more supervisory or clerical functions with salaries ranging from $30,000 to $40,000. Positions on the higher end often require advanced degrees, including the J.D., and years of administrative and court experience, while positions at the lower end may require some college course work and a minimal number of years of court experience. Here's an example of what you're more likely to encounter when researching clerk of court jobs:

Clerk of the Municipal Court: Directs administrative activities involving court records and legal document processing; prepares annual budget; develops policies and procedures for the receipt and accounting of fine payments, issuance of warrants, and scheduling of defendants and attorneys to clarify rules, regulations, and court functions. Qualifications: A minimum of five years of increasingly responsible court administration experience, with a bachelor's degree in court administration, criminal justice, public administration, or a related field. Salary: $42,000–$57,000.

In some courts the clerk of court is the chief administrative officer. In others the clerk of court may report to the court administrator.

Court Administrator

These positions are considered upper-level, require some experience, and often pay quite well. Here's a typical example from the Job Description Databank of the National Center for State Courts:

> **Court Administrator:** Duties include managing the court system and supervising all office positions. Desired qualifications: Prefer a four-year degree in business/public/judicial administration or related field. Desired experience: Five years management/administrative-level experience, with three years in a supervisory capacity. Salary range: $45,136 to $57,158. Mail, fax, or E-mail letter of application, resume, and salary history to . . .

Court administrator positions in larger courts or those overseeing court systems, such as a state court administrator, will pay more. A study by the National Center for State Courts found that as of July 1999, salaries for state court administrators ranged from $62,772 to $147,600, with an average salary of $96,454. These positions will also probably require or, at the very least, prefer additional experience and an advanced degree, either a master's or a law degree.

Paralegal

Salary levels of paralegals vary greatly and depend on geographic location, educational background, work experience, and type and size of employer. Salaries tend to be greater for people with a bachelor's or more advanced degree, and on the West Coast, in larger firms, and in metropolitan areas. The National Association of Legal Assistants (NALA) in its *2000 National Utilization and Compensation Survey Report* cites an average salary for legal assistants of $37,946 plus average yearly bonuses of $2,449, making for a total compensation of $40,395. This is an increase of more than $4,000 since 1997, the last time the survey was conducted. Employees with less experience (one to five years) averaged lower salaries and bonuses, earning $30,342.

In terms of public employment, the latest available figures from the Bureau of Labor Statistics are as of 1997. The federal government paid the highest salaries to paralegals, with a median of $43,900, while those working in local government earned around $32,200.

As you can see, paralegals earn relatively good salaries. This may be a reflection of the increased emphasis on responsibilities or tasks that previously belonged to attorneys and the correspondingly higher education and professional standards.

One final note for job seekers who already have a bachelor's degree and would like to become a paralegal: the NALA study also found that paralegals with bachelor's degrees who went on to complete a certificate in paralegal education earned an average salary including bonuses of $43,974. That's almost $5,000 more than those with specific bachelor's degrees in paralegal education.

Legal Researcher

A sampling of current job openings for legal researchers indicated an average salary range of $25,000 to $35,000. Senior and more experienced researchers could earn $45,000 to $55,000 or even more. Here's an example of an ad from a court in Florida:

Court Analyst: Analyze information and data; research court policies and procedures; assist in the design of survey instruments and data collection tools; and prepare reports of research findings. Qualifications: Bachelor's degree from an accredited four-year college or university with a major in public criminology, administration, judicial administration, political science, or statistics. Salary: $25,920–$40,176.

Lawyer

The National Association for Law Placement, in its latest annual report, *Jobs and J.D.s: Employment and Salaries of New Law Graduates—Class of 1998*, found that the median salary paid to the graduating class of 1998 for full-time jobs was $45,000. Earnings in private firms, where 55 percent of the graduates were employed, were the highest at $60,000, followed by starting salaries in business and industry of $50,000, government at $36,000, and public-interest jobs at $31,000. If you thought that *all* lawyers make a lot of money, consider this: according to the report, "the higher median in private practice notwithstanding, salaries of $35,000–40,000 were equally as common as salaries of $70,000 or more."

For all lawyers, both new and seasoned, the median salary for 1998 was $78,200, with most earning between $51,500 and $114,500. Trial lawyers, those involved in actual litigation, tend to earn more, particularly if they work in private practice as opposed to the district attorney's office. While lawyers employed by the federal government earn about what the average is for all lawyers, those working for local government (such as the city or town attorney) or state government (such as public defenders) make less, usually around $50,000 and $59,000, respectively.

CAREER OUTLOOK

Generally speaking, employment in the court system is expected to grow about as fast as the average for all occupations, which translates to an increase of 10 to 20 percent between now and 2008. Despite the increased numbers of cases before the court, budget constraints continue to limit the growth of local, state, and federal courts. So, most of the employment opportunities will come from replacing workers who are promoted, retire, or move on to other positions. To a lesser extent, jobs will become available as a result of the limited growth within the court system. Couple this limited growth with, for many people, the appeal of working in the court system, and you will find keen competition for the jobs that do exist. For the most part, court-related jobs pay relatively well, offer job security, and provide a working environment that's interesting and sometimes even exciting.

Being aware of the supply-and-demand constraints in court-related careers should motivate you now to develop skills that are desired in the field in which you're interested. You can serve in an internship in which you can gain real-world experience and get to know people who can help you in your job search. Join associations to increase your knowledge of the field as well as your network of contacts, and start early to learn where the jobs are and how to put yourself in the best position to get them.

Keep in mind that we've been talking about the career outlook in general terms. There are some exceptions to the foregoing projections, most notably among paralegals, as you will see.

Probation and Parole Officers

While the population of probationers continues to grow, funding for probation does not always follow. According to the Bureau of Labor Statistics, in 1998 the adult probation population alone increased by about 121,000, and the nation's parole population grew by approximately 10,000 individuals. Yet, only about one-tenth of the national corrections budget goes to probation and parole administration. Certainly based on need, employment of probation and parole officers is not expected to decline. It will most likely experience an average growth rate.

Probation has long been an attractive career field for many students of criminal justice and other social sciences, so expect healthy competition for jobs. Try to gain some on-the-job experience to put you ahead of other new graduates. This is an ideal area in which to pursue an internship. Not only will you gain the relative work experience you need, but you'll meet (and get to know) the important hiring officials as well.

Another tip for positioning yourself in the market is to investigate civil service exam requirements in the state in which you'd like to work. Some states require an exam for probation and parole officers, while others don't. Exams are usually scheduled on specific dates; if you need to take the test, arrange to do so at the earliest possible time. And don't forget to prepare for it!

Victim Advocate

The employment outlook for victim advocates is strong, as the government continues to sponsor grants and fund programs to aid victims of crime. In this new and growing field, opportunities are abundant. Sadly, there are thousands and thousands of victims of crime each year, from missing children to bomb victims and their families, who are in need of assistance and services. Within the first twelve years of the passage of the Victims of Crime Act of 1984, $2.2 billion in federal criminal fines were transferred to states to fund local victim assistance programs. Today, approximately ten thousand programs exist.

Getting in on the ground floor of a new career field also means that opportunities for advancement will be great as well. As you develop experience, to qualify for promotions, in most cases, you'll also need to continue your education through professional development activities such as seminars and workshops (often offered through or sponsored by your employer) and through more formalized education leading to a master's degree.

Bailiff

Bailiff jobs are expected to grow more slowly than the average for all occupations nationwide. Only an 8 percent growth rate is predicted through 2006, which means that each year on average, 1,130 bailiffs will be hired in the country. This will vary from state to state, however, and for some states, such as Florida, the growth rate is expected to be around 23 percent. The number of bailiffs hired in each state varies considerably as well. California employs approximately 5,700 bailiffs, while North Dakota employs only 50! If you're willing to relocate, you can use the on-line *America's Career Infonet*, www3.gu.com/acinet, to explore trends for various states. The variance in numbers reflects the fact that the field itself is relatively narrow. Approximately 44,000 bailiffs are employed nationwide. Compare that with the close to 700,000 lawyers in this country.

Court Reporter

According to the National Court Reporters Association, employment opportunities for this occupation are plentiful, as work in the legal field is keeping pace with increased levels of litigation. The occupation is predicted to remain stable, and significant opportunities exist for entry-level positions in particular. The high salaries received by court reporters make this an attractive career, and you will definitely encounter competition in your employment search. However, only 300 schools and colleges offer court reporting programs, and only a third of those are accredited by the NCRA. The job outlook is best for reporters who become certified by passing a state certification exam and for those achieving the distinction of registered professional reporter (RPR), which is conferred by the NCRA. Other areas of specialized certification that will enhance career opportunities include registered merit reporter, registered diplomat reporter, certified real-time reporter, and certified video specialist.

Some people have been under the mistaken impression that the field of court reporting will diminish with the advent of voice recognition equipment. The NCRA argues that current voice and speech systems have high error rates, much higher than those of court reporters who write accurately at speeds in excess of 200 words per minute. Most in the field predict that the refinements to voice recognition software that would be needed to achieve the accuracy required in legal and other proceedings is another forty to fifty years away.

Clerk of Court

All courts by design include enormous administrative responsibilities, and with the continued growth of cases coming before the courts, these administrative needs will also continue to grow. Thus, you can see why, in order for the court system to run smoothly and efficiently, there will always be a demand for clerks of court and other personnel to work in these offices. Within a clerk's office, you will often find assistant clerks, court clerks, associate clerks, deputy clerks, and so on. If becoming a clerk of court is your career goal, you will likely need to enter the field in one of these support positions. From there, you can gain the experience necessary for promotion. Ultimately, you may advance to a court administrator's position!

Court Administrator

In all likelihood, you will not be qualified for this job at this stage in your career. It's included here because the position is integral to the functioning of the court system and can provide you with a vision of a career path down the road. Not all courts have a court administrator; usually only the bigger and/or busier ones do. You will often see someone with the title "clerk of the court" who may perform the duties of the court administrator in less busy courthouses. The clerk of the court often reports to the court administrator where there is one. All states have a court administrator, or an equivalent, who oversees the court system in that state. These are appointed positions with high visibility and high salaries. They require years of experience and very often advanced degrees. If you aspire to this position, you will probably start in the clerk's office, where you will gain valuable experience as you continue your education. Opportunities are limited, though, and you will need to be a shining star among the ranks of court clerks to rise to this level.

Paralegal

As mentioned at the outset of this section, paralegals represent the most notable exception to court-related positions in terms of job outlook. The Bureau of Labor Statistics projects that employment of paralegals will have grown 62 percent between 1998 and 2000, making it one of the fastest-growing occupations among those tracked by the Bureau. This expansion is not new. It has been a steady trend in recent years and is probably best explained by the expanded role that paralegals have assumed in law offices and departments and in government agencies. More experienced paralegals are intensively involved in trial preparation and may be called on to produce interrogatories for an attorney's review, assist in trial-related motions, and even meet with clients. Also, senior-level paralegals sometimes supervise lower-level paralegals. The increasing reliance on paralegals to perform such higher-level duties is easy to explain. Paralegals help to reduce costs for law firms and agencies and promote efficiency by freeing up lawyers to concentrate on direct legal services.

Despite the tremendously positive outlook for paralegals, take note that while the field is growing, so is the competition. Paralegal programs have become so popular in America's colleges and universities that the number of graduates, combined with others who, for example, may be looking to enter the field and are learning on the job, is outpacing job growth. To be competitive for entry-level positions, you need to be an expert in computer software packages and the Internet, possess strong researching skills, and demonstrate a willingness to work extended hours as part of the legal team.

In all probability, you will need to continue your education to be considered qualified for this position. While your criminal justice curriculum might have covered some of the same areas as a paralegal studies curriculum would, it would not include all of the specialty course work. Therefore, although it's possible that a law firm or department will hire you and train you, it's more likely that you will have to complete a certificate in paralegal studies. Most certificate programs can be completed in one year if you are attending full-time. Plenty of part-time programs are also available for those who choose to continue to work while taking classes.

Legal Researcher

Similar to paralegals but much smaller in scope, the employment outlook for legal researchers is strong and for much the same reasons. Law firms and departments and other employers can decrease their costs and increase their efficiency by hiring researchers to do much of the background function or "legwork" previously done by lawyers. This is especially true in larger organizations. Some employers require legal researchers to have paralegal experience, and you may even encounter some who hire entry-level attorneys to do the job.

Lawyer

Competition is the name of the game for lawyers. It starts right from the beginning with your application to law school, where competition is fierce. If you're lucky enough to get in (and if you successfully complete the program), you're then faced with the fact that the number of law school graduates continues to outpace the growth of jobs and creates a strain on the economy to absorb them, a trend for much of the past thirty years. That said, however, the growth for employment for lawyers is still expected to hover around 19 percent over the next five years or so. Most of the gain will be due to population growth, growth in business activities in general, and increased legal action involving health care, intellectual property, the environment, international law, and sexual harassment.

Another positive finding comes from the National Association for Law Placement in its statistics for the graduating class of 1999, which demonstrate that "for the first time since 1990, employment of new law graduates exceeded 90 percent." The findings also show that the overall employment rate for law school graduates continued to increase for the sixth consecutive year, with 75.5 percent employed in full-time legal positions (the rest were either working part-time or employed outside of the direct practice of law).

STRATEGY FOR FINDING THE JOBS

You're in luck! Courts aren't hard to locate. A smart strategy is to first identify all the court settings (local, county, state, and federal) in the geographic area you have under consideration. It's not a bad idea to actually purchase a map and locate these sites, and begin to anticipate drive time, road conditions, and so forth. Make up a chart, listing each court along with its type and location. You may note, depending on where you live, that some larger cities have more than one court. Following are some techniques for locating all the court possibilities in your area:

- Local courts: To determine local court jurisdictions, you can simply call the local police department, which deals with the lower-level court every day. Another alternative is to consult the white pages under the business listing section; look up the towns in your area of interest, and you will find any courts located there. Then, contact them to find where they post their job openings. Once you know that, check on a regular basis so that you don't miss any new opportunities. You'll usually find that in addition to postings on their job bulletin boards, announcements will be placed in the local newspaper.

- State courts: Once again, the Internet has made life easier for you. Visit your state's home page to find a listing for state courts (www.piperinfo.com/state/states.html is a great on-line resource, as it connects you to every state in the country). Once you find your state's judiciary page, you will most likely see not only the locations of courts within the state system but also directions and contact information. You will also learn about the different courts that make up the state system and their areas of responsibility. Any employment opportunities are usually made available as well. Another good place to look on the Internet is the National Center for State Courts, which publishes job vacancy announcements for all state courts in the country. Jobs are updated on the first and fifteenth of each month, free of charge. They can be found at www.ncsc.dni.us/pubs/jobann .html. The site also provides links to state and some federal court sites at www.ncsc.dni.us/court/sites/courts.html.

- Federal courts: Each federal court does its own advertising and hiring for job positions, so it's important to find out where these courts are located. The Federal Judicial Center at www.fjc.gov provides links to the home pages of all federal courts when you click on "Other Court-Related Servers." You'll also find a link to www.uscourts.gov, which provides at least a partial listing of job opportunities at the federal level.

Within each court setting that you identify, you will come across most of the jobs outlined in this chapter, with some exceptions. For instance, while victim advocacy may take place as a "process" within all of these courts, in your search for a position in the field, you may also want to look in the local newspaper, where local social service agencies often advertise, or visit your town hall.

Lawyers and paralegals, on the other hand, will likely be associated with either private law firms or the state district attorney or prosecutor's office. Legal researchers may be as well. Where do these employers advertise? State positions are advertised on the state's website. Private firms and other organizations with law departments are most apt to advertise in local and regional newspapers, on their own websites, as well as on law employment–related websites such as The Legal Employment Search Site at www.legalemploy.com. In addition, you can always find listings of local law firms in the yellow pages in the phone book and on the Web. In both paralegal and law careers, your job search should also take into account any specialty of law you have in mind. Some firms specialize in litigation, for example, while others may handle real estate transactions exclusively.

Don't forget to visit your career services office, which will have information on how to find opportunities for your specific career.

POSSIBLE EMPLOYERS

For many of the positions presented in this chapter, local, state, and federal governments are the only employers. This is true for probation and parole officers, bailiffs, court administrators, and most court reporters. It also applies for some lawyers, paralegals, legal researchers, and victim advocates. There are different kinds of courts—municipal, U.S. district, superior, trial, or appeals—for matters as diverse as juvenile justice and bankruptcy, but in each of these courts you are ultimately employed by a government agency. For certain positions, however, there are some further alternatives.

Victim Advocate

As explained earlier, victim advocates often work in partnership with the court system but may or may not be direct employees of the court. Grants for victim assistance and services may be awarded to local law enforcement agencies, district attorney's offices, independent state agencies, or any other organizations that may contract with local, state, or federal authorities to provide services to victims. The types of agencies that provide the services vary according to the nature of the crime that's been committed. Victims can include those of child abuse, domestic violence, rape/sexual abuse, stalking, fraud, workplace violence, juvenile crime, hate crime, elder abuse, and discrimination. Agencies that offer such outreach are just as diverse.

Court Reporter

In addition to being employees of the court, court reporters can be independent contractors or can work for a court reporting firm. Many do choose to work outside of the courtroom. In fact, in 1998, one in four was self-employed. Given the large number of conventions, conferences, seminars, and meetings, both in the private sector and in government agencies that take place each year in which the proceedings need to be accurately recorded, court reporters can find ample work outside the court system.

Paralegal, Legal Researcher, and Lawyer

Private law firms employ the vast majority of paralegals, legal researchers, and lawyers. Most of the remainder work in corporate legal departments or various levels of government. At the local level, they may work for the city law department. At the state level, you may find them working in the offices of the attorney general, district attorney, public defender, prosecutor, or individual state departments such as a department of social services or the office of the treasurer. Most employed by the federal government are hired by the Department of Justice, followed by the Departments of the Treasury and Defense, and the Federal Deposit Insurance Corporation. Other paralegals, legal researchers, and lawyers may work for publicly funded legal services centers.

Within organizations, you may deal in all areas of law, or you may want to work within a particular area of specialization, including personal injury, litigation, intellectual property, labor law, family law, criminal law, discrimination, employee benefits, real estate, estate planning, and technology-related concerns.

POSSIBLE JOB TITLES

As you launch your search for an entry-level position in the courts, you're likely to turn up many different jobs with a variety of job titles. Are these for you? Do you meet the qualifications? Some of these job titles were introduced in this chapter. Some are simply variations of these titles. Some may be new to you. Begin to build a collection or portfolio of job postings by job title; after you have collected three to five ads in each category, many of your questions will be resolved.

Here are some job titles you are likely to come across. While the list is long, it in no way encompasses all the jobs in all the courts (or related to the courts) all across the country.

Probation and Parole

Aftercare Coordinator	Parole Officer
Chief Probation Officer	Pretrial Services Officer
Community Service Coordinator	Probation and Parole Officer
Director of Probation	Probation Counselor
Family Service Officer	Probation Officer
Juvenile Probation Counselor	Release-on-Own-Recognizance (ROR) Interviewer

Victim Services

Animal Treatment Investigator	Gender Issues Specialist
Caseworker	Housing/Tenant Representative
Child and Youth Counselor	Nonprofit Organization Advocate
Child Support Agency Worker	
Counselor	Support Services Coordinator
Crisis Counselor	Victim Advocate
Domestic Violence Counselor	Victim Restitution Coordinator
Family Service Clinician	Victim Services Specialist
Witness Protection Worker	Victim-Witness Coordinator

Law Enforcers

Bailiff	Court Security Officer
Bondsman	Process Server
Constable	U.S. Marshal
Court Officer	

Court Reporting

Court Reporter	Legal Video Specialist
Diplomat Reporter	Manager of Reporting Services
Merit Reporter	Reporting Instructor

Real-Time Reporter

Registered Professional Reporter

Stenocaptioner

Stenographer

Court Administration

Administrative Coordinator

Appeals Reviewer

Arbitrator

Assistant Clerk

Case Flow Manager

Case Manager

Chief Deputy Clerk

Clerk of Court

Court Administrator

Court Clerk

Court Executive

Court Magistrate

Court Representative

Deputy Clerk

Judicial Assistant

Mediation Specialist

Paralegal

Legal Assistant

Paralegal

Legal Research

Analyst

Conflicts Researcher

Court Analyst

Court Services Analyst

Law Librarian

Legal Researcher

Researcher

Senior Researcher

Sentencing Analyst

Law

Adjudicator

Attorney

District Attorney/Assistant
   District Attorney

Expert Witness

Judge

Law Clerk

Lawyer

Litigation Manager

Public Defender

Trial Lawyer

RELATED OCCUPATIONS

Claims Examiner	Title Abstractor
Contracts Administrator	Title Examiner
Medical Transcriptionist	Title Searcher
Patent Agent	

PROFESSIONAL ASSOCIATIONS

Listed in this section are some of the associations that relate to careers in the courts. For more information about these professional associations, either check the websites listed or consult the *Encyclopedia of Associations*, published by the Gale Group. Review the Members/Purpose notes for each organization to determine if it pertains to your interests. Membership in one or more of these organizations may gain you access to job listings, networking opportunities, and employment search services. Some provide information at no charge, but if you want to receive specific publications that list job opportunities, you may need to join. If you're still in college, check for student member rates.

American Bar Association
541 N. Fairbanks Ct.
Chicago, IL 60611
www.abanet.org/
Members/Purpose: The premier association for attorneys. Its mission is to be the national representative of the legal profession, serving the public and the profession by promoting justice, professional excellence, and respect for the law. The association provides extensive resources for its members, law students, the media, and the general public.
Publications: Numerous books, magazines, journals, and newsletters.
Training: Mid-year and annual meetings. Also sponsors the Center for Continuing Legal Education.

American Correctional Association
4380 Forbes Blvd.
Lanham, MD 20706-4322
www.corrections.com/aca/

Members/Purpose: For more than 125 years, the American Correctional Association has championed the cause of corrections and correctional effectiveness. Founded in 1870 as the National Prison Association, ACA is the oldest association developed specifically for practitioners in the correctional profession.

Publications: *Corrections Today* magazine; *Corrections Compendium* journal; publications catalog from which you can choose books, videos, or products; on-line job bank.

Training: On-line training workshops; training sessions throughout the year on specific topics; video library.

American Probation and Parole Association
P.O. Box 11910
Lexington, KY 40578-1910
www.appa-net.org/aboutappa.htm

Members/Purpose: Established to serve, challenge, and empower members and constituents by educating, communicating, and training; advocating and influencing; acting as a resource and conduit for information, ideas, and support; developing standards and models; and collaborating with other disciplines.

Publications: Issue papers on topics facing the field of community corrections; *Perspectives*, a quarterly journal; variety of books and manuscripts, many of which are aimed at career building.

Training: Training institutes; national/regional training seminars and technical assistance; professional development program.

Conference of State Court Administrators
500 S. Duval St.
Tallahassee, FL 32399-1900
www.ncsc.dni.us/cosca/coscaros.htm

Members/Purpose: Dedicated to the improvement of state court systems. Membership consists of the state court administrator or the equivalent official in each of the fifty states, the District of Columbia, Puerto Rico, American Samoa, and the Virgin Islands.

Publications: *The Justice System Journal*; variety of monographs; many on-line publications such as court technology bulletins, jury news, and job announcements.

Training: None available.

National Association for Court Management
300 Newport Ave.
P.O. Box 8798
Williamsburg, VA 23187-8798
www.nacmnet.org
Members/Purpose: The NACM is committed to improving the administration of justice and promoting the interdependence of court managers and judges.
Publications: Quarterly magazine, *The Court Manager*.
Training: Annual conference.

National Association of Legal Assistants
1516 S. Boston, No. 200
Tulsa, OK 74119
www.nala.org
Members/Purpose: A leading professional association for legal assistants, providing continuing education and professional certification programs for paralegals.
Publications: *Facts and Findings*, quarterly journal, as well as a variety of manuals.
Training: Seminars; workshops; on-line educational programs.

National Court Reporters Association
8224 Old Courthouse Rd.
Vienna, VA 22182-3808
www.verbatimreporters.com
Members/Purpose: The NCRA's mission is to create an understanding of the role of information/court reporters among customers, legislators, and regulators and to ensure that they are professionals who capture and manage the record through education, training, and state-of-the-art technology.
Publications: *Journal of Court Reporting*, a monthly magazine; *The Job Bank*; membership directory.
Training: Annual conferences; seminars; extensive professional development opportunities, including certification programs. Also offers a Virtual Mentors program to bring court reporters and students together.

National Federation of Paralegal Associations
P.O. Box 33108
Kansas City, MO 64114
www.paralegals.org/home.html
Members/Purpose: Established to advance, foster, and promote the paralegal concept; to monitor and participate in the developments affecting the paralegal profession; and to maintain a nationwide communications network among paralegal associations and other members of the legal community.
Publications: *National Paralegal Reporter*, the NFPA's magazine, printed five times a year; directory of member associations; informational brochures; on-line job listings.
Training: Annual conventions and seminars.

National Organization for Victim Assistance
1757 Park Rd.
Washington, DC 20010
www.try-nova.org
Members/Purpose: A private nonprofit organization of victim and witness assistance programs and practitioners, criminal justice agencies and professionals, mental health professionals, researchers, former victims and survivors, and others committed to the recognition and implementation of victim rights and services.
Publications: Information packets and bulletins; articles; training materials on selected topics.
Training: Crisis response training utilizing selected topics and training methods.

National Paralegal Association
Box 406
Solebury, PA 18963
www.nationalparalegal.org
Members/Purpose: An international organization offering benefits and services to individuals, law firms, corporate legal departments, independent paralegals, and paralegal training schools and colleges, as well as vendors of services or products to the paralegal profession.
Publications: Material directed to people exploring entry into the profession and to established paralegals, either employed by a firm or in independent practice. Offerings include *Career Guide, Local and/or Paralegal School and College Directory, Legal Placement Agency Directory*, and *Paralegal Employment Network* (job listings).

Pretrial Services Resource Center
1325 G St. NW, Suite 770
Washington, DC 20005
www.pretrial.org
Members/Purpose: The mission of the Pretrial Services Resource Center is to improve the quality, fairness, and efficiency of the criminal justice system at the pretrial stage by promoting systemic strategies that improve court appearance rates, reduce recidivism, provide appropriate and effective services, and enhance community safety.
Publications: *The Pretrial Reporter*, a bimonthly newsletter; monographs and reports.
Training: Pretrial Justice Institute.

Victim Offender Mediation Association
143 Canal St.
New Smyrna Beach, FL 32168
www.igc.org/voma/
Members/Purpose: Established to provide greater networking among practitioners and other interested individuals to enhance the overall credibility of victim/offender mediation and reconciliation programs within the justice community.
Publications: *VOMA Connections*, a quarterly newsletter; numerous articles.
Training: Training institute and conference (annual meeting).

CHAPTER 12

PATH 3: CORRECTIONS: LOCK UP YOUR FUTURE

THE CORRECTIONS SYSTEM

A recurrent theme in this book is the changing role of criminal justice careers in society. We, as a nation, are paying more attention to all aspects of criminal justice; we are more demanding of our police and federal officers, our courts are under intensive scrutiny for fairness and cost efficiencies, and our jails and prisons are no longer warehouses for criminals. The result is that graduates of criminal justice degree programs have never had their degree as valued as it is today, nor have they had as many opportunities to make a difference. This chapter deals with an aspect of the criminal justice system that society sometimes wants to forget but that features largely in the criminal justice curriculum: the field of corrections.

Perhaps the biggest change and the most important one for you as a criminal justice major is that the field of corrections is increasingly populated by people like you: graduates who are choosing the field of corrections, knowing they can apply their education and training to an area of criminal justice that is in the process of major reforms even as it continues to struggle with the age-old problems of budgets and overcrowding. Sure, the problems are there, but so are the opportunities. If you are looking to make a difference, corrections is worthy of your interest!

Criminal justice jobs have been a prime target for movies, novels, and television shows. Police, FBI agents, judges and lawyers, and, of course, prison and jail personnel have been depicted in numerous ways—some accurate, many not. On the whole, the image of personnel in corrections that is projected by the popular media is way off. Brutalizing, abusive staff (almost always male) are the stuff of fantasy and not today's reality.

Today's corrections professionals are men and women, most often college educated like you, and are dedicated, service-oriented personnel whose dual duty is to house lawbreakers away from society and to provide those same lawbreakers with an environment that offers those wishing to access them as well as those returning to society an instrument for positive change.

The Corrections Situation Today

From 1984 to 1994, our prison population increased by more than 250 percent. That kind of exponential growth continues today and has largely been responsible for the arrival of private prison management firms, some of which have developed modular construction programs that can erect, outfit, and staff a prison faster than the public sector. On top of the overpopulation problem, we have prisons now charged with increasingly sophisticated missions of a combination of punishment, treatment, and/or rehabilitation, depending on the sentence meted out and the nature of the criminal and the crime.

Women in Corrections

While the typical inmate is male, under thirty, and without a high school diploma, the number of women who are incarcerated is increasing at a faster rate than the male population. Though women currently make up less than 10 percent of the total inmate population, this number is expected to continue to multiply. More women inmates mean more women corrections staff and more facilities to house this growing population. Up until the 1970s, women performed a limited role in corrections. Inmate teachers, nurses, clerical positions, arsenal staff, information desk service, and gun tower duty were the principal occupational areas for women. The tide began to turn in 1982, when a federal court decision declared that women could not be barred from other duties and provided compensation to women corrections officers previously restricted from these assignments and to those who had been denied promotional advancement for lack of experience that they could not obtain. Female officers thus began to receive the training they had been denied and took up their positions in the housing units without incident.

The Corrections Setting: Prisons and Jails

Most members of the general public are not aware of the distinction that the criminal justice field makes between prisons and jails. *Prisons* are operated by the federal government or state governments; they are often large facilities with large staffs and many inmates. Sizable populations of inmates generally mean that men and women can be segregated in separate facilities and that a variety of programs and instruction for rehabilitation and treatment is available. These prisons house individuals convicted of felonies carrying a sentence of more than one year.

The small facilities run by counties, cities, and towns and that generally house only up to about fifty people are correctly termed *jails*. Prisoners in these facilities are serving shorter sentences, generally for smaller crimes or misdemeanors, or they may be awaiting a trial date for a crime for which either there is no bail or they could not post the required dollar amount. Increasingly, these jails also may be housing convicted felons who have been sentenced to a prison facility but must wait for a spot to open. Since jails are not designed for extended use and many are not used consistently or even frequently, they tend to be in disrepair. Support programs are not offered because turnover is intended to be rapid. Likewise, staff may have no special training and may be charged with many other duties in the county or city facilities that house the jail.

The jail facilities that we toured during our research for this book were, at best, functional, even those that were new. We were struck by how basic the cells were, and, of course, there is no privacy whatever. Cell design and preventing vandalism by angry offenders dictate a certain sterility in the furniture and heavily influence the cost of even the most spartan lockup unit. Open stainless-steel toilets that we saw cost more than $600 apiece. Consequently, budgets of small cities or localities can rarely extend to jail modifications and upgrades.

Prison Populations

The Web is a handy source for corrections information, and every state has a state corrections site. The site for Connecticut, www.state.ct.us/doc/facts/facts_body.htm, provides a good picture of the staff and population of one state's corrections facilities:

- 20 facilities

- Total staff of 6,279

- An incarcerated population of 16,776, of which 1,093 are women

- 910 prisoners on conditional release

- 758 in halfway houses

- 34 on reentry furloughs

- State corrections department budget of more than $400 million in 1999

Connecticut has separate facilities for men and women. Several of its state facilities serve as jails and as intake facilities for unsentenced males, though these jails will also process and confine convicted males for sentences of less than two years. Special facilities exist for sentenced and unsentenced males between the ages of fourteen and twenty-one. Five security levels have been established: level 5 is maximum security, level 4 is high security, level 3 is medium security, level 2 is low security, and level 1 comprises prisoners who have been released into the community but remain under departmental supervision.

Each state has its own complement of prisons, and they vary in age, architecture, size, and amenities. What they share is a special world of extreme regimentation and detailed structure. Within this structure, there exist any number of subcultures built around offenses, personalities, education, goals—even anger. These subcultures display hierarchies, leaders, values, codes, and behavioral patterns that can be remarkably similar from prison to prison. Some of these subcultures can exert tremendous pressure on individuals as well as groups of prisoners.

This description is not just interesting sociology about group behavior since it is within and between these groups that conflict often arises and violations of prison protocols occur. Some of the country's most dangerous and violent prison breakouts and hostage situations have had their beginnings within these subcultures. As a corrections officer, you'll develop a specialized antenna for the nuances of group behavior, membership, codes, and interactions.

DEFINITION OF THE CAREER PATH

Corrections Officer

The corrections officer is the mainstay and principal employment figure of the corrections system. The role of corrections officers is to oversee individuals who have been arrested and are awaiting trial or who have been convicted and sentenced to a jail, reformatory, or penitentiary. They maintain security and inmate accountability to prevent disturbances, assaults, or escapes. These officers have no law enforcement powers outside the institutions where they work.

There are occasionally corrections officer jobs in county jails or precinct station houses, and the people holding these posts are known as detention officers. These jobs, too, pose serious physical threats, especially in the period immediately following an individual's arrest, when the suspect may be violent and his or her background (and even name) may be unknown. This is a dangerous phase of the incarceration process.

In addition to prisons and jails, a smaller number of corrections officers may also find employment with the Immigration and Naturalization Service, which holds noncitizens and permanent residents before they are released or deported.

Regardless of the work setting, the duties and responsibilities of corrections officers are generally similar. They include:

- Ensuring that inmates are orderly and obey rules

- Monitoring inmate activities and work assignments

- On occasion, searching inmates and their living quarters for contraband and weapons

- Settling disputes between inmates

- Enforcing discipline

- Inspecting the facility for unsanitary conditions, fire hazards, or any infractions of the rules

- Reporting orally and in writing on inmate conduct

- Reporting security breaches, disturbances, and any unusual occurrences

- Keeping a daily log of corrections facility activities

- If the situation arises, helping other law enforcement officials to investigate crimes or search for escapees

Most corrections officers work unarmed if they are in facilities with direct-supervision cell blocks, although they do carry communication devices to summon help. Generally, officers work alone or in pairs in cell blocks of 50 to 100 inmates. Order is maintained through interpersonal skills on the part of the officer and progressive sanctioning, including loss of some privileges. Corrections officers walk a fine line between being friendly and firm. They must gain the respect of prisoners but not encourage a familiarity that could prove dangerous.

WORKING CONDITIONS

Make no mistake about it—working conditions are stressful and hazardous. Each year, corrections officers are injured in the line of duty. Work is indoors and outdoors, and not all correctional facilities are up-to-date with modern equipment, lighting, plumbing, and climate control. Some facilities are modern, brightly lit, and well ventilated; others are noisy, dim, overcrowded, and unpleasant. Most corrections officers begin their careers working rotating eight-hour shifts, and since prisons must be staffed twenty-four hours a day, seven days a week, these shifts are bound to coincide with holidays, special occasions, family celebrations, and other important events. Again, due to staffing imperatives, overtime may be required.

TRAINING AND QUALIFICATIONS

As with many other jobs in the criminal justice area, becoming a corrections officer now generally requires a postsecondary education of some kind, either an associate's or bachelor's degree, and your criminal justice major means you'll be highly competitive in this field. Likewise, your degree in criminal justice enhances your promotional prospects as you advance in your career. Other postsecondary degrees of bearing include psychology, sociology, police science, and criminology.

Although the application process varies from state to state, you can expect a battery of tests and interviews to determine your suitability for this work. The ability to think and act quickly in the corrections environment is paramount. You'll be screened for drug use and, in addition to undergoing a background check, you'll generally have to pass a written examination. Many states or clusters of states have training academies that you may be required to attend, and all state and local agencies provide on-the-job training that covers legal elements as well as interpersonal skills. Certain systems also require firearms proficiency and self-defense skills. In some employment settings, the officer candidate participates in months of probationary on-the-job training alongside a more experienced officer.

The following is an actual job advertisement for an entry-level corrections officer posted by the State of Florida. Note the pay differential for your associate's or bachelor's degree in criminal justice.

Corrections Officer: Immediate openings for certified Corrections Officers or noncertified Corrections Officer Recruits. Full Florida State Retirement benefits (25 years/75%, ability to retire at age 55). Vested after 10 years of service. 10 paid holidays. 18 personal leave days accrued during first year of service. Shift differential ($750–1,080 per year). State salary incentives for an Associate's/Bachelor's (up to $1,560 per year). Specialized units (CERT, K-9, Honor Guard, Road Crew, Transportation, Policy & Review). Tuition reimbursement up to $1,250 per year. In-service training (40 hours per year minimum). All equipment and uniforms provided. Medical/dental/vision/life insurance. Come join our department and work with over 1,000 officers and help supervise 4,400 inmates. Special requirements: High school graduate. U.S. citizen. Must not have been convicted of a felony or a misdemeanor involving moral turpitude. Must be able to work all shifts, weekends and holidays. Must possess and maintain a valid Florida driver's license.

Federal corrections officers must have 200 hours of formal training within the first year of employment. They also complete a 120-hour course at the federal Bureau of Prisons training center in Glynco, Georgia, within sixty days after they are appointed.

Some officers will receive additional, specialized training for assignments on tactical response teams so that they can deal with weapons, forced entries, chemical agents, crisis management, hostage events, forced cell moves, and other highly charged situations.

DEFINITION OF THE CAREER PATH

Corrections Counselor/Corrections Caseworker

Corrections provides many varied fields through which you can help others, as the listing of possible job titles later in this chapter attests. One classification of corrections worker you may want to consider is that of corrections counselor, sometimes called corrections caseworker. Other titles apply as well, such as for positions in prerelease programs and halfway houses. Because the training and day-to-day work among these jobs share the counselor/client relationship, they are discussed collectively in this section, using some of the different job titles possible in the examples and applications to give you a sense of the variety of settings possible for a corrections counselor.

The following excerpt from an actual advertisement for a counselor in the Georgia Department of Corrections makes clear the variety of work sites possible and the importance of your criminal justice degree.

Counselor: Under general supervision, provides professional counseling services to offenders at a correctional facility such as an institution, boot camp, probation detention center, transitional center, division center, or office. Completion of an undergraduate degree in criminal justice, social work, counseling, or sociology.

Corrections counselors provide intensive case management and counseling to adult offenders in corrections facilities and outreach settings (such as halfway houses). They may be employed by the state, by the county sheriff, or by their local-community department of justice. Basic duties may include intensive case management, counseling, alcohol and drug evaluations, and needs assessments. You may also lead and facilitate therapeutic and educational group sessions. In addition, you will frequently coordinate your work with related departments such as family services, alcohol and drug treatment programs, and other departmental staff. Programs with which you may be involved include probation, alternative detention, release on own recognizance, supervised release, DWI assessment, deferred prosecution, restitution, work crews, jail programs, employment, and alternative service.

Corrections counselors' duties vary by size of institution and employer (federal, state, county, or local). Following are typical key tasks and responsibilities of the corrections counselor/caseworker:

■ Supervises the distribution of caseload functions and court referrals among staff members within the assigned unit

■ Prepares the unit budget and grant applications, monitors services expenditures for program participants, and provides summary statements

■ Reviews program changes and policy mandates, assists in evaluation of unit programs, evaluates contract performance, and develops new proposals for contract work

■ Visits work crews and special project sites

■ Maintains unit records and case files in accordance with applicable laws

■ May represent the department at boards or meetings

■ Prepares a variety of reports for the courts

Rehabilitation counselors/prerelease program counselors plan and coordinate rehabilitation treatment services for adult offenders. They work with offenders during and immediately following their incarceration. While offenders are in custody, the counselor assists with programming, monitoring of behavior, and preparation of release plans. Upon their release, the counselor continues to work with the offenders during the initial transition from custody to community supervision (perhaps in a halfway house).

Halfway house managers and counselors perform duties similar to those outlined in the preceding description. Halfway houses are facilities designed to hold offenders for a limited period prior to their independent release into the community. Referrals of offenders to halfway houses are accepted from the courts, probation officers, case managers, and jail and prison staff; also, many residents are self-referred. These programs accept individuals with a history of criminal offense who are motivated to make positive changes in their lives, remain drug and alcohol free, and accept program rules and policies while living as law-abiding members of the community. Helping clients with their individual needs is a highly collaborative process involving other professional staff in order to tailor an appropriate treatment plan.

The program of services that you devise for each client is individually planned and incorporates a variety of academic and vocational studies, work assignments, recreational activities, and psychological and medical services. Counselors must also maintain extensive documentation on offenders' progress in their specific plans. Other typical functions of this type of counselor include:

- Supervise activities of subordinate staff on assigned shift; assign duties, schedule workloads, and authorize time off

- Ensure that proper security, sanitation, and safety requirements are met; maintain surveillance of residents; supervise resident counts; search for contraband; and distribute medications

- Supervise the orientation of all new facility residents; ensure that residents have been informed of rules and regulations of the facility

- Coordinate transportation of residents to and from work locations, medical appointments, and recreational activities; maintain accurate vehicle records and reports

- Review reports prepared by subordinate staff, such as resident count sheets, medication logs, and sign-out sheets; prepare and maintain records and reports of any unusual resident activities

- Provide instruction to residents and staff on emergency procedures

- May provide direct paraprofessional guidance to residents on grooming, public transportation, parole requirements, and other areas as indicated

WORKING CONDITIONS

Candidates may take jobs as lead counselor or senior staff for any of a variety of functional units (educational, recreation, therapeutic, residential, etc.).

Work is performed primarily in an office setting. However, stress comes with the territory, as counselors are frequently mandated to resolve problems of a serious and immediate nature arising from staff or offenders. You may have to defuse potentially hazardous situations involving offenders and may be pressed to carry out your assignments within extremely short time frames.

TRAINING AND QUALIFICATIONS

Most supervisory jobs go to candidates with four-year degrees in criminal justice, social work, sociology, or psychology. Additionally, most of these jobs, even at the entry level, require at least a year's experience in adult corrections casework, probation or parole, or substance abuse counseling. Some graduate work may be substituted for that work experience. In some instances, additional but less-related work experience (employment interviewing, social casework, etc.) may substitute for the education and experience requirements. More senior positions in the pay scale require commensurate experience and/or education.

Depending on the level of position for which you are applying, here are some of the skills and attributes you would be expected to possess to qualify as a candidate:

- Use of diagnostic criteria

- Understanding of the basic factors that reduce recidivism

- Developing, implementing, and facilitating groups

- Familiarity with cognitive restructuring techniques

- Dealing with noncompliant and mandated clients

- Ability to establish effective and appropriate boundaries with offenders

- Ability to work in a jail, prison, or other part of the criminal justice system

- Experience working with difficult populations, including offenders with mental disabilities, sex offenders, and substance abusers

The ability to pass a security clearance and a thorough background investigation as well as possession of a valid driver's license are also common criteria for this position. Bilingual candidates are highly valued in these positions.

DEFINITION OF THE CAREER PATH

Warden

While the distinguished position of warden would be the culmination of most people's careers in corrections, it has a definite place in a career guide devoted primarily to entry-level positions. The resumes and biographies of the country's wardens today reveal that this is a profession that truly promotes from within. The men and women serving as wardens of prison complexes almost always detail a job history beginning with corrections officer. As these individuals advanced in their careers, they typically held the job titles of corrections counselor, program supervisor, and corrections administrator. Some were selected, after several assignments, to return to teach at a corrections officers training academy or to work in staff development and training before moving into the ranks of deputy warden and warden.

WORKING CONDITIONS

Several websites feature wardens from large corrections institutions in various states showcasing their facilities. An outstanding site is that of Warden R. C. Lee of the North Carolina Department of Correction, Division of Prisons (www.doc.state.nc.us/dop/cptour/index.html). Central Prison, depicted in his site, is the oldest corrections facility in the state, and the warden supervises 777 professionals in this complex prison facility.

What is especially attractive about this site is that it is a virtual "tour" of the prison from an inmate's viewpoint, beginning with arrival at the gatehouse, receiving and processing, records, the cell block, the cell, and work assignments (license plate manufacture). Touring the prison with Warden Lee gives you an excellent sense of the multiple departments and varied concerns of the warden, from equipment maintenance to food service management, health and safety issues, and the time-consuming area of staff management. It's a big job, and you can understand why it's best done by someone who has come up "through the ranks" and understands intimately every aspect of prison life.

Just how involved prison life can be is well illustrated by some facts about the California State Prison at Sacramento. This facility has a female warden who presides over a site that covers 1,200 acres and has 896 professional staff and 262 support staff, with an annual operating budget for the year 2000 of more than $80 million. The prison was designed for a capacity of 1,728 inmates and currently houses 3,010, so you can appreciate the scope of cell and cell-block redesign necessary to accommodate such an overflow. This particular prison is a maximum-security facility for inmates who are serving long sentences or who exhibited behavior management problems at other institutions. It also has one minimum-security unit. The warden here has a variety of inmate work programs, including furniture assembly, reupholstery, and refinishing; paper products; printing; and a warehouse. Some prisoners even do computer refurbishing. There are adult basic education programs, G.E.D. programs, English as a second language, computer-assisted education, and many other academic and service-related programs for inmate participation. You can view this facility at www.cdc.state.ca.us/facility/instsac.htm.

TRAINING AND QUALIFICATIONS

Corrections institutions increasingly seek officers and top management with collegiate and graduate education, particularly in criminal justice, psychology, political science, criminology, and related fields. A number of wardens cite having a master's degree in business administration (M.B.A.) as particularly helpful in dealing with the complex facilities management, budgetary, and staffing concerns involved in maintaining a corrections facility.

The following actual advertisement for a warden of a midwestern women's corrections facility clearly demonstrates how the job is the culmination of a wide variety of work experiences in corrections combined with business, analytical, and management skills. This ad was posted (among other places) on the largest on-line resource for news and information on prisons and corrections departments, the Corrections Connection, at http://database .corrections.com.

Warden: Plans, organizes, and directs the operation of an adult female correctional facility including security, operations, and programs; hiring, evaluating, and motivating employees; developing and controlling the institution's budget; and controlling capital assets; represents the facility's program before the news media and interest groups; participates as a member of the Division's management team; develops and promotes programs that meet the unique needs of women offenders. The position serves at the pleasure of the administrator of the Division of Prisons and the Director of Corrections. Salary Range: $53,000–$78,500.

EARNINGS

If you are considering a career in corrections, you should try to determine what corrections staff are being paid in the geographic location in which you're interested. Average salaries across the country are presented in this section to give you a base from which to work; however, salaries in corrections can vary tremendously from one state or region to the next. While this type of variability occurs in most professions, it is especially applicable in corrections. In fact, a 1999 salary survey published in the *Corrections Compendium*, a professional journal of the American Correctional Association (www .corrections.com/aca/), concluded that there is no common pattern or trend in corrections salaries and that vast differences between low and high starting salaries existed across all positions and personnel at all experience levels.

The employment field in corrections is volatile, and salary levels in any given area can change quickly as state or local governments try to come up with innovative ways to fill the ever-growing number of positions they have available. Ratcheting up salaries is one of the strategies that many are closely evaluating.

So, do some homework. Consult state human resources pages on the Web; visit your town hall personnel office or county jail; check regional newspapers for current corrections job announcements. Even salaries for federal positions will vary based on locality pay, as explained in Chapter 10. Here's some information to get you started.

Corrections Officer

The most recent government labor statistics indicate that corrections officers earned a median salary of $28,540 in 1998. While most earned between $22,930 and $37,550, the differences from state to state were considerable. The lowest 10 percent of officers earned less than $18,810, while some in other states earned more than $46,320. The variance wasn't quite as great among officers at different levels of government. Average salaries at the federal level were highest at $32,600, followed by local government with an average of $29,700, and finally the state level (where most officers are in fact employed) with average earnings of $27,300. Remember that these are average salaries for *all* corrections officers and that starting salaries will be less. Also, a small number of corrections officers are employed by privately operated prisons, and their median salary is the lowest at $18,500.

Effective January 2000, entry-level federal corrections officers are being hired at the GS-5 level, which pays $26,354 to $32,762, excluding local pay. In addition, officers assigned to night duty are paid a percentage of their basic hourly rate above regular pay, and officers earn 25 percent above regular pay for all work on Sundays.

Employees of the government also receive a good benefits package and usually an allowance to purchase uniforms if they are not already provided. Tuition reimbursement may also be included, which can be a tremendous financial help if you intend to further your education. And don't forget the federal retirement coverage, whereby if you enter employment in your twenties, then you may be able to retire in your forties.

Corrections Counselor/Caseworker

Counselors in the field of corrections can be generalists, such as case managers, or they can be specialists, such as substance abuse counselors. They can even be a combination of a corrections officer and a counselor. Take an example from Massachusetts:

> **Correctional Program Officer:** Maintain a dual function by performing casework while providing custodial care and control of inmates. Conduct counseling interviews with inmates, inform them about rehabilitative services available, and confer with agency staff regarding treatment plans. Salary: $31,542.

We sampled listings from around the country for a variety of counseling positions in corrections. Advertised salaries ranged from a low of $21,000 to a high of $39,785. A new graduate with a bachelor's degree will most likely qualify for positions with average salaries in the mid-$20s. The higher salaries generally require some experience and graduate study; in some situations certification is also needed. Let's take a look at some recent ads to illustrate this:

> **Correctional Center Rehabilitation Counselor:** Conducts initial classification interviews. Provides individual counseling to each inmate on caseload. Facilitates inmate treatment program(s). Prepares annual/parole progress reports. Qualifications: Bachelor's degree from a college or university in a field related to social services. Salary: $25,881.

Here's one for a substance abuse counselor. Notice the two pay ranges depending on the degree you hold.

> **Addictions Counselor:** Responsibilities include management and individual and group counseling. For those with a B.S. or B.A., pay range will be $23–29 K; master's level is $25–33 K. We offer a competitive salary and an excellent paid benefits package.

And finally, with a little experience, you could qualify for the following position:

Corrections Counselor, Department of Community Justice and Sheriff's Office: Provide intensive case management and counseling to adult offenders in the County's correctional facilities and in community outreach settings. Basic duties include counseling; alcohol and drug evaluations; needs assessments; and leading and facilitating process and educational groups. Minimum of two years of social counseling and/or case management experience; specific experience with the criminal justice system is preferred. Bachelor's degree with major course work in criminal justice, psychology, or sociology. Salary: $31,737–$45,998.

Salaries are somewhat higher in federal government, but the qualifications are higher as well. The Bureau of Prisons, which oversees all federal corrections facilities, requires that "correctional treatment specialists" (case managers) and "drug treatment specialists" have two full years of graduate study in behavioral or social sciences, or one year of supervised casework experience, or an equivalent combination. Entry-level salaries for these positions are at the GS-9 level, $32,380 to $42,091, not including locality pay increases where applicable.

Warden

Most wardens are promoted from within, so by the time you reach the position, assuming this is part of your career plan, you will have received multiple promotions and salary increases. Wardens are the chief operating officers in corrections facilities and are, in almost all cases, the highest wage earners as well. Recent ads for wardens cited salaries in the $50,000 range and continuing upward to $98,999.

CAREER OUTLOOK

You are in luck in terms of employment outlook if this is the field you have chosen. Corrections facilities process more than 22 million people a year, and that figure is expected to rise. As inmate populations grow and mandatory sentencing guidelines (calling for longer sentences) are adopted, the need for corrections facilities and workers to staff them will grow as well. Employment growth is also anticipated in the private sector as government authorities contract with private industry to create and staff additional facilities. Moreover, the government continues to fund community-based corrections programming such as halfway houses and alternative sentencing programs to ease overcrowding and better accommodate and rehabilitate certain types of offenders. Because of this employment growth, you can also expect layoffs to be rare and job security to be strong.

Corrections Officer

The outlook in this occupation is especially promising. It was one of the fastest growing careers in the '90s, and that trend looks to be ongoing. The Bureau of Labor Statistics estimates that employment of corrections officers will increase by at least 36 percent between 1998 and 2008. One ad for a Florida county corrections department stated that the department would be creating more than 160 corrections officer positions within the next two years alone.

While this overall employment growth rate is one reason for the positive outlook, another reason cannot be ignored: the high turnover rate for corrections officers. This is a tough job. Perhaps Princeton Review Online (www.review.com) says it best when it opens its profile of the career with "This is no day at the beach. Ever." Corrections officers wear multiple hats and put their lives on the line every day they go to work. Not only are they required to work different shifts, but also, because of staffing shortages, they may need to work extra shifts to maintain appropriate security levels. You can see, then, how stress can affect a corrections officer's decision to transfer into other areas, retire, or change careers altogether.

For those who stay in the field, there are many opportunities for promotion and advancement. A corrections officer with experience, education, and additional training can move up to corrections sergeant, directing the activities of corrections officers. This path could extend all the way up to warden.

Corrections Counselor/Caseworker

As new facilities are built and community corrections efforts expand, employment for counselors and caseworkers will remain favorable. Here too are opportunities for promotion and advancement, providing that you continue your training and education. You may start as a counselor and go on to become a unit manager, case management coordinator, or director of therapeutic services. Or, perhaps you'll decide to specialize in alcohol and substance abuse, in vocational guidance, or in juvenile rehabilitation. If you're more interested in working in a community-based facility, maybe you'll become the program's director or regional administrator. In summary, not only is the outlook good for entering the career, but also, once you're there, many and diverse options are available to you.

Warden

Wardens will be hired mainly as new facilities are built or, in some cases, to replace wardens who retire. A salient difference between this occupation and the others that have been mentioned is that the field is much narrower. Each institution has one chief administrator, and at the federal level, for example, there are only ninety-six institutions. Wardens and superintendents do have assistants, who usually have moved up through the ranks of the corrections system and are in line for a warden position. Wardens themselves may go on to become state corrections administrators, overseeing entire state systems.

STRATEGY FOR FINDING THE JOBS

Since the vast majority of positions are with the government, an ideal place to start looking is on-line at the Corrections Connection website, www.cor rections.com. Here, when you click on "Corrections Links," you can select links to federal agencies, state departments of correction, county sheriff departments and jails, and corrections facilities, including prerelease and community residential programs, all presented by state, along with links to every state's home page. Pretty much all the information you'll need is in one place. Some states include employment opportunities on their department of corrections websites. For others, you may need to visit the state's home page to obtain personnel information. Some county sheriff's offices also list openings directly on their sites; at the very least, you'll be given contact information such as phone, address, and E-mail addresses so that you can check with prospective employers personally.

Many positions require civil service testing, so don't forget to inquire about that as well. There are books and guides to help you prepare for this exam, such as the recently published *Corrections Officer Exam: The Complete Preparation Guide*, by Learning Express Editors. These can be ordered on-line at amazon.com or barnesandnoble.com or through your local bookstore.

If you are interested in working in a federal corrections facility, you will need to follow these application guidelines:

- Submit form OF 612, Optional Application for Federal Employment, or a resume. The form is downloadable from the Bureau of Prisons website at www.bop.gov/recruit.html. You're advised to keep your original application or resume in case you are contacted for an interview since applications and resumes received in the Examining Section (where your application is evaluated and rated against the required and preferred eligibility) are not retrievable by the candidate.

- Submit OPM Form 1203-AW, Form C, Qualifications and Availability Form, if you are applying for a corrections officer position. This form is not on-line, so you'll need to call your regional office to request one. A list of regional offices with phone numbers is included in the Bureau of Prisons website.

- Submit an Applicant Availability Statement if you are applying for a corrections treatment (case manager) or drug treatment specialist position.

- The Supplemental Qualification Statement to be submitted will depend on the specific job as well. You can call the Bureau of Prisons Career Information Service Line at (800) 347-7744 to request a complete application package.

- Have your official college transcript sent.

Additional paperwork may be required if you have served in the military. For complete application information, visit the Bureau of Prisons website.

If you are seeking a position in a community-based facility or program, don't neglect to look in the local newspapers or visit one of your state's unemployment offices. You can locate the office closest to you by checking the white pages in the phone book or on-line. In the state's listing of offices, you will usually find them under "Employment Security Department."

You can also visit America's Job Bank at www.ajb.dni.us, which connects you to all state employment offices. You will be asked to select a job category; choose "Community and Social Services." Then you enter the zip code of the area you want to search (the site will help you identify a zip code if you're not sure), and the service will display jobs that meet your criteria. You can view complete job descriptions and even some benefit information. This is a helpful site to review on a regular basis.

As you begin to interview for jobs in corrections, heed these words of advice from corrections officials who conduct interviews and review applications for employment:

- The most basic advice is to arrive for the interview on time. It shows dependability, which is imperative in this field.

- Be able to articulate your goals, and be proud of the profession you have chosen.

- Prepare for the interview by doing basic research on the institution. Know something about the facility. Know what forms of testing your state requires.

- A bachelor's degree will help not only because the applicant pool is big and your degree makes you more competitive but also because it reflects a willingness to commit to and complete responsibilities.

POSSIBLE EMPLOYERS

Employees in the field of corrections are most likely working for the government at some level, be it local, county, state, or federal. More than half of all corrections officers work at state corrections institutions such as prisons, detention centers, prison camps, and youth corrections facilities. Most of the remainder work for city and county jails or other local corrections programs and centers. Some are employed by the federal Bureau of Prisons and work in a federal penitentiary, corrections institution, prison camp, or medical center.

Some corrections workers are employed by community corrections centers or detention facilities that contract with the Bureau of Prisons to provide these services. State departments of corrections also fund such programs. So, even if you are working in a social service agency providing substance abuse counseling services to prerelease inmates, your employer may be a local agency, but your position is in all likelihood ultimately funded by the government.

As noted, a small but growing number of privately owned and managed prisons also employ corrections workers.

POSSIBLE JOB TITLES

As you read through this list, remember that different job titles can mean very different job responsibilities. Also, job responsibilities may not always be reflected in the job title. This is particularly true in the case of the corrections officer, who sometimes has responsibilities similar to those of a counselor, teacher, or work supervisor. Although the job titles here are grouped into three categories—Corrections Officer (protective/security services), Counselor (social services), and Administrator (management services)—titles may sometimes overlap areas.

Corrections Officer

Classification Officer

Correctional Officer

Correctional Officer Trainer

Correctional Program Officer

Correctional Sergeant

Corrections Officer Trainee

Detention Officer

Guard

Jailer

Prison Tactical Response Team

Transport Officer

Counselor

Addictions Counselor

Alcohol and Substance Abuse
Counselor

Case Manager

Caseworker

Community Service Caseworker

Correctional Rehabilitation Counselor

Correctional Treatment Specialist

Corrections Counselor

Drug Treatment Specialist

Education Counselor

HIV Specialist

Prerelease Program Correctional
Counselor

Prerelease Program Employment
Counselor

Recreational Counselor

Release Counselor

Social Worker

Substance Abuse Specialist

Vocational Counselor

Administrator

Chief of Programs

Classification and Treatment Director

Corrections Facilities Manager

Inmate Records Coordinator

Penologist

Prerelease Program Halfway
House Manager

Superintendent

Warden

RELATED OCCUPATIONS

Academic Teacher

Director of Community Education

Education Specialist

Private Security Specialist

Recreation Leader

Store Detective

PROFESSIONAL ASSOCIATIONS

Listed in this section are some of the associations that relate to careers in the field of corrections. For more information about these professional associations, either check the websites listed or consult the *Encyclopedia of Associations*, published by the Gale Group. Review the Members/Purpose notes for each organization to determine if it pertains to your interests. Membership in one or more of these organizations may gain you access to job listings, networking opportunities, and employment search services. Some provide information at no charge, but if you want to receive specific publications that list job opportunities, you may need to join. If you're still in college, check for student member rates.

American Association for Corrections Psychologists
West Virginia Graduate College
College of Graduate Studies
Institute, WV 25112
Members/Purpose: Membership comprises practitioners, academicians, and researchers interested in community and institutional programs for juvenile and adult offenders and their victims.
Publications: *The Correctional Psychologist*, a quarterly newsletter; *Criminal Justice and Behavior*, a quarterly review.

American Correctional Association
4380 Forbes Blvd.
Lanham, MD 20706-4322
www.corrections.com/aca/
Members/Purpose: A multidisciplinary organization of professionals representing all facets of corrections and criminal justice, including federal, state, and military correctional facilities and prisons, county jails and detention centers, probation/parole agencies, and community corrections/halfway houses.
Publications: *Corrections Today* magazine; *Corrections Compendium: The National Journal for Corrections*; major catalog of additional publications.
Training: National training conventions; certification seminars; on-line workshops; video lending library.

American Jail Association
2053 Day Rd., Suite 100
Hagerstown, MD 21740
www.corrections.com/aja/

Members/Purpose: The American Jail Association is a national nonprofit organization dedicated to supporting those who work in and operate our nation's jails.

Publications: *American Jails* magazine; *Write It Right* quarterly; *Jail Operations Bulletin*; *Who's Who in Jail Management*.

Training: Annual conferences; Jail Manager Certification Program; on-line national training schedule.

American Probation and Parole Association
P.O. Box 11910
Lexington, KY 40578-1910
www.appa-net.org/aboutappa.htm

Members/Purpose: The American Probation and Parole Association is an international association composed of individuals from the United States and Canada actively involved with probation, parole, and community-based corrections, in both adult and juvenile sectors. All levels of government, including local, state/provincial, legislative, executive, judicial, and federal agencies, are counted among its constituents. By taking the initiative, APPA has grown to become the voice for thousands of probation and parole practitioners, including line staff, supervisors, and administrators. Educators, volunteers, and concerned citizens with an interest in criminal and juvenile justice are also among APPA's members. The association represents a strong, unified voice for the field of community corrections.

Publications: *Perspectives*, quarterly journal; complete library of books, magazines, and periodicals.

Training: Training institutes; national/regional training seminars and technical assistance; professional development program.

Association for the Treatment of Sexual Abuse
4900 S.W. Griffith Dr., Suite 274
Beaverton, OR 97005
www.atsa.com

Members/Purpose: ATSA is strongly committed to the elimination of sexual victimization, the protection of our communities through responsible and ethical treatment of sex offenders and their victims, and the prevention of sexual assault through effective management of sex offenders.

Publications: *Sexual Abuse: A Journal of Research and Treatment*, quarterly.

Training: Annual conference.

Association of Halfway House Alcoholism Programs
5 Ridgeview Rd.
P.O. Box 610
Kerhonkson, NY 12446
www.ahhap.org
Members/Purpose: AHHAP represents more than 1,500 residential
facilities providing long-term, cost-effective recovery services to more than
120,000 individuals each year. AHHAP members have successfully affected
millions of lives for almost thirty years, returning individuals to sober,
productive living within their families and communities.
Publications: On-line newsletter.
Training: National Certified Recovery Specialist Certification program.

Correctional Education Association
4380 Forbes Blvd.
Lanham, MD 20706
www.sunsite.unc.edu/icea
Members/Purpose: The purpose of the CEA is to increase the
effectiveness, expertise, and skills of its members and to represent the
collective interest of corrections education before the government, the press,
and the public on the national as well as on the state, provincial, and local
levels.
Publications: *The Journal of Correctional Education*; *CEA News and Notes*;
Yearbook; *Directory of Continuing Educators*.
Training: Annual national conference.

Correctional Industries Association
1420 N. Charles St., Suite CH-415
Baltimore, MD 21201-5779
www.correctionalindustries.org
Members/Purpose: Provides, promotes, aids, serves, and encourages
individuals and agencies, both public and private, engaged in and concerned
with correctional industries as a meaningful employment program for
inmates of correctional institutions.
Publications: *CIA Newsletter*; *Executive Director's Report*.
Training: Prison Industries Enhancement (PIE) Certification; training
conferences and regional meetings.

Council of Juvenile Correctional Administrators
Stonehill College
16 Belmont St.
South Easton, MA 02375
www.corrections.com/cjca/
Members/Purpose: The Council of Juvenile Correctional Administrators, incorporated in 1994 to bring together juvenile justice leaders, is dedicated to the improvement of juvenile corrections services and practices. The CJCA promotes and facilitates three major activities: the exchange of ideas and philosophies at the top administrative level of juvenile corrections planning and policy making, the advancement of juvenile corrections and juvenile justice techniques, and the education of the public about juvenile justice and corrections systems.
Publications: Quarterly newsletter; yearbook survey.
Training: Summer meetings.

International Community Corrections Association
P.O. Box 1987
La Crosse, WI 54602-1987
www.iccaweb.org
Members/Purpose: ICCA's mission and purpose is to promote and enhance the development of community corrections programs. It also provides information and training to enhance the quality of services, to promote effective management practices, and to promote the effectiveness of community corrections programming.
Publications: *ICCA Journal on Community Corrections*; *ICCA Justice Committee News*; *Research Conference Proceedings*; membership newsletter.
Training: Extensive year-round conference schedule.

Mental Health in Corrections Consortium
9140 Ward Pkwy., Suite 200
Kansas City, MO 64114
www.mhcca.org
Members/Purpose: A leading voice for mental health providers within the criminal justice system, primarily corrections, providing high-quality training related to mental health issues in criminal justice.
Publications: Members share publications with the American Association for Corrections Psychologists and receive the journal *Criminal Justice and Behavior* and the newsletter *The Correctional Psychologist*.
Training: Annual conference.

National Institute of Corrections
1860 Industrial Circle
Longmont, CO 80501
www.nicic.org/inst/
Members/Purpose: Established to advance and shape effective corrections practice and public policy that respond to the needs of corrections, through collaboration and leadership and by providing assistance, information, education, and training.
Publications: Extensive on-line publication database of more than 1,200 titles in jails, prisons, community corrections, and general-interest categories.
Training: Corrections staff training; regional training events and teleconferences.

CHAPTER 13

PATH 4: JUVENILE JUSTICE: YOUR FUTURE IS THEIR FUTURE

The current dilemma of whether to try adolescents as children or adults is just one symptom of the complexities and difficulties that surround and infuse the area of juvenile justice. The previous three chapters outlined various career paths that would apply to juvenile justice. For example, certain police and federal law enforcement positions offer specialties in areas of juvenile justice. The career paths of corrections officer, probation officer, parole officer, and counselor also can focus on the activities germane to juvenile court.

This chapter is devoted to two broad categories of employment that represent the challenging and rewarding career opportunities in juvenile justice. First we will review positions that are involved with the daily rehabilitation of juveniles in a particular setting, including caseworkers; counselors; group home workers; juvenile justice counselors; and child, youth, and runaway counselors. The second employment category discussed is that of juvenile probation officers, who are responsible for case management of juvenile offenders in conforming and fulfilling the probationary dictates of the court.

THE JUVENILE COURT SYSTEM

Background

The juvenile justice process varies from community to community, depending on local practice and tradition, but the justice process for juveniles in general is distinguished by some common decision points, regardless of the system. The first decision point pertains to the question that opened this chapter: youth or adult? At the time of the arrest of a juvenile, a decision is made by the courts to either send the matter on to the justice system or divert the case out of the justice system to some alternative program. This decision incorporates the youth's criminal record (if any), conversations with parents or caregivers, and a review of any past contact with the law enforcement system. About a third of juvenile subjects are released by the police back to the parents or caregivers, while the remainder are sent to juvenile court. Law enforcement referrals account for 85 percent of all delinquency cases referred to juvenile court. Other referrals are made by parents, caregivers, victims, schools, and probation officers.

Federal law has traditionally frowned on holding juveniles with adults, so there have been strict guidelines on where and for how long a juvenile can be detained in a nonjuvenile detention facility. However, the number of people under eighteen years old who are sentenced to adult state prisons each year more than doubled between 1985 and 1997—from 3,400 to 7,400, according to the Justice Department's Bureau of Justice Statistics. At the end of 1997 (the most recent year for which data are available), approximately 5 percent of incarcerated offenders under age eighteen were serving in state prisons, which hold mostly adults who have been sentenced to terms of more than a year for felony convictions.

Generally, the court intake function is the responsibility of the juvenile probation department and/or the state prosecutor's office. They decide to either handle the situation informally and dismiss the case or take it to juvenile court. Generally this decision involves the degree of sufficiency of evidence in the case, although half of all cases referred to juvenile court are handled informally by dismissal.

Those that are not dismissed outright may still be handled informally by setting some specific conditions that the juvenile voluntarily agrees to observe for a specific time. This set of conditions is formally drafted and signed and is often termed a *consent decree*. Conditions may include restitution to the victim, school attendance, drug counseling, or curfew restrictions. In most cases, no informal disposition is possible unless the juvenile admits to having committed the act. Though informal, the decree may still be monitored by a juvenile probation officer, a procedure often referred to as *informal probation*. If the juvenile complies with this consent decree, the case is dismissed. If the juvenile fails to meet the conditions of the consent decree, then the case reverts to the other option: formally prosecuting the juvenile. The case would then be referred for an adjudicatory hearing.

While awaiting the hearing, the juvenile may be held in the nearest local juvenile detention facility (if that action is determined by the court to be in the best interest of the community). Juvenile probation officers or detention workers review the case to decide if the juvenile should be held pending a hearing by the judge. In all fifty states, a detention hearing must be held within twenty-four hours. A judge decides between continued detention or release. About one-fifth of cases remain in detention. If a juvenile facility is not available (usually because of crowded conditions), the detention may extend beyond the adjudicatory and dispositional hearings.

Prosecutors may file a case in either juvenile or criminal court. Of course, debates over which court should hear such cases have been much in the news. In some states, the legislature has determined that certain crimes are so egregious that the perpetrator will be treated as a criminal offender. Some states have given the prosecutor discretionary power to decide which court will hear the case of a juvenile.

Juvenile Court

If the case is handled in juvenile court, two types of petitions may be filed. If a *delinquency petition* is filed, the allegations are stated, and the prosecutor requests that the juvenile become a ward of the court and requests the judge to adjudicate the juvenile as a delinquent. This language and the disposition of the case are very different from criminal court, where an offender is convicted and sentenced.

The response to the delinquency petition is a hearing with a judge, at which the facts of the case are presented and witnesses may be called. In most of these cases, the judge makes the final determination of responsibility for the offense, although in some states the juvenile has the right to a jury trial. In 1999, about 60 percent of juveniles were judged delinquent in cases petitioned to juvenile court for criminal violations.

Criminal Court

The other petition possibility in juvenile court is a *waiver petition*, filed when the prosecutor or intake officers feel that the case is more appropriate for criminal court. If *probable cause* that the juvenile committed the act is determined by the court, the court will then decide if the matter should be waived and transferred to criminal court.

Generally, in making this decision the court is concerned with how amenable to treatment the offender would be in the juvenile court system. Arguments against staying in the juvenile court system (by the prosecutor) may be based on a record of past offenses in juvenile court or the seriousness of the current offense. If the judge approves the waiver, the case is filed in criminal court.

Possible Disposition Recommendations from Juvenile Court for Young Offenders

If the case stays in juvenile court and a petition of delinquency is adjudicated, several possible recommendations may be put before the bench either by probation staff or by the prosecutor. The court may also entertain pro-posals by the offender. Before this disposition plan is presented, probation staff have usually thoroughly interviewed the youth; ordered diagnostic eval-uations, including psychological evaluations; and assessed available support systems. Possible outcomes include:

- Probation and other provisions. Most dispositions are a combination of requirements that may incorporate drug counseling, weekend confinement, victim restitution, or community restitution in addition to probation. Probation itself may be either for a specific period or open ended. Once probation conditions are met in full, the case is terminated by the judge. In 1999, about 60 percent of adjudicated delinquents were placed on formal probation.

- Commitment to residential placement. This, too, may be either for a specific period or open ended. About a third of adjudicated delinquents are assigned to residential placement, which may be publically or privately operated, and conditions vary from a prisonlike setting to more homelike atmospheres. In some states, the state department of juvenile corrections determines the placement; in other states, it is the judge's decision.

- Juvenile aftercare. Following release from detention, confinement, or a residential facility, the juvenile is ordered to court-supervised aftercare, which is, in effect, no different from adult parole conditions. Violation of the aftercare conditions may result in recommitment.

Corrections Officer/Corrections Counselor

In juvenile justice employment, you will often encounter variations on the job title of corrections officer. Frequently this position is referred to as coun-selor, corrections caseworker, corrections residence counselor, or some vari-ant of any of those. These may, in fact, be different positions, depending on the setting. The corrections officer in a detention facility, for example, has different duties from those of the corrections officer in a residential unit for juvenile delinquents. To add to the confusion, one residential unit may call that position corrections officer, and another residential unit (in a different state or county) may term the very same position juvenile counselor. Make it a practice to read job descriptions for any of these positions carefully to understand what the job is, regardless of what it is named. Here's a good example of this nomenclature confusion. Both of the ads quoted are seek-ing two- and four-year college graduates in criminal justice or other social science majors:

> **Correctional Officer (Michigan):** To serve as Assistant Resident Unit Supervisor providing guidance for juvenile delinquents in the Department of Child and Family Welfare Protective Services.
>
> **Counselor (Georgia):** Under general supervision to provide a variety of services (including counseling) for juveniles at a transitional center.

Though the titles are different, the jobs sound very similar, both have the same requirements, and both indicate salaries in the same range ($30,000 to $40,000). So, as you read the job descriptions provided in this chapter, be aware that what's important is the job and not the title of that job. Increasingly, residential treatment centers are staffed by counselors, caseworkers, and teachers, and all function as disciplinarians when called upon, but technically no positions are labeled as "corrections officer."

Here's a job ad for a "Youth Worker" at a private rehabilitation center for young boys in Montana structured in a military format:

> Responsible for the supervision of cadets during their daily activities, to include all aspects of daily living, treatment, and education. Provides daily structure for the platoon cadets, provides discipline, and holds cadets accountable for their actions. Follows strategies as established to assist the teachers in the classroom. Responsible for the safety and security of cadets. Supervises barracks maintenance and recreational activities and is responsible for teaching the cadets hygiene and cleanliness. Issues instructions and provides direction to cadets. Provides on-the-spot counseling and correction to cadets, implements intervention strategies, and completes programmatic reports as necessary.

Though couched in the language of the military setting, the functions of this position are representative of the juvenile corrections counselor whose main role is to provide a combination of care, treatment, and custody for juvenile offenders.

DEFINITION OF THE CAREER PATH

One essential part of your job is daily hands-on implementation of the programs designed to habilitate, remediate, and divert young offenders from a life that has included some dysfunctional or maladaptive behavior, which has led to their involvement with the juvenile justice system.

A second area of responsibility is to attend to juveniles with overtly negative rehabilitative records and to provide programs for their personal growth and social development. Generally, juvenile corrections officers working with offenders with more serious rehabilitative issues would be sited at a medium-security facility. These inmates might have done poorly in their previous placements or escaped from a lower-security site and been assigned to the medium-security facility by the juvenile justice authorities.

A third aspect of this job embraces a larger context. As you grow in your position and develop experience in juvenile justice, you will participate in a variety of cooperative ventures. These may be collaborations among state, local, and county agencies and private concerns to share your combined resources and perhaps develop new initiatives to prevent or inhibit juvenile crime. Juvenile justice experts like you will be called on to share age-appropriate strategies with school, child welfare, medical, and mental health professionals to assist at-risk children in mastering key development tasks. Experts agree that fostering the strengths of at-risk children as they progress from birth to adulthood holds the greatest promise for reducing juvenile crime. As your own expertise develops, you will become skilled in helping others to explore better ways of delivering treatment and aftercare programs to juvenile offenders.

Following are some of the services for which you may be responsible:

Academic: Depending on your population's age, you may be helping students earn the G.E.D. certificate or a high school diploma in a cooperative program with a local public school. You may be helping teaching staff to implement an I.E.P. (individualized educational plan) for students with special educational needs.

Vocational: Most rehabilitative settings provide some vocational work experience as a mechanism for learning cooperative behavior and team responsibility, building trust, and, of course, developing workplace skills. Typical program offerings include upholstery, horticulture, welding, optical lab work, graphic design, auto body and mechanics, electrical and building trades, machine shop, small engine repair, and radio and television communications. All of these programs help the resident population learn to set realistic life and career goals for themselves.

Social Services: You may be required to provide individual, group, and crisis counseling. Substance abuse services are often contracted out to Alcoholics

Anonymous or Narcotics Anonymous trainers, either in-house or off-site. Some residential programs offer specialized housing units for residents needing treatment for substance abuse.

Aftercare: *Aftercare* is the term used for the treatment plan that begins almost immediately upon the offender's arrival at the facility. The goal is to ensure that all the ingredients of a successful rehabilitative stay are met and that the offender is fulfilling his or her responsibility to commit to the program. A team approach is standard, often involving the offender's family and all support staff, who meet regularly to plan and prepare for the eventual return of the juvenile to his or her home and community.

Medium-Security Sites

The difference for corrections officers working at medium-security sites is that the population tends to be youths with more serious emotional and behavioral disorders who require a more structured and secure environment. Within this structure, many of the services previously described are the same, although the supervision of residents is more intensive. The goal is still rehabilitative, with efforts directed to returning the juveniles to the community.

Counseling in the medium-security setting is also more intensive, and counseling services are provided most often by licensed clinical social workers supervised by a clinical psychologist, in recognition of the population's more complex emotional and behavioral profile.

Voluntary Sites

Some states offer juveniles the opportunity to sign (with the court's recommendation and approval) a voluntary agreement to participate in a structured residential program of limited duration designed to rehabilitate juvenile offenders whose histories do not warrant a lengthy sentence in a corrections facility.

These voluntary reintegration programs usually take less than six months to complete and involve many of the services previously detailed, including drug and alcohol counseling, general counseling services, educational programming, and an emphasis on a highly regimented daily routine, involving considerable physical activity.

Because these programs are of limited duration, aftercare planning is pivotal and begins right after the offender's arrival to help ensure a successful transition back to the community. Usually, corrections staff, family, teachers, social workers, and the juvenile's probation officer would all be involved in monthly team meetings.

WORKING CONDITIONS

You have a wide choice of work settings in this position. Corrections facilities range from an almost summer camp atmosphere to relatively restrictive institutional settings. You could work in a juvenile "boot camp," a probation detention center, a transitional center, or an office. Perhaps in working with troubled youth, you would prefer to be in an outdoor setting, perhaps riding horses and doing some farming. Check out the website of the Idaho Youth Ranch at www.youthranch.org. This remarkable institution provides residential treatment, group homes, adoption, and other services to troubled, disturbed, delinquent, or abused children and adolescents. It's unique as a facility, but it exemplifies the variety of settings possible in working with juveniles.

Regardless of the setting, your job as a juvenile corrections worker is a hands-on, energy-intensive, patience-demanding role that will put enormous physical and emotional demands on you and deliver comparable rewards for your efforts. You are, first and foremost, a role model. You become a teacher through your day-to-day conduct, your behavior toward your charges, your language, and your reactions to situations. It's not a job for those who want to stand back and observe nor for those with defensive personalities or who have not achieved some level of stability in their lives. To do this job well, you need to be focused, natural, versatile, and able to communicate.

Each day, you'll share confidences and concerns, provide advice, and help solve a wide assortment of problems. Since many of the settings for juveniles involve some degree of structure and rule setting, your ability to work within those rules and remain consistent will be fundamental to your efforts to exert leadership over your charges.

Because these facilities operate twenty-four hours, you will work in shifts, and entry-level job holders generally do not have shift preference until they achieve some seniority. More frequently, your personal schedule will be subjected to some buffeting as your shifts vary from 8 A.M. to 5 P.M., or 4 P.M. to 1 A.M. and midnight to 9 A.M. Shifts frequently overlap an hour so that incoming staff can be thoroughly briefed and updated by the previous shift to ensure continuity of treatment. Though these jobs generally offer excellent benefits, including holidays, because of the year-round nature of the work, you will frequently work holidays that others (friends and family) have off.

It is important to note here that depending on where you work and the background of the offenders under your supervision, there can be some physical risk. Among older adolescents and in medium-security facilities, particularly, inmates may expose corrections staff to a considerable degree of danger of injury or assault.

TRAINING AND QUALIFICATIONS

Many job ads indicate that they are seeking criminal justice majors. Occasionally, you will see a corrections position requesting previous work with a juvenile population in any capacity. Those employers know that if you have served in a parks and recreation program, coached junior or senior high school sports teams, or worked at a summer camp, you will have a better appreciation of the developmental dynamics of this population. It's a legitimate job demand and one that you may want to take into account when you are pursuing part-time or summer jobs if you feel that a career in juvenile justice is in your future.

In some positions, you will start as a trainee in corrections counseling and be promoted from trainee status after a two-year period of satisfactory work and training experience.

DEFINITION OF THE CAREER PATH

Juvenile Probation Officer

The previous discussion on juvenile corrections officers stressed that the job title is undergoing a "softening" and being replaced more frequently by titles such as juvenile counselor, juvenile caseworker, corrections counselor, and other terms that may read more supportively and therapeutically than the word *corrections*. In reviewing job postings in the career path of a juvenile probation officer, however, it is not the job title that demands your caution but the description (if any) of the duties and responsibilities of the position.

Let's begin with one of the briefest job ads:

Juvenile Probation Officer (Ohio): Bachelor's degree in criminal justice or other behavioral science area. Must be twenty-one years old and have a valid Ohio driver's license. Submit resume to Judge . . .

Not a very illuminating job description, is it? And since there are some significant differences in the duties and responsibilities possible within this classification, you'll want to have a sense of the specific job *before* you apply, if possible.

Let's look at a more complete job advertisement—this one from Arizona:

Juvenile Probation Officer: Bachelor's degree in criminal justice or related field with one year of work experience with youth. Bilingual (Spanish/English) a plus. No criminal background. Must successfully complete a criminal history check relevant to employment since persons convicted of a felony may not be child-care workers in Arizona. Must be twenty-one, have a valid Arizona driver's license, and be able to work some flexible hours. Final job offer will be contingent upon a satisfactory five-year Arizona Motor Vehicle Report.

Duties: Under general supervision performs social investigations and evaluation of assigned offenders, including interviews with relatives, members of social agencies, employers, and others; prepares required reports and assessments and makes recommendations to the court; advises and supervises offenders as ordered by the court in order to enforce compliance with court directives; develops and implements client-based programs and refers offenders for placement in needed services; appears and testifies in court; conducts visits with offenders at the office and at various sites; performs searches, makes arrests, and provides crisis intervention; enters data and provides statistical data for computer-based management; maintains written and computerized records, runs reports, and verifies statistics with central records; keeps track of client payments; consults with attorneys and works with victims and community agencies; may transport offenders; may counsel offenders; works in partnership with the community for input, planning, and accountability (Restorative Justice); trains other officers; makes most case decisions independently.

Essential functions of this position include: Searching for files, etc.; working with and around other clients, community contacts, child-care advocates, and staff; dealing with interruptions; repetitive motion (hand-wrist) for report writing, computer input, and documentation; vision acuity (near) for reading and computer input; vision acuity (far) needed for surveillance and driving; hearing and speech (ordinary conversation) for interviews, fieldwork, and communicating with staff and the public.

While states often publish detailed job specifications, we cite this example from Arizona because it is among the most detailed. More important, it's a very helpful set of clues to the criminal justice job seeker interested in juvenile justice because it so thoroughly details the different tasks and occupations of the probation officer's job. Using this particular job as a basis, here's a breakdown of the different tasks and skills required of a juvenile probation officer:

- Interviewing (clients, parents, social service personnel, employers, etc.)
- Report writing
- Making assessments and recommendations
- Knowledge of court directives and protocols
- Development and implementation of client-based programs
- Serving as a court witness
- Transporting offenders
- Performing searches; making arrests
- Counseling, including crisis intervention
- Computer proficiency (data entry, report writing, database management)
- Consulting (with attorneys, victims, and social agencies)

If you are strongly interested in juvenile justice, and especially in the position of parole/probation officer, and reading this job description and the list of skills required inspires both excitement *and* a bit of apprehension, that's OK! You've just come to the realization that the job is a highly responsible position with significant demands. Even more good news, as you will see in the following section on earnings, is that the salary for these positions tends to be among the best for entry-level jobs and is commensurate with the demands of the work.

You will be managing a caseload of probationers. What this means in your day-to-day work is that you assess each client to identify and monitor what risks the individual may present, you attempt to ensure his or her compliance with the judge's sentence, and you do all you can to encourage positive behavior changes.

Behind the scenes, you act as one of many probationary consultants to the courts, providing direction, services, and information on possible treatment plans, sentencing protocols, and alternatives for each offender. Because of this relationship to the court, many of the ads for juvenile probation officers require that you submit your application packet directly to the judge or to the judge's administrative aide.

WORKING CONDITIONS

Though some "desk time" is required with this job, you probably aren't delivering the best service if you are behind a desk much of the time. This job carries intensely competing demands of paperwork/record keeping and personal contact with offenders and members of their support systems.

You may be transporting your client to the doctor or to a job interview or to a group counseling session with parents and social workers. There will be conferences with lawyers, judges, and other court officials. You will have a full calendar of your own court dates as a witness as well as appointments to visit treatment and residential centers.

In any job this busy and this hectic, organizational skills are the key to successful performance. Your own skills and how you employ them will directly affect the quality of your working conditions. Good time management and record keeping; clear communications with others; and follow-up, follow-up, follow-up will go far to keeping your stress level down and the job manageable.

TRAINING AND QUALIFICATIONS

Because of the responsibilities (and the good salary) that this job offers, the position is not as readily available as many others. Review the self-assessment exercises in Chapter 1, and be honest with yourself about your skills and experience. Can you demonstrate competency in oral and written communication technique? How can you assure prospective employers that you have the required ability to work independently and exercise good judgment? Many of these positions (though not all) demand some familiarity and work experience with a youth population. If you are still in school and have not had this kind of experience, through either summer camp counseling, church or community youth groups, or parks and recreation programming, then consider an internship in some area of juvenile justice before you graduate. Not only will it allow you to meet the requirements of working with youth, but also it will give you the advantage of insight into the criminal justice system through the experiences you will have enjoyed.

Each job and each employer will have unique demands. The lengthy job ad quoted in this section, for example, put particular emphasis on your state driving record, specifying evidence of five years of blemish-free driving. Other employers will require firearms experience and/or some training in self-defense. All of them will require that you undergo a thorough background investigation and will not consider any candidate with a felony conviction or evidence of any past moral turpitude.

EARNINGS

The juvenile justice system parallels the adult judicial process, with salary levels among corrections officers and counselors/case managers at juvenile facilities similar to those at adult prisons. The same can be said for probation officers in juvenile courts, whose salaries correspond to their counterparts associated with adults in the criminal court system throughout the country.

Corrections Officer/Corrections Counselor

As noted in Chapter 12, the median annual salary for all corrections officers in 1998 was $28,540. In other words, among *all* officers employed in the field, in both adult and juvenile facilities and at the entry level as well as after many years of experience, half earned above that amount and half earned below it. Our informal sampling of current employment ads for just entry-level juvenile corrections officer positions tends to support this earnings level. An ad for a detention officer in Arkansas specified a salary of $16,145. However, this position did not require a college degree. At the opposite end of the spectrum, an opening for a corrections counselor trainee in Connecticut was advertised at a high starting salary of $30,587. Here a college degree was required, and you could expect to earn $32,589 after your first year of training. Neither of these positions required experience. The majority of positions carried minimum salaries in the mid-$20s and many approached $30,000.

With some experience, even as little as six months in some circumstances, salary potential increased. Take a look at this recent ad from Ohio.

Youth Services Residential Unit Manager: Directs and coordinates all custodial and treatment phases (group living social services, safety, security, academic, and special services) of one living unit on all three shifts; determines staffing orientation of new employees and staff training, and supervises all youth leaders and social workers assigned to living units; prepares and submits budgets for living units; attends meetings, court hearings, and training sessions. Qualifications: Completion of undergraduate core program in behavioral science (e.g., juvenile justice, psychology, sociology); six months' training or six months' experience in counseling; six months' training or six months' experience in security measures and safety practices associated with detention of incarcerated individuals. Salary: $31,387.

Juvenile Probation Officer

According to the *Probation and Parole Directory (1998–2000)*, the most recent edition issued by the American Correctional Association, starting salaries for juvenile probation officers working in state-administered systems ranged from $13,000 to $40,000, with the majority of entry-level salaries falling in the $20,000 to $30,000 range. In systems run by local or county government, most beginning salaries were between $20,000 and $25,000.

Since salaries in one state or region of the country can differ vastly from those in another, you may want to check out the website maintained by the National Center for Juvenile Justice at www.ncjj.org/stateprofiles. This is one of the best sites on the Web for up-to-date, comprehensive information at the local level. Select a state, and you will be given a complete profile of the juvenile justice system in that state, including information on probation, detention, and state institutions, along with beginning salaries and caseload averages for probation officers. It is definitely worth investigating whether you want to learn about your local area or explore other locations. If that's not enough, the site gives you contact information and, in most instances, directly links you to the juvenile departments and/or agencies responsible for hiring probation and other youth workers.

CAREER OUTLOOK

As long as there are juveniles being arrested, there will be a need for corrections officers, probation officers, youth workers, and other professionals to provide services for them. Sadly, those numbers are rising. According to the most recent statistics from the U.S. Department of Justice's Office of Juvenile Justice and Delinquency Prevention, in 1998, there were 8,570 arrests for every 100,000 youths ages ten to seventeen in the United States. Between 1988 and 1997, the total number of delinquency cases handled by juvenile courts increased 48 percent. This figure has bearing for employment prospects because virtually every one of those approximately 2 million cases in 1997 would have had contact with a probation officer at some point. Moreover, this increase in juvenile court cases has not occurred just since 1988; in fact, the 1997 juvenile court delinquency caseload was more than four times what it was in 1960! You can easily see how marked increases such as these necessitate an increase in staffing as well.

As a previous section explained, juvenile courts sometimes hold youths in secure detention facilities while the court is processing their cases. Between 1988 and 1997, the number of cases involving such detention increased 35 percent. Some of these juvenile offenders were referred to residential placement facilities. According to the *Census of Juveniles in Residential Placement*, which provides a one-day count of all juvenile offenders in residential facilities, on October 29, 1997, there were 125,805 youths assigned beds in 1,121 public and 2,310 private facilities across the country. Depending on the specific mission and the types of services offered, these facilities need some combination of counselors, caseworkers, instructors, trainers, security officers, recreation leaders, treatment specialists, and managers and other administrators. If your career goal is in the field of juvenile justice, the odds are very good that you will find a job that matches your interests and skills.

STRATEGY FOR FINDING THE JOBS

An important point to keep in mind as you begin your job search is that there is no comprehensive juvenile justice system in this country. Instead, there are separate, individual systems in each state and the District of Columbia. In some states, for example, probation is administered by local juvenile courts; in others, state executive agencies oversee probation services. Most often, these executive agencies are separate juvenile corrections agencies. However, they may also be welfare/social service agencies, children and youth agencies, or, in a few instances, adult corrections agencies. Probation services can also be run by the judicial agency of the state, such as a court administrator's office, or by a local executive agency. Some states even employ a combination of the foregoing, whereby local courts administer probation services in some parts of the state while the state oversees services in other parts, usually the more rural areas. So, to find out where the jobs are within a given state, you must first determine how the state's juvenile justice system is organized.

The best way to do this is through the website www.ncjj.org/stateprofiles. There you will be able to view complete profiles of juvenile justice systems by state. You'll then know what agencies to target. You'll be provided with resources and contact information and, in the majority of cases, direct links to those agencies and organizations. Many of the linked sites list job openings and application procedures clearly, while for others you may need to navigate around a bit to find the human resources Web page. You may not always be able to locate employment announcements, but you will at least be given a phone number and contact name. One site stated that its job vacancies are posted in its office every Wednesday and that you could call the office to receive a copy.

If you can't find any employment information at the site, you can call or E-mail the website contact person to ask when and where job openings are advertised.

Paperwork Tip

The application and hiring process in public employment is often heavily dependent, especially in the early stages, on the careful submission of paperwork. Therefore, pay particular attention to the application forms and their completion. Make several copies of every form you receive, and use them to work up a preliminary draft before submission. You'll discover that many application forms demand frustratingly long responses in very small spaces, often requiring that you attach additional sheets. You'll want to work out your responses on a copy of the original form before completing the finished product. Remember that appearance is important, as is the thoroughness of your information.

Other Sources of Job Leads

Not all positions in juvenile justice are with government agencies. Many opportunities are available in private and nonprofit youth agencies that contract with government agencies to administer and operate juvenile justice programs. To find these positions, you will need to go to other sources, some of which have already been mentioned, such as local and regional newspapers and local employment offices. Others are described here.

Your College's Career Office. Virtually all college career offices maintain some system of posting the job advertisements that they receive daily via fax, phone, mail, or E-mail. Ads may be posted on a website (either the school's own or a national jobs database aimed at college students, such as Job Direct at www.jobdirect.com), in three-ring binders, or on jobs boards. Most of the jobs will be entry level and targeted to recent college graduates. These postings change quickly as new ones arrive each day, so be sure to check the site or office at least weekly. You may also want to check with the criminal justice department at your college or university. Sometimes employers send postings to the relevant academic department, where they may be maintained on a bulletin board.

Internet Job Searching. Chapter 3 emphasized the importance of developing a list of employment websites to monitor. (Don't forget to include any state or local sites you've found, along with on-line newspaper classifieds in your area; www.careerpath.com is a link to newspaper classifieds nationwide.) Some of the more popular employment sites are www.monster.com, www.careermosaic.com, www.headhunter.net, and www.careerbuilder.com. You may want to prepare an activity log, with the name of each site listed in one column and dates to check across the top of the page. This will help to organize your Internet job search and ensure that you check each site at least once a week. Develop a list of keywords for searches based on your area(s) of interest, such as *youth counselor, youth worker, juvenile probation officer,* and *juvenile corrections.*

Another worthwhile Web-based search function is the Web yellow pages found on many search engines (dogpile.com is one service). Using keywords more suited to employers, such as *juvenile, social service,* or *youth centers,* you can search your own locale and surrounding areas where these hiring organizations may be listed.

Professional Associations. Associations are the best-kept secret of the job search. A listing of some that are appropriate to the field of juvenile justice is included at the close of this chapter. Some of these associations will provide you with actual job listings; others may provide links to related sites with employment information. For the most part, you will have to join an association to take full advantage of its services, such as professional journals and newsletters. Some may offer a student membership rate. Consider any expense an investment in your future. It's worth it! This book lists national associations, but many have local affiliates that may be cheaper to join and more in line with your needs.

A Final Tip: Build Skills and Gain Some Direct Experience with Youth

Many, if not most, of the want ads for juvenile justice worker that you encounter will ask for some kind of documented experience dealing with youth. So, don't dismiss the camp counselor job you had during your summer breaks in college. Be sure to include the job on your resume and highlight any responsibilities that involved supervision, leadership, program or activity planning, or counseling support. Volunteer work counts as well. Are you a Big Brother or Big Sister? Have you coached youth sports teams? How about any involvement with youth church groups? Record any of these on your resume, and be prepared to discuss them in an interview.

If you haven't had any experience with youth programs, now is the time to get some. An internship would be the best way. These professional experiences give you an opportunity to test the reality and see if juvenile justice work is a good fit given your interests and abilities. Sometimes, you can earn academic credit for an internship if it fits into your curriculum. Check with your criminal justice academic department or college career office to find out what opportunities are available to you. Start the process early, as internships can be very competitive. Once you complete an internship, you'll have that all-important experience to put on your resume, and you will have established some professional contacts in the field.

If an internship is not possible, consider volunteer work. Many nonprofit and government agencies are short-staffed and would welcome the additional support. You can also contact youth organizations in your area and ask what their volunteer needs are. Also ask what kind of training they may provide. This can be a great way to enhance your skill base at no cost. These same organizations may even offer part-time and/or summer opportunities.

EMPLOYERS

State and local governments are the primary employers of juvenile justice workers. Unlike the situation with some of the other careers already discussed, the federal government is not a major employer here. That's because very few juvenile offenders are processed through the federal criminal justice system. Almost all juvenile offenders go through state and local courts.

Since each state has its own system for handling juvenile delinquency, how services are organized and, therefore, who does the hiring will depend on the state. Nevertheless, some generalities apply. To understand the system, it's helpful to break down juvenile delinquency services into front end and back end. The front end includes **probation**, defined as intake, investigation, and supervision of delinquents, and **detention**, which refers to the temporary custody of juveniles awaiting final court disposition. The back end includes **delinquency institutions**, sometimes called training schools, where delinquents are securely housed, and **aftercare** services, when the juvenile has been conditionally released but is being supervised in the community.

Generally speaking, front-end services (probation and detention) tend to be local responsibilities, while those at the back end (delinquency institutions and aftercare) tend to be state responsibilities. Most state systems, however, are hybrids, with some services being the responsibility of local government and others administered at the state level. The hiring agencies, therefore, may be the local courts (often the case with probation services), local executive agencies (most often a county juvenile bureau), or state-level executive agencies (for example, a state's department of youth services or office of court administration).

In *every* state, delinquency (residential) institutions and aftercare services are administered by a state executive agency (such as a department of youth services). In most cases, the agency that oversees the delinquency institutions is the same one that oversees aftercare services. As you look from state to state, you will notice varying names for these agencies. The ones most often seen are Department of Youth Services, Department of Juvenile Corrections, Youth Authority, Department of Children and Families, Juvenile Justice Authority, and Department of Health and Human Services (usually with a specific division for handling youth services). Sometimes the state's department of corrections will handle both adult and juvenile cases.

While state and local authorities may be charged with administering juvenile delinquency services, that doesn't mean that they always provide these services directly. Many states contract with private providers to operate detention centers, residential sites, and aftercare services. Nonprofit agencies and organizations also receive funding for residential and nonresidential services such as education programs, wilderness camps, recreation programs, vocational training, and treatment-specific programs for alcohol and substance abuse and sexual misconduct, to name a few.

POSSIBLE JOB TITLES

This career path is directed at a specific target population, so you will often see the words *youth* or *juvenile* in the job title. Sometimes the word *counselor* is in the title, and these jobs are often considered entry-level positions. Once you gain some related experience, you may begin to qualify for positions with *coordinator* or *supervisor* in the title. With additional years in the field and increased administrative responsibilities, such as training and supervising new workers, monitoring overall caseloads, and preparing and maintaining budgets, your options for jobs will include terms such as *director* and *executive director*.

Corrections Officer/Corrections Counselor

Aftercare Counselor

Alcohol and Substance Abuse
  Counselor

Case Manager

Corrections Residence Counselor

Cottage Manager

Counselor

Detention Officer

Employment Specialist

Group Counselor

Juvenile Detention Counselor

uvenile Rehabilitation Coordinator

Program/Project Director

Reentry Counselor

Residential Facilities Manager

Residential Treatment Counselor

Runaway Counselor

Support Services Coordinator

Team Leader

Training Specialist

Youth Advocate

Youth Counselor

Youth Services Group Worker

Youth Worker

Probation Officer

Chief Juvenile Probation Officer

Community Program Specialist

Court Advocate

Deputy Probation Officer

Director of Juvenile Court Services

Intervention Officer

Juvenile Probation Officer

Juvenile Services Assistant

Juvenile Services Officer

Parole Officer, Juvenile Justice

Probation Officer

RELATED OCCUPATIONS

Beyond the preceeding list, your educational background and interest in working with youth can be combined with other skills or interests you may possess. Some postitions of this type may be found within the corrections system; some may support the system in some way. Examples include:

Adoption Caseworker

Recreation Center Director

School Attendance Officer

School Resource Officer

Teacher

Vocational Instructor/Specialist

Wilderness Instructor

PROFESSIONAL ASSOCIATIONS

Listed in this section are some of the associations that relate to careers in the field of juvenile justice. For more information about these professional associations, either check the websites listed or consult the *Encyclopedia of Asso-*

ciations, published by the Gale Group. Review the Members/Purpose notes for each organization to determine if it pertains to your interests. Membership in one or more of these organizations may gain you access to job listings, networking opportunities, and employment search services. Some provide information at no charge, but if you want to receive specific publications that list job opportunities, you may need to join. If you're still in college, check for student member rates.

American Bar Association
Juvenile Justice Center
541 N. Fairbanks Ct.
Chicago, IL 60611
www.abanet.org/crimjust/juvjus/
Members/Purpose: Dedicated to monitoring legislative, fiscal, policy, and administrative changes emerging in juvenile justice systems across the nation. The website contains more than 500 links to other juvenile justice sites.
Publications: *A Call for Justice*; *Beyond the Walls*; *More Than Meets the Eye*; reports; *IJA/ABA*, twenty-four volume set.
Training: Mid-year and annual meetings. Also sponsors the Center for Continuing Legal Education.

American Correctional Association
4380 Forbes Blvd.
Lanham, MD 20706-4322
www.corrections.com/aca/
Members/Purpose: A multidisciplinary organization of professionals representing all facets of corrections and criminal justice, including federal, state, and military corrections facilities and prisons; county jails and detention centers; probation/parole agencies; and community corrections/halfway houses.
Publications: *Corrections Today* magazine; *Corrections Compendium: The National Journal for Corrections*; major catalog of additional publications.
Training: National training conventions; certification seminars; on-line workshops; video lending library.

American Jail Association
2053 Day Rd., Suite 100
Hagerstown, MD 21740
www.corrections.com/aja/

Members/Purpose: The American Jail Association is a national nonprofit organization dedicated to supporting those who work in and operate our nation's jails.

Publications: *American Jails* magazine; *Write It Right* quarterly; *Jail Operations Bulletin*; *Who's Who in Jail Management.*

Training: Annual conferences; training seminars throughout the year on a variety of topics; Jail Manager Certification Program.

Council of Juvenile Correctional Administrators
Stonehill College
16 Belmont St.
South Easton, MA 02375
www.corrections.com/cjca/
Members/Purpose: The Council of Juvenile Correctional Administrators, incorporated in 1994 to bring together juvenile justice leaders, is dedicated to the improvement of juvenile correctional services and practices. The CJCA promotes and facilitates three major activities: the exchange of ideas and philosophies at the top administrative level of juvenile corrections planning and policy making, the advancement of juvenile corrections and juvenile justice techniques, and the education of the public about juvenile justice and corrections systems.
Publications: Quarterly newsletter; yearbook survey.
Training: Summer meetings.

Juvenile Justice Trainers Association
930 Coddington Rd.
Ithaca, NY 14850
www.jjta.org
Members/Purpose: A founding partner of the Alliance for Juvenile Justice, the Juvenile Justice Trainers Association provides a structure for collaboration on initiatives and projects for improved services to at-risk youth throughout the nation. It's devoted to the development and advancement of a specialized system of education and training for juvenile justice professionals.
Publications: *Juvenile Justice Training Notes*, newsletter.
Training: Annual conferences.

National Association of Community Action Agencies
1100 Seventeenth St. NW, Suite 500
Washington, DC 20036
www.nacaa.org

Members/Purpose: It is the mission of the National Association of Community Action Agencies to be a national forum for policy on poverty and to strengthen, promote, represent, and serve its network of member agencies to assure that the issues of poor people are effectively heard and addressed.

Publications: *Community Action Digest*; technical assistance manuals.

Training: Annual conference; training seminars; Certified Community Action Professional Program.

National Association of Family-Based Services
1824 Fifth St. NW
Washington, DC 20012
www.nafbs.org

Members/Purpose: A nonprofit organization promoting effective, culturally appropriate services to families.

Publications: *Empowering Families*, a quarterly newsletter and on-line job postings.

Training: Annual conference.

National Center for Juvenile Justice
710 Fifth Ave., Suite 3000
Pittsburgh, PA 15219-3000
www.ncjj.org

Members/Purpose: The research division of the National Council of Juvenile and Family Court Judges, the NCJJ is dedicated to improving the quality of justice for children and families. Its primary means of accomplishing this is by conducting research and providing objective, factual information that is utilized to increase the juvenile and family justice systems' effectiveness.

Publications: Numerous publications are available for download on topics such as juvenile protection, juvenile and family courts, substance abuse, and statistical information.

Training: Resource center for telephone consultation, technical assistance, preparation of informational packets, and custom database searches/bibliographies of the Center; on-site visits.

National Center for Youth Law
405 Fourteenth St., Fifteenth Floor
Oakland, CA 94612
www.youthlaw.org

Members/Purpose: The Center uses the law to protect children from the harms caused by poverty and to improve the lives of children living in poverty. An advocacy group, it aims to protect abused and neglected children, expand access to health care for children and youths, secure public benefits to meet the special needs of children and youths, and improve child support collection.

Publications: Articles; manuals; books; bimonthly journal, *Youth Law News.*

Training: Technical assistance and training.

National Council of Juvenile and Family Court Judges
1041 N. Virginia St.
P.O. Box 8970
Reno, NV 89507
www.ncjfcj.unr.edu/

Members/Purpose: Focuses attention on the concept of a separate tribunal for children and encourages the development of essential treatment programs for children with special needs.

Publications: Materials such as *Juvenile and Family Court Journal, Juvenile Justice Today Magazine,* and *Juvenile and Family Law Digest,* a variety of textbooks, and some full-text on-line publications.

Training: Annual conferences, institutes, and training sessions; technical assistance.

National Council on Crime and Delinquency
685 Market St., Suite 620
San Francisco, CA 94105
www.nccd-crc.org

Members/Purpose: The National Council on Crime and Delinquency promotes effective, humane, and economically sound solutions and criminal justice strategies for family, community, and justice problems. The group conducts research, promotes reform initiatives, and seeks to work with public and private organizations and the media to prevent and reduce crime and delinquency.

Publications: Quarterly journal; crime and delinquency special reports.

Training: Conferences.

National Juvenile Detention Association
301 Perkins Building
521 Lancaster Ave.
Richmond, KY 40475-3102
www.njda.com

Members/Purpose: Promotes adequate detention services for juveniles through such means as delivery of first-class products to the field of juvenile justice and detention services; interpreting and promoting the concepts of juvenile detention services at the national, state, and local levels; and defining the mission of and interpreting the detention services process.
Publications: *The Journal for Juvenile Justice and Detention Services*; *Juvenile Detention Careworker Curriculum*; videos such as *Services to Female Juvenile Offenders*, *Communicating the Write Way*, *Implementing Medication in Youthcare Correction Settings*, and *Explosion of Gang Violence in the United States.*
Training: Annual conference; training and technical assistance provided through the association's Center for Research and Professional Development.

CHAPTER 14

PATH 5: ALLIED BUSINESS: CAREERS FOR THE CRIMINAL JUSTICE ENTREPRENEUR

Criminal justice has been a great major for you: hard work, demanding faculty, but lots of fun and interesting areas of study. You've enjoyed school, and you've liked the people you've met in the classroom (both teachers and students) and out in the field. You believe in the field of criminal justice and you've grown to appreciate its vital role in our social fabric. You have no doubts that criminal justice is the career field for you, but you are still wondering just where you may fit in.

Perhaps the career paths described in the preceding chapters all have their appeal, but none of them completely satisfies your career interests and demands. Perhaps you have high income aspirations, or, through your work experience, you've learned that you have strong management or business skills that you would like to put to use in a job. Maybe you are a highly creative systems-thinker—always coming up with new and better ways to do things. You may be wondering, Can I stay in the criminal justice work arena if I don't see myself as a law enforcement officer, or a corrections professional, or a court or juvenile justice worker? Of course! A career in one of the many possible businesses outlined in this chapter may be the blend that satisfies you.

Every job in the areas examined in this path brings its own environment and its own "package" of associated values. If you've worked through some of the self-assessment exercises in Chapter 1, you likely have begun to build a mental picture of your particular personality dimensions, work attributes, and values. When you combine that growing self-awareness with your work experience, you begin to realize that different jobs deliver different atmospheres and interactions with others; varying degrees of remuneration; and often exceedingly different work experiences in terms of pace, location, energy, and so forth.

So, while this may all sound intriguing and attractive, you may be asking yourself, "What's the catch?" What else do I need to know about working in the area of private enterprise? You're correct in thinking that there will be other expectations beyond your criminal justice expertise. Other attributes that will be helpful include, but are not limited to, the following:

- Interest in and familiarity with the commercial marketplace

- Appreciation for the competitiveness of the marketplace

- Willingness to assume management responsibilities, including staff supervision, budgets, and hiring and evaluation of employees

- As your career progresses and you start to be promoted, willingness to shed your technical abilities (sales skills, technical writing, etc.) and take on the increasingly conceptual responsibilities of management for strategic concerns, planning, and evaluation

This is a career path in which you are hired for your criminal justice degree and "something more"; you will use your criminal justice degree every day, but you'll use many other aptitudes as well. In these jobs, you may be expected to assume the mantle of management responsibility in your preparation of business reports, memorandums, and other correspondence; in your training and supervision of employees; and in your representation of the organization in a responsible and professional manner.

DEFINITION OF THE CAREER PATH

Private Security

Many insurance companies, banks, and other businesses utilize private security to protect private property above and beyond what can be easily safeguarded by the police. Many corporations and virtually all banks use private firms to guard and patrol their premises. In some instances, representatives of these firms may be called on to investigate crimes by employees and customers. Independent private security companies also hire investigators for work on a contract basis. The field of private security is reflecting the same changes and upgrades in professionalism that are influencing the entire field of criminal justice. There was a time in the not too distant past when a book such as this would probably not have included private security as a possible employment field. Firms were small and not particularly well managed, and the jobs were just that—jobs—not careers.

Things have changed much for private security, both as an industry and as an individual career path for criminal justice graduates. One of the most notable shifts has been in the "blurring" of private security into a sometimes public law enforcement job. Private security professionals are now seen working in the public sector, specifically townships, counties, and smaller towns where the fiscal authorities find it more economical to supplement the regular police department with private security professionals instead of hiring, training, and permanently employing a larger public workforce.

Each of the jobs featured here falls into one of the many broad occupational areas within the general rubric of private security. In addition to the job of security services, those occupational areas include the following:

- *Consulting and investigation.* Consulting services available to clients can include help in the areas of competitive intelligence, computer and systems intelligence, crisis management, disaster preparedness, engineering services, intellectual property programs, threat analysis and security surveys, kidnap/extortion/incident management, product contamination protection, and workplace violence.

- *Systems integration.* This growing area includes closed-circuit television (CCTV) systems, intrusion detection, access-control systems (using the latest access card and "open architecture platform" technology), electronic imaging (badging), optical turnstiles, and custom security consoles.

- *Global intelligence.* Professionals in this specialty monitor and report on international security threats and events related to terrorism, crime, and civil unrest and help protect executives, office staff, and property around the world.

WORKING CONDITIONS

Working conditions in private security vary by assignment. While security officers spend considerable time on their feet and frequently work different shifts, growing numbers sit at large electronic consoles to monitor security or surveillance devices. The only general statement that can be made about security officer positions is that they tend to be relatively routine in terms of duties and responsibilities, although the person fulfilling this role must be ever vigilant. Even in the case of uniforms, there is little consensus anymore. The types of duties as well as the environments in which officers work are changing. Some employers seek a "military" look, while others prefer what is termed the "soft" look, whereby officers blend less conspicuously into the social milieu.

But security officer is not the only entry-level position available, especially for a bachelor's degree graduate of a criminal justice program. The range of private security occupations makes generalizations about working conditions almost meaningless.

TRAINING AND QUALIFICATIONS

Good judgment, common sense, physical fitness, observational skills, leadership, conscientious application of company principles and policies, ability to provide credible testimony in a courtroom, professional appearance and attitude, and strong interpersonal skills are some of the general qualities looked for during the hiring process for private security professionals.

Most states require private security officials to be licensed. If you enter this work as a security officer (a typical entry-level position for a criminal justice graduate) you must pass a background check and complete classroom training in areas such as property rights, emergency procedures, and detention of suspected criminals. Drug testing is frequently required and may be ongoing and random. The Montana Department of Commerce, Division of Professional and Occupational Licensing, has a Board of Private Security Patrol Officers and Investigators licensing unit (www.com.state.mt.us/license/ pol/pol_boards/psp_board/board_page.htm) that provides an excellent example of licensing requirements for a variety of private security positions, including:

- Private investigator

- Private security guard

- Security alarm installer

Many jobs also require a driver's license. In addition, if your position mandates that you carry a firearm, you will be required to be licensed by the appropriate authority; frequently, you will be required to be certified additionally as a special police officer so that you are empowered to make arrests while on duty. Obviously, armed positions have more stringent background checks and entry requirements due to the potential liability to the hiring organization.

As an indication that private security is rapidly becoming as demanding and professional as every other criminal justice occupation, many states are making ongoing training for private security professionals a legal requirement for the retention of certification. This training encompasses topics such as protection, public relations, report writing, crisis deterrence, and first aid, as well as any specialized training relevant to the individual's assignments.

DEFINITION OF THE CAREER PATH

Private Investigator

This employment field is difficult to categorize. It is not law enforcement, and it is not criminal justice, nor is it, strictly speaking, private security. It is, however, a possible employment site for criminal justice majors in the private sector. Because most private investigators operate alone as independent agents, they come to this work with considerable experience gained elsewhere. Only the larger private investigatory hiring organizations offer entry-level jobs and will provide the training necessary. Since most of the firms that offer investigative services are small (often entrepreneurships) and their time is contracted in discrete units for pricing purposes, this field can be grouped within the category of products and services.

Let's dispel the myths about this job right now. It's not about glamour; it's mostly about divorces and missing people, generally family members. A considerable amount of detective work is done on the computer, and that is why many private investigators successfully advertise their services on the Internet—they can work from anywhere.

Your days are spent researching birth and death records, marriage licenses, real estate transactions, tax filings, news reports, and legal findings. You investigate, produce results, and write up a report. If you are working for yourself, you will also need to spend considerable time generating clients in order to maintain a steady stream of income.

If you are associated with a large private investigatory firm, you may be involved in investigations of internal security or other internal problems of large organizations whose potential risk or dollar loss is such that they can afford to contract with your employer.

WORKING CONDITIONS

Working conditions for "private eyes" are generally solitary. You'll spend considerable time on the computer searching records, spend some time on telephone work, and travel rarely—generally, only in the final stages of an investigation. A high degree of isolation exists in this job, in which many practitioners are self-employed or employed by very small agencies. Income can be unpredictable if you are self-employed or work on a contingency basis. Many independent private investigators describe a situation in which they have a full roster of clients and are so busy that they can't take on any more clients, and then, one by one, they resolve all of their clients' business only to find that they have no new clients. They then must spend precious time recruiting new business, advertising, and telemarketing to get a full client load again. The cycle starts anew.

Much of your time may be occupied doing library research, or searching courthouse or city hall records, and writing reports for clients. Hours can be long, and most work is done "behind the scenes."

In summary, the specific dynamics of the private investigator's work environment are:

- Solitary work

- Significant computer desk time

- Outside research of courthouses, city halls, large libraries

- Limited caseload (divorces, missing persons, credit checks)

- High degree of interaction with lawyers and legal issues

TRAINING AND QUALIFICATIONS

Most employers look for some strong background in any specific field (law, business, etc.). Most private investigators learned their skills in local law enforcement, the military, federal law enforcement, or private security firms.

Some states have specific licensing requirements, including examinations, and may require you to post a bond to ensure compliance with state regulations.

The following attributes are also important:

- Appropriate demeanor. Can you work alone, think logically, react quickly to changing circumstances, use sound judgment, and keep professionally distant from your work? Maturity is a must.

- Excellent research skills, including familiarity with credit checks, Lexis/Nexis, and Dow Jones searches, and strong skills in Internet research.

- Strong work ethic, with an independent style.

- Good budgeting and record-keeping skills.

- Excellent client-relations skills.

- Ability to prioritize.

CYBERCRIME

A New Threat

The scene of the crime: a twelve-year-old girl is at home on her computer writing in a "chat room" to someone she thinks is a fifteen-year-old boy in the next town who wants her to meet him at a local mall . . .

The reality of this situation is that the "young boy" may, in fact, be an adult sexual offender trying to lure the girl out of her home and to a public place where her abduction would be less likely to be noticed.

The vulnerability of our children on the Web is not the only hot issue in computer crime. A review of just a week's worth of newspaper and television news brings items such as:

- Millions of bogus messages flooding websites or Internet service providers, blocking access to networks and servers and "freezing" the systems

- Computer break-ins by malicious hackers who violate the confidentiality and integrity of data and systems by exploiting security holes or poor procedures (including lack of "firewalls" and passwords)

- Internal computer attacks, often by disgruntled or dismissed employees

- Development and proliferation of destructive viruses

- Simple physical attacks on computer hardware in which criminals or terrorists damage or unplug critical components of a computer system to disrupt operations

As the United States and the world community begin to confront cyber-crime, efforts have perforce begun to classify and codify these crimes. A basic breakdown might look something like this:

Crimes Against Property

- Hacking: Using programming abilities with malicious intent

- Cracking: Using programs to gain unauthorized entry into a computer or network

- Spreading viruses: Creating and disseminating harmful computer programs

- Software piracy: Illegally copying and distributing software

Crimes Against Persons

- Electronic dissemination of obscene material/pornography: trafficking in, posting, or distributing pornography, child pornography, or indecent-exposure materials over the Web

- Cyber-harassment: using electronic mail, chat rooms, or programs to harass individuals

- Cyber-stalking: using the Internet to track the movements and behavior of individuals

Cyber-Terrorism

- Most cryptographic systems depend on secrecy since it is not yet a crime to break those codes; however, the U.S. government has set standards for the strength of encryption programs. Hackers breaking these cryptographic codes remain a threat to some governments and private businesses that employ them.

- As our lives become more involved with and recorded by computers, the possibilities of "crackers" using this collective information to terrorize governments, businesses, or groups of individuals become ever more a reality.

DEFINITION OF THE CAREER PATH

The investigation of any crime involves the painstaking collection of clues and forensic evidence and requires attention to detail. This is particularly true of today's "white-collar crime," in which computer-linked evidence frequently plays a pivotal role as documentary evidence. With the advancing number of households now using computers and the reliance on computers by businesses large and small, coupled with easy Internet access, it is almost inevitable that at least one electronic device will be found during a crime investigation. It could be a computer, but it could also be a printer, mobile phone, personal organizer, and so on. The electronic device may figure prominently as evidence in the investigation, or it may be just on the periphery. No matter which, the information must be retrieved and investigated in the proper manner, especially if any of this evidence is to be relied on in a court of law.

Examples of the evidence you may find on a computer system that could assist the prosecution or defense of a case include:

- Use/abuse of the Internet

- Production of false documents and accounts
- Encrypted/password-protected material
- Theft of computer time
- Abuse of systems
- E-mail contact between suspects or conspirators
- Theft of commercial secrets
- Unauthorized transmission of information
- Records of movements
- Malicious attacks on computer systems
- Names and addresses of contacts

Roles you might play in an entry-level career investigating computer crime include advising on how to initiate an investigation in which computers are involved and, related to this, advising on how best to secure any possible evidence. In other situations, investigators visit sites to secure data, either overtly or covertly, using the latest in forensically sound imaging techniques. Investigators detecting cyber-criminals become skilled in examining data captured and retrieved from the deepest files and lowest levels of discs that the owner or operator might have thought were long discarded. They also must record, report, and summarize all of this information in a professional format.

WORKING CONDITIONS

Case: Your client suspects misuse of its computer system. Your job is a covert, on-site examination of more than 100 machines to uncover use of the employer's equipment for downloading child pornography. Result: the ultimate conviction of an employee and disciplinary action of others for related offenses.

Case: Sensitive files are missing from a central computer system. Your work uncovers a former employee dialing in, using a long disused (but not deleted) phone access code, to delete these files.

Case: An insurance company has received a huge claim for the loss of all data on an insured firm's mainframe computer due to interaction with an industrial magnet. While you confirm major damage to the motherboard and casing by magnetic interaction, you are able to reclaim all data from the hard disk and thus nullify the claim.

Case: In the course of only a couple of days of consulting time, you are able to establish that an employee is downloading valuable client information to start his own company. Resulting savings to your client could be in the millions of dollars.

Case: You are called as an expert witness in a court case to testify to specific facts regarding your knowledge and examination of specific technology and to state your opinion as to why certain events did or did not occur.

This is real detective work, and on many of your assignments you will be on-site at the client's place of business. Other times, you can work from your own terminal and patch into the client's system on a shared drive. From the few sample scenarios described, you can see that each day, each client, and each investigation is very different. Of course, each client's hardware and software will be different as well. So, while there are few overriding similarities in working conditions, one constant is that this is not a boring nine-to-five desk job!

Because some of your work will be on-site and your presence is sometimes acknowledged and other times hidden, you will need to be conscious of your appearance and demeanor. At times, you may have to make subtle adjustments in your wardrobe and manner to more easily go unnoticed as you collect evidence.

TRAINING AND QUALIFICATIONS

The field of cybercrime represents new territory in law enforcement, and many procedures, jurisdictions, laws, and even investigative and evidentiary techniques have yet to be worked out. That's compelling because we are seldom offered an opportunity to get in on the emergence of some aspect of our chosen calling. Look around at some of the other majors graduating with you. Psychology, foreign language, social work, accounting—all are good and worthwhile majors leading to productive jobs and satisfying lives but, perhaps, fewer chances than you have to experience the cutting edge of a career.

Right now, the ideal qualifications for entry-level positions in the cybercrime field would be a dual major in criminal justice and accounting. Accounting courses (which involve considerable and sophisticated computer use) teach students how a business is structured, and that knowledge combined with your investigative procedures course work in criminal justice can be a powerful combination. A close second is a criminal justice major with a computer science minor. A third and also viable combination is a criminal justice major with significant electives in computer science and perhaps some strong work experience with computer systems.

If you can take advantage in any way of the courses offered at your college or university in the computer science department, do so. Focus on courses in information technology, which would include the functioning and workings of hardware and software systems in an organizational setting. This is just what you'll need on your resume for an entry-level position in computer crime work.

In addition to your academics in criminal justice and your computer skills, you'll hopefully be able to document either internships, practicums, or solid work experience using either or both of these specialties. Through these experiences, you will be able to meet and interact with the computer professionals on staff. By all means, tell them about your career plans and ask them to share as many insights as they can (and the work day allows) about systems analysis and information retrieval. This kind of on-the-job training will prove invaluable, and you may develop enough of a relationship with those professionals to request a recommendation at some point in your job search. Even better, if your part-time employer has some deleted files that need to be rescued, or hidden files that need to be found, or data in free space that may contain deleted or overwritten files to be retrieved, you may be asked to undertake this project. What great experience for your future career!

Other important skills and attributes for this job include report writing, systems analysis, patience, and enjoyment of problems. In this career you need to "wrestle" with the problem and see it from different perspectives to find a creative way to acquire your evidence. You can't be the kind of person who finds tough challenges defeating; rather, you need to approach solving problems as intriguing and fun.

An additional requisite is interviewing skills. Working with clients in a variety of office and corporate settings, you need to become skilled at understanding how their systems function and how people perform their duties and interact so that you can get inside the situation for yourself and deduce where evidence might lie. Good questioning, probing, and restatement skills are what put you on the right evidentiary trail.

EARNINGS

This career path tends to present the greatest variance in earnings among occupations. Much of the reason for this is that options in the private sector are so diverse that they cover a wide stretch of income levels. The two specific occupational areas highlighted in this chapter will provide you with a good sense of just how wide the ranges can be. On the lower end of earnings, you have many private security jobs. On the higher end, you have one of the highest-paying fields among all occupations: computer specialists. These, of course, are all general statements. Many private security jobs pay quite well, but computer security specialists represent the one area for which the general statement may apply across the board; salaries for those with computer expertise rank relatively high. Let's take a look inside each of these areas.

Private Security

Most men and women who choose this career begin as security or protection officers. Entry-level salaries can be somewhat low compared with other criminal justice occupations. The latest Bureau of Labor Statistics report shows that in 1998, most security officers earned an annual salary of $13,430 to $20,110. While this level of remuneration may be discouraging to aspirants who are working toward or have completed a bachelor's degree, some additional factors should be brought to bear before you dismiss private security as a viable career option.

First, the field has been experiencing a rapid upgrade in professionalism. As our society becomes more and more security conscious, and as private industry responds with demands for increased and sophisticated security in its operations and systems, this trend is expected to continue. Add to this the fact that the private security field is continually expanding and taking on roles and responsibilities previously held by public law enforcement officials, and you can see why the level of professionalism has been elevated. In fact, special certification such as the certified protection professional (CPP) is now preferred or required for some positions. As the need for security professionals to become more sophisticated, better educated, and specially trained increases, so will the salaries.

Salaries vary with the type of employer. Many security officers are employed by private security agencies that then contract with companies or organizations to provide security services for them. The hiring organization benefits by having a dedicated security force without having to recruit, hire, train, and supervise personnel. The downside for you is that it may mean less income than you might receive if the company employed you directly. Because your employer (the security firm) is, in effect, a middleman, you sacrifice some income for the firm's profit margin.

Many companies and organizations do hire their own security staff. In these cases, salaries (and the opportunity for advancement) may be higher. The American Society for Industrial Security, on-line at www.asisonline.org, offers some relevant demographic information, including salary ranges, for security professionals working in various specialty areas. Their "Typical Lodging (hotel) Security Professional," for example, with some experience is earning between $30,000 and $50,000 per year. Security professionals employed in the gaming/wagering industry are earning $30,000 to $60,000 plus.

The industry or specialty area itself can be a key determinant in salary levels. Those requiring higher levels of security, such as nuclear power plants, require higher standards in employment and involve longer and more intense periods of training, but salaries typically are higher as well. The size, location, and financial stability of the employer also influence salary levels. A large, established hospital in a major metropolitan area is more likely to pay its administrators and security staff alike a salary higher than is a small, suburban community hospital. Many larger organizations also offer a ranking system whereby opportunity for advancement in position and salary is clearly outlined.

Many entrants who start as private security officers will go on to become investigators. Here, earnings may be considerably higher, as this recent ad from California demonstrates.

Investigator: Bachelor's degree in criminal justice, business, public administration, or related field. Two years' experience in security or law enforcement. Must pass a Department of Security background investigation. May be required to travel to various locations and work irregular hours. Salary: $40,491.

You can see how with as little as two years of experience you can qualify for other positions that may more than double your salary. This can be said of other options too. Many officers advance to positions as supervisors, managers, and directors. Some become protection specialists, guarding and protecting the lives of corporate executives or celebrities traveling around the country and the world, and meeting interesting people. Others are more entrepreneurial and eventually establish a business, such as a contract security agency or a security consulting firm, or even one that specializes in a particular product, such as security alarm systems. In all cases, you can expect your salary to grow as the demand for your experience, knowledge, and services increases.

Private Investigators

Most private detectives and investigators come to the profession with some work experience, usually in private security, the military, or the insurance industry. Your criminal justice degree may help you to become one of the few who enter the field without any related experience. Earnings will depend on the size of the employer, the area of specialty, and the geographic area. On average, you can expect to earn about $30,000. Here's a recent ad that is a good example of what you may encounter.

Undercover Employment: Seeking highly motivated, career-oriented individuals for the position of undercover investigator. Starting salary is $30,000 per year, with second-year pay of $35,000 and third-year pay of $40,000. Applicants must possess one or more of the following: A bachelor's degree; a current police academy certificate; an associate's degree in criminal justice; or four years of military police experience. Benefits include medical and dental insurance, life insurance, and 401(k). Applicants must be willing to temporarily relocate throughout the United States.

With experience, you may eventually establish your own private detective agency. One out of four detectives is actually self-employed. In most cases, pay is per project, with limitations on the time that any fee will cover. Incomes for self-employed detectives therefore are indexed to the number of projects they have at any given time. The number of projects they receive and accept is determined by the amount of time they are willing to work, their reputation for results, their areas of specialty, and their location.

Cybercrime

If you have the advanced computer skills required for entry into the cyber field, you can expect significant income. Among new college graduates, those with computer expertise are often the highest paid of all. Computer security is a growing specialty within the computer field, so future salary potential is difficult to predict. However, the potential seems strong, as evidenced by a recent report by Robert Half International Consulting published in the company's *2000 Salary Guide*, which indicates salaries for security administrators of between $50,000 and $73,000.

While those figures are impressive, the vast majority of job seekers will not be able to step into a position such as security administrator straight out of college with a degree in criminal justice. You will need to demonstrate advanced computer skills, including network design and integration, and a working knowledge of state-of-the-art computer hardware and software technology (particularly technology used in information security). Careers in computer crime investigation will demand additional experience, such as computer investigative techniques, application, and legal aspects related to computer evidence recovery, including procedures for collection, preservation, and presentation of computer evidence.

This is not to imply that you are not qualified for some positions in the field of cybercrime. Many entry-level positions are available to you if you can establish that you have technical aptitude and a desire to learn the employer's systems and software. Course work in computer science and mathematics that supplements your criminal justice curriculum will be extremely helpful, as will a summer job or internship in the field. Basically speaking, you can expect to earn a salary commensurate with your experience and technical skills. In entry-level support positions, you stand to earn somewhere between $27,000 and $42,000. And, keep in mind that to attract good employees in the information technology industry, companies are sometimes willing to provide such benefits as stock options and equity incentives, as well as signing bonuses, flexible work schedules, and telecommuting opportunities.

CAREER OUTLOOK

You read in the preceding chapters about the promising employment outlook for the majority of jobs presented in those four career paths. How encouraging to see such strong evidence of the value of your criminal justice degree as you plan your career. And the news for the occupations outlined in this path is the best of all! In every category, you can expect to witness employment growth into the foreseeable future. In many other career fields, new employment is primarily a function of replacing workers in that field who retire or move on to other careers. In the case of the careers in this chapter, the growth in new employment is the result of explosive growth in the field itself.

Much of it can be attributed to the development of new and more sophisticated technologies. The best example of this can be seen with the expansion of Internet technology, which, for many companies, has resulted in a whole new way of conducting business: E-commerce. As popular as it has become, E-commerce would not be viable without built-in security systems in which consumers have confidence. Workers are needed to develop, monitor, upgrade, and investigate failures in these systems. Beyond those functions are the personnel needed to promote and sell the systems to companies and organizations.

The development of new technologies and products comes at a time when the public is experiencing a heightened awareness and fear of crime. These concerns are most often expressed by demands for increased security in all areas of people's lives. The private sector is listening and responding.

Private Security

The outlook for employment in this field is terrific. In fact, within the next five years, you can expect to see employment of security officers alone advance by about 23 percent. This translates to almost 42,000 job openings each year! Rapid growth shouldn't come as a surprise when you consider how important security has become in so many circumstances. One example is the extensive publicity about campus crime and the level of violence in and around all educational institutions, including elementary and secondary schools. This has naturally led to demands for increased security in all of these facilities. Hotel security similarly has greatly expanded in response to the flood of lawsuits filed against hotels based on charges of security breaches. As fears of terrorism grow, airlines and airports heighten security. These are just a few illustrations of how demand—in the form of crime and the fear of crime—affects supplies needed for additional security personnel.

Another driver of employment in this field is the necessity to staff multiple shifts. In many instances, security is a twenty-four-hour business, so that instead of one person to fill a position, you actually need three.

Private Investigators

It is projected that private detective agencies will grow in number and size during the next ten to fifteen years. The news is especially good for you, as opportunities for entry-level jobs will be the best. Through 2008, it's anticipated that employment of private detectives and investigators will increase by 21 percent or more. The reasons for this expected growth include a demand for investigatory services related to increased litigation involving civil and criminal cases. Add to that a growing need to protect confidential information; a continuing focus on protecting property of all kinds; and increased efforts by companies to control internal and external financial losses, prevent industrial espionage, and monitor their competitors.

While the employment outlook is healthy, the competition for these jobs will be equally strong. You will be in contention with other recent college graduates in addition to candidates who have experience in law enforcement, the military, private security, or a specialty area such as finance or insurance.

Cybercrime

The fastest growing of all occupations through 2008 will be those that involve computers. The expansion of computer applications and the development and integration of new technologies fuel the tremendous demand for skilled professionals, including those with expertise in communications security.

It is easy to see why the employment outlook is expected to be extremely strong in the area of computer crime when you consider that companies are increasingly using the Internet and intranet applications to expand business operations and make them more lucrative and efficient. As business in cyberspace grows, unfortunately the likelihood of cyber-attacks grows along with it. The Computer Security Institute (with participation from the San Francisco FBI Computer Intrusion Squad) released its fifth annual Computer Crime and Security Survey in March 2000, and the findings were discouraging. Ninety percent of those responding to the survey (primarily large corporations and government agencies) reported incidents of cyber-attacks within a twelve-month period. Seventy percent reported that the nature of these attacks was serious: cases involved theft of proprietary information, financial fraud, system penetration from outsiders, sabotage of data or networks, and denial-of-service attacks. Forty-two percent quantified what these attacks meant in financial terms: the losses from these 273 organizations alone totaled $265,589,940 for a one-year period.

What makes this state of affairs even more remarkable is that annual total losses for the previous three years averaged $120,240,180, leading Computer Security Institute director Patrice Rapalus to state, "The trends the CSI/FBI survey has highlighted over the years are disturbing. Cybercrimes and other information security breaches are widespread and diverse. . . . Clearly, more must be done in terms of adherence to sound practices, deployment of sophisticated technologies, and most importantly adequate staffing and training of information security practitioners in both the private sector and government." So long as the threat from computer crime and security breaches continues unabated, not only is the financial toll mounting but also businesses and organizations may witness disastrous results from loss of consumer confidence and downstream liability. How can they not then continue to supplement staff and resources to protect assets?

STRATEGY FOR FINDING THE JOBS

In strategizing your job search, it's important to make use of a variety of tactics. For example, reading the help-wanted ads in the Sunday paper is a must, but not all job announcements are published. In fact, for most general employment openings, only 20 percent nationwide are published. If you were to rely on this method alone, you would be missing up to 80 percent of the opportunities. Devise a plan consisting of some general approaches as well as some more specific to your chosen field. The following general avenues are good ones to include.

Alumni Career Connections. Either the career office or alumni office on your campus can put you in touch with former graduates of your college who are now working in the particular job markets of interest to you. These alumni connections can be very helpful, offering informational interviews, background on the firms that employ them, and general insights into the retail job market. Your school's alumni database may be able to actually isolate those who are working in private security versus public law enforcement. Remember, when contacting these individuals for career guidance, that you are representing your college *and* every other student who may someday want to make use of this valuable referral service. Be prepared with a list of questions, and use their time wisely. You'll make a good friend and have increased insight into your chosen career field. Many alumni will invite you to visit their places of business, and some may even offer to assist with your resume or job search strategy.

On-Campus Recruiting. Employers who visit your campus are giving you a strong indication of their interest in your school's students. Sign up for every recruitment interview that seems appropriate. On-campus interviewing can and does lead to actual job offers. Even when it doesn't, it's excellent interview practice. Most important, you will begin to develop a sense of what each employer is offering to make distinctions about what would be the best "fit" for you in a criminal justice career offering. Unlike job fairs, these are private interviews, one-on-one with a senior representative from the organization. Even better, the interviews are held on campus in familiar surroundings, which should help you in controlling those interview jitters. Your campus career office probably maintains files on all the recruiting firms to allow you to thoroughly prepare for your session.

Job Fairs. Job fairs are valuable job search tools for students. First, they are very efficient. How else would you be able to meet and talk with so many possible job contacts in one day? In addition, the process of walking up to employment representatives, greeting them, and giving them a one-minute "infomercial" about who you are and what you have to offer a given organization is a perfect example of the specific people skills that security employers seek. Most of these employers are looking for evidence of assertiveness, confidence, ingenuity, and persistence. They're seeking candidates with solid communication skills and those who aren't afraid of confrontation. The job fair provides you with an opportunity to demonstrate all of these.

Recently, you might have noticed "virtual job fairs" advertised at your college or on the Internet. These are becoming more popular, as they offer job candidates access to many more employers than they would be able to meet in a specific physical space. Plus, they usually run for a week or longer, giving you more time to explore and communicate with employers of interest to you.

Your Career Office. Your college career office not only will hold subscriptions to numerous job posting newsletters offering entry-level jobs but also will be on the mailing lists of many employers that recruit on college campuses to fill these positions. Employers looking for graduates with criminal justice backgrounds naturally target their recruitment efforts to colleges or universities that offer criminal justice programs.

Your Resume and Cover Letter. Be sure that your resume and cover letter reflect the skills and capabilities that employers in your field are looking for. This means that you'll have to spend some time reviewing actual ads for your field. For example, if you continually see ads that state the need for excellent people skills, be sure to highlight any previous jobs in which you had significant contact with customers or coworkers, or experience working as part of a team. Likewise, if you see that computer knowledge is often required (and you most definitely will), be sure to list your level of expertise with various hardware and software.

These are only a few of the general aids that you should consider putting to use in your venture. Other resources that have been mentioned elsewhere in this book are Internet searching, state employment offices, newspapers, and even the phone book. Now let's move on to ideas for your particular area of interest.

Private Security

You don't have to wait until you graduate to find a job in private security. There are many opportunities for part-time or seasonal work while you are still in college. Your campus security force can be a good place to start. You could also contact a security services agency in your locale. They're easy to find—just look under "Security" in the yellow pages—and they almost always have part-time assignments to fill. Another possibility is a nearby department store, often a great training ground for a career in security. While security personnel are hired year-round, typically there is a need for increased staffing starting in late October as stores gear up for the holiday shopping season.

Whichever you choose, the point is that you can begin to establish a resume for a career in security now. Working part-time or during the summer will enable you to try out the job to see if it's really the direction in which you want to go. You'll build the valuable experience needed for more advanced positions, and you'll meet people working in the field who can be instrumental to you when you graduate.

Remember that for most security positions, you will need to undergo a complete background check; be vigilant about keeping your record clean. You will be expected to provide solid character references. Think carefully about people in your life who can attest to your dependability, trustworthiness, maturity, work ethic, and emotional stability—professors, your faculty adviser, former supervisors, or religious leaders. Usually, you'll need to provide three to five references. Be sure to ask your prospective references first if they would be willing to speak on your behalf, and let them know whenever you have provided their names to a potential employer.

Private Investigators

The National Association of Investigative Specialists (NAIS) provides a top-notch resource on how to become a private investigator. On the Web at www.pimall.com/nais/beapi.html is almost everything you would need to know, including what the licensing requirements are in your state and how to contact your state's licensing authority, with direct links in most cases. While you're at it, learn about the latest trends in the field and even review a short, on-line course on private investigation. If that's not enough, you can search by state for NAIS member investigative agencies and pull up names, contact information including websites where available, and any specialty areas of the agency. The site also contains an on-line bookstore where you can order manuals such as *The Private Investigative Agency Business Start-Up Manual* and *PI—A Self-Study Guide*. This is definitely a site to peruse if private investigation is in your future.

You may want to conduct an informational interview with a private investigator, maybe one chosen from the NAIS site. This is a great way to really get the inside story on a specific occupation. Most people are flattered that you're interested in their work and are happy to consent to the interview. But remember to keep the meeting brief since time is money, especially in the case of self-employed investigators. Come prepared with a list of questions (your college career office may have a handout or other resource on informational interviewing), and be open to learning about both the good *and* the bad aspects of the job. You are, after all, looking for the "real" story.

Because almost all private detectives and investigators have some experience in a related field, the same advice offered earlier for private security applies here. Get some experience as soon as you can by working in private security or, perhaps, an insurance or collections agency. Another option is a position as a department store detective in which you can develop investigative and observation skills and acquire real-world experience in conducting surveillance and apprehending and prosecuting suspects.

Cybercrime

The most important strategy for attaining employment in the cybercrime field is to gain, strengthen, and be prepared to demonstrate strong computer skills. You can do that by adding a minor in computer science, by selecting a significant amount of electives in that area, and by gaining hands-on experience through part-time and summer jobs, internships, and practicums. This is not to say that other skills you have developed as a criminal justice major won't be valued. In fact, according to the Robert Half *2000 Salary Guide*, 68 percent of the 1,500 chief information officers surveyed said that "soft" skills such as business acumen and interpersonal skills were very important. Only 3 percent said that these skills were not. When asked which capabilities they considered most important for reaching management levels in the information technology profession, respondents cited interpersonal skills most often, followed by advanced technical skills. It makes sense in a field where project teams predominate and technical staff need to be able to communicate complex information to employees at all levels with varying degrees of sophistication.

The point is that you need both of these skill areas, along with the investigative skills that you have developed in your major, to best position yourself in the cybercrime job market. Be patient and willing to accept a more entry-level technical or customer support position as you continue to learn and develop the skills that will be necessary. You will be entering a career field that is still in its developing stages. Think of how bright the future is!

POSSIBLE EMPLOYERS

While this chapter features the private sector, don't think that the only opportunities for these positions are in the business arena. Many local governments employ private security to supplement their law enforcement staffs, and the federal government is in the forefront of cybercrime. Also, public and private utility companies must provide security services, particularly in the event of a natural disaster, resource shortage, or civil disturbance.

In contrast to the previous paths, for which the bulk of employment possibilities presented is within the public sector, the purpose of this chapter is to give you a better sense of the other, very broad side of the employment picture—the private sector.

Private Security

If you are working in the private security field, chances are that you are either employed by a security services agency or an industrial security firm, or directly employed by the organization whose building or property you're responsible for securing. The difference lies in who your actual employer is—who issues your paycheck and assigns and supervises your work—not the actual location to which you report every day or the kind of work you do.

For example, if you are a security officer at a community hospital, your work is the same whether you're employed by the hospital or by an agency that contracts with the hospital to provide security services.

The variety of industries that utilize security services include:

Construction	Manufacturing
Crisis management	Nuclear plants
Education	Office building management
Entertainment	Pharmaceutical
Executive protection	Proprietary/information
Government operations	Real estate management
Health care	Retail
High tech	Special events
Hotel/hospitality	Terrorism counteraction
Insurance	Transportation

Within these industries are numerous possibilities, yielding a wide variety of employment options. For example, transportation includes positions in airports and airplane hangars, trucking, rail terminals, armored cars, and sea operations. Entertainment includes shopping malls, museums, art galleries, theaters, parks, nightclubs, restaurants, gambling casinos, and sporting events. And for each of these, you have a variety of security services. In addition to protective services, there are opportunities for security consulting, design and engineering, education and training, investigations, and, of course, sales of products and services.

Private Investigators

One out of four private investigators and detectives is self-employed. Of the rest, another 25 percent work for private detective agencies, 25 percent work for department and specialty stores, and the remaining fourth work in industries such as lodging, insurance, and legal services. Many private investigators have an expertise and interest in a specific area that will determine who their employer is. A lawyer or law firm will hire an investigator who specializes in cases involving the courts. A corporation may employ a private investigator to do preemployment background checks, to conduct internal (e.g., drug use in the workplace) and external (e.g., billing fraud) investigations, or to provide protection for the corporation's chief executive. Private detective agencies often specialize in one or several areas. The National Association of Investigative Specialists lists the following top twenty private investigative specializations as of 1998:

1. Insurance claims investigations

2. Service of process (serving legal papers for attorneys)

3. Background checks

4. Locating missing persons

5. Surveillance

6. Executive protection

7. Countermeasures (focusing on information security)

8. Fraud investigations

9. Criminal investigations

10. Accident investigations

11. Assets searches and checks

12. Corporate investigations

13. Domestic investigations

14. Auto repossession

15. Preemployment screens

16. Bail enforcement

17. Computer security

18. Nanny investigations and child abuse

19. Corporate security services

20. Information brokerage (providing research service)

While much of the work involved in private investigation is computer or research based, with limited opportunities (except for some types of investigations) for fieldwork, the foregoing list and descriptions of specializations possible suggest that the most effective and cost-efficient detectives would be those who develop a specific area of expertise. Through actual experience in the field, you will gain exposure to many of these specializations and be better able to gauge the best fit for you.

Cybercrime

Any company, organization, or government agency that does any business on-line is a potential employer. From a corporation conducting E-commerce; to a small nonprofit organization using E-mail as a communication tool; to the Federal Bureau of Investigation, the lead agency for a variety of the nation's security concerns; and everywhere in between, lies potential for employment in this field.

Add to these the firms that specialize in computer security and/or crime investigation. Many of these firms are referenced on some of the criminal justice and law enforcement sites already mentioned, such as www.crime spider.com and in the library at www.talkjustice.com.

A growing number of computer-savvy professionals are self-employed, consulting with organizations or providing direct services to businesses on a contract basis. They may, for example, set up a new communications security system for a company and train the in-house information technology staff to monitor it. They may also handle any troubleshooting or upgrading that needs to be done.

At one time, you would almost always find the responsibility for computer security tacked on to the systems administrator's job duties, and it is still that way in many cases. However, as concern for information security grows in scope and as incidents of cyber-attacks continue to mount, more and more employers are turning to hiring full-time computer security and crime investigative specialists or contracting with firms to provide that service.

POSSIBLE JOB TITLES

Because the scope of employment is so large in the private sector, the list of potential job titles could never be exhausted on these few pages, but this sampling should give you a good idea of the possibilities:

Private Security

Armored Car Guard	Hotel Security Director
Bank Office	Security Officer
Bodyguard	Loss Prevention Agent
Security Alarm Installer	Plant Protection Officer
Corporate Security Specialist	Private Security Specialist

Protection Officer

Protection Specialist

Security Agent

Security Consultant

Security Systems Technician

Special Police

Store Detective

Undercover Investigative Trainee

Private Investigator

Corporate Investigator

Legal Investigator

Private Detective

Private Investigator

Store Detective

Surveillance Specialist

Undercover Investigator

Cybercrime

Computer Crime Investigator

Computer Forensics Operator

Computer Security Specialist

Customer Support Specialist

Firewall and VPN Lab Analyst

Information Security Analyst

Information Security Specialist

Internet Enforcement Officer

Investigations Manager

Malicious Code Lab Analyst

Manager of Information Systems Security

Product Developer

Security Architect

Security Systems Technician

Systems Analyst

Systems Developer

Technical Consultant

Technical Support Specialist

PROFESSIONAL ASSOCIATIONS

Listed in this section are some of the associations that relate to careers in the field of businesses allied to criminal justice. For more information about these professional associations, either check the websites listed or consult the *Encyclopedia of Associations*, published by the Gale Group. Review the Members/Purpose notes for each organization to determine if it pertains to your interests. Membership in one or more of these organizations may gain you access to job listings, networking opportunities, and employment search ser-vices. Some provide information at no charge, but if you want to receive spe-cific publications that list job opportunities, you may need to join. If you're still in college, check for student member rates.

American Society for Industrial Security
1625 Prince St.
Alexandria, VA 22314-2818
www.asisonline.org
Members/Purpose: An international organization for professionals responsible for security, including managers and directors of security; attorneys; and federal, state, and local law enforcement.
Publications: *Security Newsbriefs*; a database, The Security News Abstracts Archive; books; magazines; newsletters; other resources including the certified protection professional (CPP) information package.
Training: Annual seminar; professional development programs.

Computer Security Institute
600 Harrison St.
San Francisco, CA 94107
www.gocsi.com
Members/Purpose: The Computer Security Institute is specifically dedicated to serving and training information, computer, and network security professionals.
Publications: *The Computer Security Journal; Frontline End-User Awareness Newsletter.*
Training: Numerous information security seminars, annual conferences, and sessions.

High Technology Crime Investigation Association
1474 Freeman Dr.
Amissville, VA 20106
www.htcia.org
Members/Purpose: Designed to encourage, promote, aid, and effect the voluntary interchange of data, information, experience, ideas, and knowledge about methods, processes, and techniques relating to investigations and security in advanced technologies among members.
Publications: On-line job postings; newsletter; *Legislative and Legal Update.*
Training: International conference; local chapters sponsor training opportunities.

Independent Armored Car Operators Association, Inc.
102 E. Avenue J
Lancaster, CA 83535-3521
www.iacoa.com
Members/Purpose: An association for the growing number of privately owned armored car companies. The organization's purpose is to establish high standards of operation and insurance.
Publications: On-line newsletter.
Training: Annual convention.

International Association for Computer Crimes
6 Swarthmore Ln.
Dix Hills, NY 11746
www.iacss.com
Members/Purpose: The first organization in the world to certify an individual's qualifications as an associate or senior-grade computer systems security professional (CSSP), based on a rigorous review of the candidate's work experience and education and the results of a two-part, seven-hour written examination. The program began in 1983, and today many organizations specify this type of qualification as a prerequisite in hiring for positions that protect information resources.
Publications: *Security and Control of Your PC/Micro Network.*
Training: Workshops; seminars; certification program for computer systems security professional, four-day workshops open to anyone.

International Association of Computer Investigative Specialists
P.O. Box 21688
Keizer, OR 97307-1688
www.cops.org
Members/Purpose: Dedicated to the education and certification of law enforcement professionals in the field of computer forensic science, IACIS exists to create and establish procedures, train personnel, and certify forensic examiners in the recovery of evidence from computer systems.
Publications: Newsletter; software.
Training: Forensic examiner course; forensic issues course.

National Association of Investigative Specialists, Inc.
P.O. Box 33244
Austin, TX 78764
www.pimall.com/nais/nais.menu.html

Members/Purpose: The National Association of Investigative Specialists is an American trade association of private investigative professionals that focuses on marketing investigative services, developing new investigative techniques, and providing training and resources to members.

Publications: *PI Bites*; books; hundreds of manuals on a variety of topics and software; articles.

Training: Interactive CD-ROM programs; numerous training packages and courses.

National Association of Legal Investigators
6109 Meadowwood
Grand Blanc, MI 48439
www.nalionline.org

Members/Purpose: This association's primary focus is to conduct investigations related to litigation. NALI is open to all professional legal investigators who are actively engaged in negligence investigations for the plaintiff and/or criminal defense.

Publications: *The Legal Investigator*.

Training: Midwinter and national conferences.

World Association of Detectives, Inc.
PMB #301
2767 S. Parker Rd.
Aurora, CO 80014
www.wad.net

Members/Purpose: The primary purpose of the association is to promote and maintain the highest ethical practice in the profession and to foster and perpetuate a spirit of cooperation among members and similar organizations.

Publications: *W.A.D. News*, which contains articles of interest to the membership.

Training: Annual conferences.

INDEX